Prayers
for all seasons
book 2

NICK FAWCETT

Prayers
for all seasons
book 2

*A comprehensive resource
for public worship*

**kevin
mayhew**

First published in 2001 by
KEVIN MAYHEW LTD
Buxhall, Stowmarket
Suffolk IP14 3BW

9 8 7 6 5 4 3

ISBN 1 84003 700 8
Catalogue No 1500414

Edited by Katherine Laidler
Typeset by Louise Selfe
Cover design by Sara-Jane Came

CONTENTS

MISSION AND OUTREACH

INFANT BAPTISM/DEDICATION

BELIEVERS' BAPTISM/CONFIRMATION

CHRISTIAN MARRIAGE

CHRISTIAN BURIAL

PART THREE – ORDINARY SUNDAYS

PRAYERS OF APPROACH

ABOUT THE AUTHOR

Nick Fawcett was born in 1957. He studied Theology at Bristol University and Regent's Park College, Oxford. His early years of ministry were spent in Somerset and Lancashire, and from 1989 to 1996 he was Minister of Gas Green Baptist Church, Cheltenham. From November 1996 to June 1999 he served as Toc H Chaplain and Development Officer for Wales and the West of England.

He is now concentrating full time on his career as a writer and editor. His books to date are *No Ordinary Man* (1997), *Prayers For All Seasons* (1998), *Are You Listening?* (1998), *Getting It Across* (1999), *Grappling With God*, Books 1-4 (2000), *No Ordinary Man 2* (2000), *The Unfolding Story* (2000), *To Put It Another Way* (2000) and *Decisions, Decisions* (2000), all published by Kevin Mayhew. He has also written the texts for *Classic Melodies for Choirs* (Books 1 and 2, 1999 and 2000) and had four hymns chosen for inclusion in the Churches Together Millennium Hymn Book *New Start Hymns and Songs* (1999), these also published by Kevin Mayhew.

He lives with his wife, Deborah, and their two young children, Samuel and Katie, in Wellington, Somerset.

ACKNOWLEDGEMENTS

As always, this book owes much to many. I wish to thank especially my wife, Deborah, for typing up so much of the manuscript; Katherine Laidler for her thoughtful work as editor; Peter Dainty for his searching and instructive criticisms; and Kevin Mayhew Publishers for the opportunity to put this and other material into print. Also, my special thanks once again to Gas Green Baptist Church, where so many of these prayers first took shape.

To Mary Edwards and Daphne Dawes
with thanks for your invaluable support and encouragement

INTRODUCTION

When I began my training for ministry some twenty-five years ago, the last thing I envisaged was writing a book of prayers. As a Baptist, I was schooled in a tradition of extemporary prayer, where the idea of reading prayers in worship was generally regarded with suspicion. That was fine, so long as I exercised an itinerant preaching ministry, but when I settled into my first church it soon became apparent to me that I was repeating the same ideas in prayer week in and week out, even occasionally using the same words! Of more concern still, many prayers lacked any sense of structure or direction, jumping from one idea to another as the mood took me. In personal devotion that may not matter but in the context of public worship I felt it mattered very much. Entrusted with the responsibility of leading prayer on behalf of the gathered congregation, I was selling both them and myself short.

The result was that I took to preparing in advance the prayers I would use each Sunday, a practice which was to lead ultimately to the first collection of prayers published under the title *Prayers for All Seasons*. This new collection is offered as a complement to that volume. It includes further prayers written during the course of my ministry, together with new ones written specifically for this book. Like the first volume, it is divided into three sections. 'The Christian Year' offers prayers for the principal days of the Christian calendar from Advent through to All Saints' Day. 'Life and Faith' focuses on life's passage from birth through to death, and on significant events in the life of the Church and the individual believer. 'Ordinary Sundays' offers a range of prayers for use in worship generally, as well as the Lord's Supper in particular.

I have purposely kept prompts and responses simple so that the congregation can memorise them without them needing a copy of the words. If preferred, responses can be omitted. Flexibility and sensitivity in the use of these prayers are essential, and there will be times when you will want to add to them or leave material out. The prayers that jointly cover Infant Baptism/Dedication and Believers' Baptism/Confirmation are necessarily broad, and you may well feel some additional words of your own are needed to bring out the theological significance of these events.

There is, of course, no right way to pray. Sometimes words are appropriate, sometimes not. Sometimes a degree of formality seems fitting, at other times quite the opposite. Much depends on the person and situation in question. This book does not pretend to be an example of how we should pray, for I will always be a learner in that myself. I offer it simply as a resource to those leading worship. It is my hope that this new collection may prove of value to those who lead worship and to all on whose behalf they pray.

NICK FAWCETT

PART ONE

THE CHRISTIAN YEAR

ADVENT

1

PRAISE
THE ASSURANCE OF ADVENT

Loving God,
    we rejoice in this season of good news and good will,
        we celebrate once more the birth of your Son,
        our Saviour Jesus Christ,
        the Prince of Peace
        the Lord of lords,
        the Word made flesh,
        and we praise you for the assurance of his final triumph.
    As you came through him,
    so you shall come again.

For coming among us through Jesus,
    for bearing our flesh and blood,
    for living our life and sharing our humanity,
    for entering our world,
    loving God, we praise you!
As you came through him,
    so you shall come again.

For suffering and dying among us,
    for your victory over death,
    your triumph over evil,
    and your promise that the kingdom will come,
    loving God, we praise you!
As you came through him,
    so you shall come again.

For the wonder of this season,
    for its message of love and forgiveness,
    its promise of peace and justice,
    and the gift of life everlasting of which it speaks,
    loving God, we praise you!
As you came through him,
    so you shall come again.

Loving God,
 we rejoice again in this season of good news and good will,
  and we look forward to that day
  when the Jesus of Bethlehem will be the Lord of all.
 As you came through him,
  so you shall come again.

 In Christ's name we praise you!
 Amen.

2

PETITION
THE CHALLENGE OF ADVENT

Lord of all,
    you tell us to wait and pray for that time
        when Christ shall come again to establish his kingdom;
        that time when your purpose shall be fulfilled
        and your name made known and worshipped on all the earth!
    You challenge us to live in the light of that promise –
        help us to respond.

Teach us, we pray, never to lose sight of your purpose,
        never to stop believing that you are at work,
        never to lose confidence in your kingdom.
Teach us that, as Christ came, so he shall come again.
You challenge us to live in the light of that promise –
        help us to respond.

But teach us also not to waste the present moment,
        not to place all our hope in the future,
        or to imagine that you are unconcerned
        for us and your world now!
Teach us to recognise that Christ is with us always,
        by our side to the end of time.
You challenge us to live in the light of that promise –
        help us to respond.

Help us to live and work for you always,
        rightly and responsibly enjoying your many gifts,
        and seeking to do your will and follow your ways.
Help us to live each day
        as though Christ were coming back at that moment,
        until that day when he returns in glory
        and you are all in all.
You challenge us to live in the light of that promise –
        help us to respond.

For his name's sake.
Amen.

3

INTERCESSION
THE HOPE OF ADVENT

Lord Jesus Christ,
   we remember today
      how so many looked forward to your coming,
      but we remember also
      how it became harder to go on believing
      as the years went by;
      how hope started to splutter and dreams began to die
      until, finally, you came –
      the fulfilment of prophecy,
      the culmination of God's purpose,
      the definitive expression of his love.
Lord of all,
   the Word made flesh,
   bring hope to your world today.

We remember with gladness
      how you brought hope throughout your ministry,
      a sense of purpose to those for whom life seemed pointless –
      the poor, sick, outcasts and broken-hearted –
      light shining in their darkness,
      joy breaking into their sorrow,
      new beginnings in what had seemed like the end.
Lord of all,
   the Word made flesh,
   bring hope to your world today.

Hear now our prayer for those caught today in the grip of despair –
      those for whom the future seems bleak,
      optimism seems foolish,
      and trust seems futile.
Reach out in love,
      and may light shine into their darkness.
Lord of all,
   the Word made flesh,
   bring hope to your world today.

Hear our prayer for those whose goals in life have been thwarted,
   whose dreams have been shattered,
   who have grown weary, cynical and disillusioned.
Reach out in love,
   and rekindle their faith in the future.
Lord of all,
   the Word made flesh,
   bring hope to your world today.

Hear our prayer for those who mourn,
   or who wrestle with illness,
   or who watch loved ones suffer.
Reach out in love,
   and grant them your strength and comfort.
Lord of all,
   the Word made flesh,
   bring hope to your world today.

Hear our prayer for those whose lives are blighted by injustice,
   crushed by oppression, poverty, hunger,
   and encourage all who work against the odds
   to build a better world.
Reach out in love,
   and grant the assurance of your coming kingdom.
Lord of all,
   the Word made flesh,
   bring hope to your world today.

Lord Jesus Christ,
   we remember your promise to come again in glory,
      the culmination of God's purpose,
      the ultimate victory of love.
   May that conviction bring new faith,
      new vision,
      and new purpose wherever life seems hopeless.
   Lord of all,
      the Word made flesh,
      bring hope to your world today.

In your name we pray.
Amen.

4

PRAISE
RECEIVING THE WORD

Gracious God,
 we praise you today for the power of your word,
  the way you have spoken to so many people
  throughout history.

 You called the universe into being –
  heaven and earth,
  night and day,
  the sea and the dry land,
  life in its multitude of manifestations.
 You spoke,
  and it was done,
  our world and our very existence owing to you.
 For your word of life,
  we praise you.

 You called Abraham, Isaac and Jacob,
  Moses and Joshua,
  judges, kings and prophets,
  Apostles, disciples, preachers and teachers –
  a great company of saints,
  each testifying to your sovereign purpose,
  your awesome power
  and your merciful love;
  each hearing your voice and responding in faith.
 For your word of life,
  we praise you.

You came in Jesus Christ, the Word made flesh,
    identifying yourself with our humanity,
    sharing our joy and sorrow,
    experiencing our life and death.
You came in fulfilment of your promises of old,
    revealing the extent of your love
    through everything he said and did,
    demonstrating your gracious purpose for all.
For your word of life,
    we praise you.

You speak still through the pages of Scripture;
    through their record of your involvement in history
    and their testimony to your will for the world.
You speak through dialogue between Christians,
    through the witness of your Church and personal testimony,
    through study and reflection,
    and through the sharing of fellowship.
You speak through the grandeur of the universe
    and the wonder of life,
    your still small voice breaking into our experience
    to challenge and inspire.
For your word of life,
    we praise you.

Gracious God,
    we rejoice at the ways you have spoken to us in the past
        and the way you continue to speak today.
We receive your word with joyful thanksgiving,
        and we pray for strength to make it so much a part of us
        that your voice may be heard through all we are and do,
        to the glory of your name.
For your word of life,
    we praise you.

Through Jesus Christ our Lord.
Amen.

5

CONFESSION
REDISCOVERING THE WORD

Sovereign God,
  we thank you for your word –
    recorded in Scripture
    and handed down over countless generations;
    heard through reading, preaching, fellowship and worship;
    glimpsed in the beauty of our world and the mysteries of life;
    brought to life through prayer and meditation,
    embodied through Jesus Christ, the Word made flesh.
  Speak again now,
    and give us ears to hear.

Forgive us that we are sometimes slow to listen.
We do not make time to read the Scriptures as we should,
  allowing instead the pressures and responsibilities of life,
  our many interests, pleasures and concerns,
  to crowd out the time we spend with you.
Speak again now,
  and give us ears to hear.

We become casual or complacent in our worship,
  no longer expecting you to challenge us,
  no longer moved to a sense of awe,
  no longer hungry for spiritual food.
Speak again now,
  and give us ears to hear.

We neglect the opportunity for fellowship,
  turning in on ourselves,
  imagining we know all there is to know of you,
  more concerned with our own insights
  than those we can gain from others.
Speak again now,
  and give us ears to hear.

We grow deaf to your voice in creation,
    our senses dulled by over-familiarity;
    no time to pause and ponder,
    to reflect on deeper, eternal realities.
Speak again now,
    and give us ears to hear.

We believe we have listened and responded,
    but our focus is on the written word
    rather than the Word made flesh,
    the letter rather than the spirit of your revelation in Christ.
Speak again now,
    and give us ears to hear.

Sovereign God,
    speak afresh through the pages of Scripture,
        through the worship that we share,
        the experience and insight of other Christians,
        and, above all, through the inner presence
        of the living Christ in our hearts.
Teach us, when your voice seems silent,
        to listen again more carefully,
        and to rediscover your word.
Speak again now,
    and give us ears to hear.

Through Jesus Christ our Lord.
Amen.

6

INTERCESSION
PROCLAIMING GOD'S WORD

Loving God,
    we thank you today for the Scriptures,
        and the opportunity we have each day
        of reading and studying them for ourselves.
Hear now our prayer for all those denied that privilege.

We pray for those who have not heard the challenge of the Bible,
    who do not possess a copy of it in their own language,
    or who are denied the right to own a Bible or study it freely.
Lord, in your mercy,
    hear our prayer.

We pray for those who have heard but closed their minds,
    for those who read but do not understand,
    and for those who have read the Bible so often
    that it fails to challenge as it used to.
Lord, in your mercy,
    hear our prayer.

We pray for those who work to make the Scriptures known
    and available to all –
    those who translate the Bible
    into modern language and other tongues,
    who print and distribute it across the world,
    who strive to open its message afresh
    to each and every generation;
    and who preach from it, witnessing to Christ from its pages.
Lord, in your mercy,
    hear our prayer.

Loving God,
   may your word be made known
      with clarity, wisdom, faithfulness and power,
      so that many hear its challenge
      and respond in faith to your loving purpose.
   Lord, in your mercy,
      hear our prayer.

Through Jesus Christ our Lord,
   the Word made flesh.
Amen.

7

PRAISE
ADVENT COMMISSION

Lord Jesus Christ,
   we praise you today for all those
      who prepared the way for your coming;
      all who made a straight path in the wilderness
      so that the hearts of many were ready to receive you.

We praise you for Abraham
      who, centuries before your coming, ventured out in faith,
      journeying into the unknown,
      trusting in God's promise that all generations
      would be blessed through his descendants.
   You call us to prepare your way in turn:
      gladly we respond.

We praise you for the prophets –
      those who foretold your birth,
      who looked forward to your kingdom,
      and who anticipated your saving grace,
      their words bringing hope to countless generations
      and still having power to challenge and inspire today.
   You call us to prepare your way in turn:
      gladly we respond.

We praise you for Mary and Joseph –
      for their obedience to your call,
      their confidence in your purpose,
      their faith that, with you, nothing is impossible.
   You call us to prepare your way in turn:
      gladly we respond.

We praise you for John the Baptist –
 for his willingness to speak the truth
 no matter what the cost,
 his readiness to point away from himself
 and towards your light,
 and the integrity of his lifestyle
 which testified to the truth of his message
 in a way that words alone could never begin to.
You call us to prepare your way in turn:
 gladly we respond.

We praise you for the Evangelists and Apostles –
 those who recorded the events of your ministry,
 who testified to their experience of your grace;
 and who offered guidance in the early days of your Church,
 so preparing their own and subsequent generations
 to respond to your coming
 and to look forward in faith to your coming again.
You call us to prepare your way in turn:
 gladly we respond.

We praise you for your invitation to continue their ministry –
 to witness to your renewing power,
 to demonstrate your unfailing compassion,
 and to lead others to a knowledge of your redeeming love.
We thank you that, as you have used others,
 so now, despite our numerous faults and failings,
 you want to use us
 to promote the growth of your kingdom here on earth.
You call us to prepare your way in turn:
 gladly we respond.

Lord Jesus Christ,
 help us to make a straight path in the wilderness,
  so that the hearts of many may be ready to receive you today.
 Help us to prepare your way.

In your name we ask it.
Amen.

8

CONFESSION
ADVENT OMISSION

Loving God,
    the great festival of Christmas is drawing nearer
        and we are busy preparing for it –
        choosing presents,
        writing cards,
        planning get-togethers,
        buying food –
        so much that has become an accepted
        and expected part of this season.
    Yet, in all the bustle, we so easily forget
        the most important thing of all:
        responding to the wonderful gift of your Son.
    You have come to us in Christ:
        forgive us when we fail to receive him.

We tell ourselves that *we* are different –
    that we will be worshipping you Sunday by Sunday,
    sharing in services of lessons and carols,
    hearing again familiar and well-loved verses of Scripture,
    but we know that this isn't enough in itself,
    for these too can become just another part
    of our traditional celebrations,
    washing over us
    rather than communicating the great message of the Gospel.
We become so concerned with the wrapping
    that we fail to recognise the gift concealed underneath.
You have come to us in Christ:
    forgive us when we fail to receive him.

Forgive us for relegating Jesus to the periphery of our celebrations,
   rather than placing him at the centre where he belongs;
   for turning this season into a time for material extravagance,
   rather than an opportunity for spiritual fulfilment;
   for doing so much to prepare for Christmas on the surface,
   yet so little to make ourselves ready within.
You have come to us in Christ:
   forgive us when we fail to receive him.

Loving God,
   open our hearts now to hear again your word,
      to welcome the living Christ,
      and to reflect on our response to his call.
   May this Advent season teach us
      to welcome him afresh into our lives
      and to rejoice in his love not just at Christmas
      but always.
You have come to us in Christ:
   forgive us when we fail to receive him.

We ask it for his name's sake.
Amen.

9

INTERCESSION
ADVENT MISSION

Loving God,
 accept our glad thanksgiving for all you have given us,
  and hear now our prayers for your world.

We pray for those for whom there is no celebration –
  the poor and the hungry,
  the homeless and the sick,
  the lonely and the bereaved,
  the oppressed and the persecuted.
 Lord, you call us to respond to their need:
  help us to reach out in love.

We pray for all those whose celebration is marred by fear –
  those who are anxious for themselves or a loved one,
  who see no hope in the future,
  or who live under the constant threat of danger.
 Lord, you call us to respond to their need:
  help us to reach out in love.

We pray for all who wrestle with grief –
  those whose lives have been broken by tragedy,
  who live each day in perpetual shadow,
  crushed by the burden of sorrow.
 Lord, you call us to respond to their need:
  help us to reach out in love.

We pray for all who feel isolated –
  those who feel unloved, unwanted,
  who find it hard to show love towards others,
  or whose relationships have been broken
  by cruelty, discord, division.
 Lord, you call us to respond to their need:
  help us to reach out in love.

Loving God,
   may your light reach into the darkest places of the world,
      so that there may be hope rather than despair,
      joy rather than sorrow,
      and love rather than hatred.
   Come now to our world through Jesus Christ,
      to bring good news to the poor,
      release to the captives,
      recovery of sight to the blind,
      and to let the oppressed go free.
   Lord, you call us to respond to their need:
      help us to reach out in love.

In his name we pray.
Amen.

10

PRAISE
ADVENT PROMISE

Lord Jesus Christ,
  we rejoice today that you came in fulfilment of age-old prophecy,
    vindicating at last the long-held expectations of your people.
  After so many years of frustrated hopes,
    so many false dawns and disappointments,
    you dwelt among us,
    the Prince of Peace,
    the promised Messiah,
    Son of David,
    Son of man,
    Son of God.
  You have shown us that what God promises shall be accomplished:
    we praise you for that assurance.

  We rejoice that we are heirs to those promises of old,
    for you came not only to your own people
    but to the whole human race,
    born to set us free from everything that enslaves us
    and to open the way to eternal life
    to anyone willing to follow you.
  You have shown us that what God promises shall be accomplished:
    we praise you for that assurance.

  We rejoice that your purpose for the world continues,
    and that the time will come
    when your kingdom shall be established
    and your victory be complete.
  We thank you that, as you came once, so you will come again;
    as you departed into heaven, so you will return in glory,
    to establish justice throughout the earth,
    and to reconcile all creation through your love.
  So we look forward in confidence
    to that day when there will be no more sorrow or suffering,

hatred or evil,
darkness or death;
that day when you will be all in all.
You have shown us that what God promises shall be accomplished:
we praise you for that assurance.

Lord Jesus Christ,
we rejoice in this season, so full of promise;
this time which reminds us of all that has been
and all that is yet to be.
May the words we hear today,
the worship we offer
and the events we remember
teach us to trust you completely,
knowing that, whatever else may happen,
your saving purpose will be fulfilled.
You have shown us that what God promises shall be accomplished:
we praise you for that assurance.

In your name we pray.
Amen.

11

PETITION
ADVENT WITNESS

Loving God,
  we remember today how prophets foretold the coming of Christ –
    how they declared their faith in your purpose,
    their confidence in your love,
    their assurance of your final victory.
  They did not keep their faith to themselves;
    they shared it with others:
    teach us to do the same.

We remember how shepherds responded
    to the message of the angels –
    how they hurried to Bethlehem
    and found the baby lying in a manger,
    and how they went on their way praising and glorifying you
    for everything they had seen and heard.
  They did not keep their faith to themselves;
    they shared it with others:
    teach us to do the same.

We remember how John the Baptist
    prepared the way of Christ in the wilderness –
    how he proclaimed a baptism of repentance,
    a new beginning,
    the coming of one far greater than he could ever be.
  He did not keep his faith to himself;
    he shared it with others:
    teach us to do the same.

We remember how you came to us in Christ –
    how he brought light into our darkness,
    hope into our despair,
    joy into our sorrow.
He did not keep his faith *to* himself.
He did not live his life *for* himself;
    he shared it with others:
    teach us to do the same.

In his name we pray.
Amen.

12

INTERCESSION
ADVENT SERVICE

Loving God,
    we thank you for the hope you have given us in Christ,
        the meaning and purpose,
        joy and fulfilment you bring us through him.
    Hear now our prayer for those who find it hard to hope,
        those for whom life is hard.
    Reach out to them in their need,
        and may the light of Christ break into their darkness.

We think of those we label as the Third World –
    the hungry and undernourished,
    homeless and refugees,
    sick and suffering –
    human beings just as we are,
    deprived of their dignity in the desperate struggle for survival.
Reach out to them in their need,
    and may the light of Christ break into their darkness.

We think of those who are caught up in war –
    overwhelmed by fear and hatred,
    their homes and livelihoods destroyed,
    each day lived under the threat of violence.
Reach out to them in their need,
    and may the light of Christ break into their darkness.

We pray for those who feel overwhelmed by life –
    lonely,
    frightened,
    sad,
    weary –
    many dreading what the next day might bring.
Reach out to them in their need,
    and may the light of Christ break into their darkness.

Loving God,
   may the message of hope which Advent brings
      burst afresh into our world,
      bringing help, hope and healing.
   And may we, as those who profess the name of Christ,
      play our part in showing his love,
      displaying his care,
      and fulfilling his purpose,
      so that he might come again this Christmas
      to all who have lost hope.
   Reach out to them in their need,
      and may the light of Christ break into their darkness.

For his name's sake.
Amen.

CHRISTMAS

13

PRAISE
A TIME OF JOY

Gracious God,
    this is a time which means so much to us
        and which says so much in so many different ways,
        but if there is one thing which stands out above all others,
        it is the joy you brought through the birth of Jesus.
    A child is born for us,
        a son is given –
        with joy we greet him!

When Mary learned she was to be the mother of the Saviour
    she sang out her praises,
    and when Elizabeth greeted her,
    the baby in *her* womb leapt for joy.
When the multitude of angels appeared to the shepherds,
    they proclaimed news of great joy for all people,
    and when both shepherds and wise men
    had seen the Lord for themselves,
    they were overwhelmed by the wonder of it all,
    going on their way rejoicing.
Time and again it was the same story of spontaneous celebration.
A child is born for us,
    a son is given –
    with joy we greet him!

Gracious God,
    in all the hustle and bustle of Christmas,
        the ceremony and tradition with which we surround it,
        we can lose sight, sometimes, of the joy at its heart.
    We can put so much energy into having a good time,
        that we forget what it is we are meant to be celebrating,
        only, when it is over, to be left with a sense of emptiness,
        a feeling that it hasn't been like Christmas at all.
    Help us to enjoy all the fun and festivity,

the love and laughter,
the giving and receiving,
but help us also to keep in mind
the reality at the heart of this season,
the message which it is finally all about.
A child is born for us,
a son is given –
with joy we greet him!

May the glad tidings of the angels,
the news of great joy for all people,
stir afresh our imagination,
so that we may experience and understand for ourselves
the great truth of Christmas –
that a Saviour is born who is Christ the Lord.
A child is born for us,
a son is given –
with joy we greet him!

Gracious God,
this is a time for rejoicing,
for celebration,
for exulting in your goodness.
We praise and thank you for the wonder of your love
and for the supreme demonstration of that love
in Jesus Christ.
A child is born for us,
a son is given –
with joy we greet him!

Amen.

14

PRAISE
A TIME FOR WORSHIP

Loving God,
  at this time of giving and receiving,
    of showing our love and gratitude to others
    through the exchanging of cards and presents,
    we are reminded of the great gift you have given us in Christ
    and of how little we have to offer in return.
  You have blessed us in so much:
    receive our worship.

Whatever we might bring, it can never repay you.
Whatever we might sacrifice,
    it can scarcely begin to express our thanks,
    but what we *can* offer and gladly bring
    is our praise,
    our homage,
    our adoration,
    offered in the name of Jesus.
  You have blessed us in so much:
    receive our worship.

Like the choir of angels on the night of his birth
    we sing your praise and tell out the good news.
Like the shepherds, returning from the manger,
    we give you the glory for all that we have heard and seen.
Like the magi, kneeling in wonder,
    we offer our gifts as a token of our love
    and sign of our commitment.
  You have blessed us in so much:
    receive our worship.

Loving God,
>   at this time of giving and receiving
>>   we do not have much to bring to you,
>>   but we offer this time together –
>>   our songs,
>>   our reading,
>>   our thinking, speaking and listening –
>>   and we offer ourselves, such as we are,
>>   in reverent praise and joyful celebration.
>   You have blessed us in so much:
>>   **receive our worship.**

In the name of Christ.
Amen.

15

PETITION
A TIME OF NEW BEGINNINGS

Lord Jesus Christ,
    we celebrate today your birth in Bethlehem –
        a birth that changed the course of history for ever.
    We rejoice that the future of the world
        was shaped by your coming,
        irreversibly transformed
        by your life, death and resurrection.
    A new chapter had begun:
        help us, in turn, to start again.

We remember how you brought a new beginning to so many –
    not just to Mary and Joseph on the night of your birth,
    but to countless others throughout your ministry
    and to innumerable generations since,
    offering the opportunity to put their mistakes behind them,
    to let go of the past and embrace the future,
    secure in your forgiveness,
    transformed by your grace.
A new chapter had begun:
    help us, in turn, to start again.

So we come now, this Christmas-time,
    acknowledging our faults and repeated disobedience.
We come recognising our need for help
    and our dependence on your mercy.
We come to hear the good news of your birth,
    the glad tidings of the dawn of your kingdom,
    and, in the light of that message,
    to seek your renewing touch upon our lives.
A new chapter had begun:
    help us, in turn, to start again.

Lord Jesus Christ,
    we have no claim on your love,
        no reason to expect your goodness,
        for we fail you day after day, week after week.
    Yet we celebrate today the glorious truth
        that you came into our world,
        you lived among us,
        you died our death,
        and you rose again, victorious over sin and death!
    A new chapter had begun:
        help us, in turn, to start again.

In your name we ask it.
Amen.

16

CONFESSION
A TIME FOR RECEIVING

Lord Jesus Christ,
    we recall today how you entered your world
        and the world did not know you;
        how you came to your own people,
        and they would not receive you;
        how you were born in Bethlehem,
        and there was no room for you in the inn.
    From the beginning it was the same old story –
        your love rejected,
        your grace ignored.
Lord have mercy,
    and teach us to receive you with gladness.

We remember that you came to set people free
    and to offer a new relationship with God –
        breaking down the barriers which keep us apart,
        bearing the price of our disobedience,
        opening up the way to life.
Yet we remember, too, that though some listened for a moment,
    few followed you to the end.
Time and again it was the same old story –
        your love rejected,
        your grace ignored.
Lord have mercy,
    and teach us to receive you with gladness.

We know we are no better,
    each of us guilty, day after day, of spurning your guidance,
    forgetting your goodness and abandoning your way.
We talk of commitment, but our faith is weak;
    we speak of following you, but follow only our own inclinations;
    we claim to be a new creation,
    but it is the old self that still holds sway.
Time and again it is the same old story –
    your love rejected,
    your grace ignored.
Lord have mercy,
    and teach us to receive you with gladness.

Lord Jesus Christ,
    we marvel that, despite it all –
    the world's hostility and our own faithlessness –
    still you reach out in love,
    never giving up,
    refusing to write us off.
We thank you that you are always ready to offer a fresh start,
    a new beginning,
    to anyone willing to receive it.
Come what may, it is the same old story –
    you continue seeking us out,
    however often we thrust you aside,
    your love rejected,
    your grace ignored.
Lord have mercy,
    and teach us to receive you with gladness.

In your name we ask it.
Amen.

17

THANKSGIVING
A TIME OF PROMISE

Loving God,
    we remember today the birth of Jesus Christ –
        your gift to humankind,
        your coming among us as flesh and blood,
        your honouring of age-old promises
        spoken through the prophets.
    The Word became flesh and dwelt among us,
        full of grace and truth:
        thanks be to God!

We do not remember those promises alone,
    but so many others associated with this time –
        your promise to Mary that she would bear a son,
        to Simeon that he would not taste death
        before seeing the Messiah,
        and, above all, your promise
        to anyone who receives Christ and believes in his name
        that they will become your children,
        born not of human will,
        but through your gracious purpose
        sharing in your eternal life.
    The Word became flesh and dwelt among us,
        full of grace and truth:
        thanks be to God!

Loving God,
we praise you that all you promised to do
was wonderfully fulfilled in Christ,
that through him your faithfulness
was most marvellously demonstrated;
the ultimate proof of your love and mercy.
We praise you for the reminder this Christmas season brings
that you are a God we can always depend on,
one in whom we can put our trust, though all else fails.
The Word became flesh and dwelt among us,
full of grace and truth:
thanks be to God!

So now we look forward in confidence
to the ultimate fulfilment of your word,
that day when Christ will be acclaimed
as King of kings and Lord of lords.
Until then, we will trust in you,
secure in your love,
confident in your eternal purpose,
assured that, in the fullness of time, your will shall be done.
The Word became flesh and dwelt among us,
full of grace and truth:
thanks be to God!

Amen.

18

THANKSGIVING
A TIME OF LIGHT

Loving God,
    we thank you for the great truth we celebrate at Christmas,
        the fact that, in Christ, your light shines in the darkness
        and that nothing has ever been able to overcome it.
    Despite hostility and rejection,
        the combined forces of hatred and evil,
        still the radiance of your love continues to reach out.
    The people that walked in darkness have seen a great light:
        thanks be to God!

We thank you for the light that dawned
    in the life of Zechariah and Elizabeth,
    that transformed the future for Mary and Joseph,
    and that lit up the sky on the night of the Saviour's birth.
The people that walked in darkness have seen a great light:
    thanks be to God!

We thank you for the light that flooded into the lives of shepherds,
    that guided wise men on their journey
    to greet the newborn king
    and that answered the prayers of Simeon and Anna.
Always you are with us,
    in life or in death leading us through the shadows.
The people that walked in darkness have seen a great light:
    thanks be to God!

We thank you for the light you brought
    through the life and ministry of Jesus –
    freedom for the captives,
    sight to the blind,
    healing for the sick,
    comfort to the broken-hearted,
    peace after confusion,
    acceptance after condemnation,
    hope after despair,
    joy after sorrow.
The people that walked in darkness have seen a great light:
    thanks be to God!

We thank you for the light that illuminates our lives today
    and which leads us step by step on our journey through life –
    the lamp of your word,
    the beacon of prayer,
    the glow of fellowship,
    the tongues of fire of your Holy Spirit,
    and the living reality of Jesus by our sides,
    the dawn from on high.
The people that walked in darkness have seen a great light:
    thanks be to God!

Loving God,
    you came to our world in Christ, bringing life and light for all.
    Shine now in our hearts
    and may the flame of faith burn brightly within us,
    so that we, in turn, may bring light to others,
    and, in so doing, bring glory to you.
The people that walked in darkness have seen a great light:
    thanks be to God!

Amen.

19

PETITION
A TIME OF ACCEPTANCE

Gracious God,
    we thank you today for your extraordinary gift of Christ
        and all that it points to –
        the wonder of your love,
        the extent of your love
        and the constancy of your purpose.
    And we thank you for the most extraordinary thing of all,
        that you came in Christ not simply to a few but to all –
        to good and bad, saints and sinners,
        to ordinary, everyday people like us.
    You reached out and accepted us as we are:
        teach us to accept others in turn.

We thank you that you chose Mary,
        representative of the powerless,
        to be the one to bear your Son;
        that you chose shepherds,
        examples of the socially marginalised,
        to be the first to hear the good news;
        that you chose Bethlehem,
        symbol of the least and lowest,
        to be the place where you were born.
    Through the manner of your coming among us,
        and through the life you lived in Christ,
        you repeatedly overturned this world's values and expectations,
        demonstrating your special care
        for the poor, the needy, the weak and the humble,
        all those ready to admit their dependence on you
        and seek your help.
    You reached out and accepted us as we are:
        teach us to accept others in turn.

We do not find it easy to accept others –
  we are biased towards the attractive and the successful,
  taken in by appearances,
  blind to the reality beneath the surface.
Our attitudes are shaped
  by deep-rooted prejudices and preconceptions
  which make us wary,
  suspicious,
  even hostile towards those
  who do not conform to our flawed expectations.
We jump to conclusions which all too often
  say more about ourselves than anyone.
Though we claim it is wrong to judge,
  in our hearts we not only judge but condemn.
Forgive us, and remind us of the example of Christ
  whom the so-called righteous repeatedly condemned
  for associating with the unacceptable.
You reached out and accepted us as we are:
  teach us to accept others in turn.

Gracious God,
  you have a place in your heart not just for the few but for all,
    not only for the good
    but for the unlovely, the undesirable, the undeserving.
  You look deep into the hearts of all,
    and where we see ugliness, you see someone infinitely precious,
    so valuable that you were willing to endure death on a cross
    to draw them to yourself.
  Help us to recognise that no one,
    no matter who they are,
    is outside the breadth of your love or the scope of your mercy.
  You reached out and accepted us as we are:
    teach us to accept others in turn.

Through Jesus Christ our Lord.
Amen.

20

Petition
A time for reflection

Gracious God,
    there are so many lessons we can learn from this season,
        but none more important than that shown to us by Mary.
    After the events leading up to the birth of Jesus –
        the shock,
        the excitement,
        the uncertainty,
        the celebration –
        we read that she 'treasured all these words
        and pondered them in her heart'.
    While shepherds made their way home
        exulting in all they had seen and heard,
        she made time to stop
        and think
        and take stock;
        time to reflect on what it all might mean
        for herself
        and others.
    You come still,
        you speak still:
        teach us to make space to listen,
        to understand
        and to respond.

We remember how Jesus, in turn, throughout his ministry,
  made time for you –
  time amid all the pressures and demands
  to be still in your presence,
  to discern your will,
  and to understand his calling.
He went into the wilderness,
  he drew aside from the crowds,
  he agonised alone in Gethsemane,
  giving *you* the opportunity to speak,
  and *himself* the opportunity to hear your voice.
You come still,
  you speak still:
  teach us to make space to listen,
  to understand
  and to respond.

We are not good at making such time to reflect,
  so easily becoming caught up in the fervour of the moment
  or bogged down in the routine of life.
We flit from this to that,
  pursuing now this goal, now another,
  our lives long on activity but short on substance.
Deep down we are scared of looking inwards,
  afraid of the hollowness we might see there,
  the emptiness that might be exposed.
Yet until we are ready to be honest,
  both with ourselves and with you,
  true peace and fulfilment will always elude us.
You come still,
  you speak still:
  teach us to make space to listen,
  to understand
  and to respond.

Gracious God,
   teach us this Christmas-time,
      like Mary, to ponder all that you have said and done;
      to listen again to familiar readings and carols,
      to hear again the story we know so well,
      but to consider what it all might mean,
      what you are saying not just to others but also to us.
   In all the celebrations and rejoicing,
      the praise and the worship,
      help us to be still before you,
      so that our lives may be opened to your living Word,
      your renewing love
      and your redeeming power.
   You come still,
      you speak still:
      teach us to make space to listen,
      to understand
      and to respond.

Through Jesus Christ our Lord.
Amen.

21

INTERCESSION
A TIME FOR CHANGE

Lord of all,
    we have heard again the good news of Jesus Christ,
        the glad tidings of his coming,
        and we have rejoiced in the wonder of this season.
    But we pray now for those for whom it brings no joy,
        serving only to remind them of their pain.
    Come again to your world,
        and turn tears into laughter,
        sorrow into gladness.

We pray for the poor, the hungry, the homeless –
    those for whom this Christmas
    will simply be another day in the struggle for survival;
    for those caught up in war, violence and persecution –
    those for whom this Christmas might be their last;
    for the unloved, the lonely, the homeless –
    those for whom Christmas merely heightens their sense of isolation.
Come again to your world,
    and turn tears into laughter,
    sorrow into gladness.

We pray for the anxious, the troubled and the fearful –
    those for whom Christmas will be swamped by worries;
    for the sick, the suffering, the broken in body and mind –
    those for whom this Christmas means only another day of pain;
    and we pray for the bereaved, the divorced, the estranged –
    those for whom Christmas brings home
    the memory of happier times.
Come again to your world,
    and turn tears into laughter,
    sorrow into gladness.

Lord of all,
   you give us a vision through the song of Mary
      of the way the world ought to be
      and one day shall be:
      a world in which you show the strength of your arm
      and scatter the proud,
      in which you bring down the powerful
      and lift up the lowly,
      fill the hungry with good things
      and send the rich away empty;
      a world of justice,
      in which good will triumph,
      evil be ended
      and the meek inherit the earth.
Give us confidence to believe that day can come
     and the resolve to make it happen.
Stir the hearts of your people everywhere
     to work in whatever way possible for change –
     to bring the dawn of your kingdom closer
     and so translate that vision into reality.
Come again to your world,
     and turn tears into laughter,
     sorrow into gladness.

In the name of Christ we ask it.
Amen.

22

INTERCESSION
A TIME FOR GIVING

Gracious God,
  we say that it is more blessed to give than to receive
    but in practice we rarely give any indication of believing that.
  We claim that Christmas is a time for giving as well as receiving,
    but our gifts are usually reserved for family and friends,
    the chosen few.
  Gratefully, we remember today
    that your gift of Christ is so very different –
    good news *for* all,
    the Saviour *of* all,
    given *to* all.
  God of grace, you have given us so much:
    teach us to give in return.

We thank you that you offered yourself freely,
    not for any reward, save that of sharing your love,
    and you gave everything,
    even life itself,
    so that anyone and everyone might come to know your goodness,
    irrespective of creed, colour or culture.
  God of grace, you have given us so much:
    teach us to give in return.

We pray now for your world in all its need –
    those in lands racked by poverty,
    crushed by debt,
    overwhelmed by famine or natural disaster.
  God of grace, you have given us so much:
    teach us to give in return.

We remember those who are persecuted,
    denied justice,
    or falsely imprisoned.
  God of grace, you have given us so much:
    teach us to give in return.

We remember those whose land is torn by hatred,
    scarred by violence,
    broken by war.
God of grace, you have given us so much:
    teach us to give in return.

We remember those afflicted by sickness,
    struggling with disability,
    or crushed by suffering.
God of grace, you have given us so much:
    teach us to give in return.

We remember those overcome by depression,
    bereavement or broken relationships,
    all for whom the present brings trouble
    and the future seems uncertain.
God of grace, you have given us so much:
    teach us to give in return.

Gracious God,
    at this time of giving and receiving
        reach out in love to your aching world.
    Bring comfort in distress,
        courage in adversity,
        confidence in uncertainty
        and compassion in suffering.
    Strengthen all those who work to build a fairer society
        and a more just world,
        and challenge each of us, who have so much
        to share from our plenty with those who have so little.
    May we not just talk in this season about goodwill to all,
        but do something to show what it means.
    God of grace, you have given us so much:
        teach us to give in return.

Through Jesus Christ our Lord.
Amen.

23

BIDDING PRAYER
A TIME FOR US

Gracious God,
  we come to hear the glorious message of this season,
    the glad tidings of great joy,
    ever old,
    ever new.
  We come to recall the faith of Mary,
    the commitment of Joseph,
    the response of shepherds,
    the pilgrimage of wise men,
    their experience of that life-changing day in Bethlehem.
  But it is not just their story this season speaks of;
    it is ours too!
  A Saviour has been born to us which is Christ the Lord:
    thanks be to God!

  You told Joseph that the words of the prophet would be fulfilled:
    that a virgin would conceive and bear a son,
    and that he would be called Emmanuel,
    meaning 'God is with us'.
  It was good news not for one but for all,
    and not simply for then but for now.
  A Saviour has been born to us which is Christ the Lord:
    thanks be to God!

  You proclaimed news of great joy to shepherds out in the fields,
    the glad tidings that in the city of David a Saviour had been born
    who was Christ the Lord,
    the promised Messiah,
    the one so long awaited.
  It was good news not only for them but for all the people,
    not just for *that* day but *every* day.
  A Saviour has been born to us which is Christ the Lord:
    thanks be to God!

You revealed to John the Apostle the meaning of these great events,
    the astonishing truth that you had taken on flesh and blood,
    your light, your word, coming into the world,
    so that all those who receive him,
    who believe in his name,
    can be called your children,
    children born not of blood,
    nor of the will of the flesh,
    but of God.
It was a promise not confined to the past but for the present also,
    not merely for the chosen few but the whole world.
A Saviour has been born to us which is Christ the Lord:
    thanks be to God!

Gracious God,
    we thank you for this time,
        this season which speaks so powerfully of your love,
        which reveals so wonderfully your purpose,
        and which demonstrates so clearly your grace.
    A time for praise,
        a time for joy,
        a time for thanksgiving . . .
        a time for us!
A Saviour has been born to us which is Christ the Lord:
    thanks be to God!

Amen.

24

CLOSING PRAYER
A TIME FOR OTHERS

Gracious God,
  we have heard the good news of this season,
    the glad tidings of the birth of your Son,
    our Saviour, Jesus Christ,
    and we have rejoiced in everything which that means.
  Yet we know that this message is not just for us but for everyone –
    your love for all the world,
    your concern for all people,
    your purpose without limits.
  Help us then to go now with joy in our hearts
    and wonder in our eyes,
    to share the love that you have shown,
    and to make known the great thing that you have done in Christ.
  May Jesus be born again in our hearts
    and made known through our lives.

Through the words we say and the deeds we do,
    the love we share and the compassion we show,
    the faith we proclaim and the people we are,
    may his light shine afresh in the world,
    bringing hope, healing, joy and renewal.
  Grant that all may come to know you for themselves,
    and so celebrate the news of great joy,
    your coming among us in Christ
    to bring us life in all its fullness.
  May Jesus be born again in our hearts
    and made known through our lives.

In his name we go,
    to live and work for him,
    with joyful thanks and grateful praise.
  Amen.

EPIPHANY

25

PRAISE
LIGHT IN OUR DARKNESS

Everlasting God,
    we celebrate your coming to our world in Jesus Christ,
        your light that continues to shine
        in the darkness of our world.

We praise you for the way your love shone
    in so many lives during his ministry;
    through the healing he brought to the sick,
    comfort to the distressed,
    promise to the poor,
    and forgiveness to the lost.
Receive our worship,
    and shine in our lives today.

We praise you for the light
    that has shone in so many lives since,
    the faith you have nurtured in innumerable hearts;
    new beginnings,
    new purpose,
    new life born within them.
Receive our worship,
    and shine in our lives today.

We rejoice that you are at work in our lives here and now,
    inviting us to bring our hopes, fears and concerns
    before you in the knowledge
    that you will always meet our needs,
    no situation beyond your power to transform and redeem.
Receive our worship,
    and shine in our lives today.

We praise you for the assurance that evil will be overcome;
   that hope will replace despair,
   joy come after sorrow,
   and life triumph over death –
   that even the deepest darkness shall be turned to light!
Receive our worship,
   and shine in our lives today.

Fill us now with the light of Christ.
May it illumine our worship and guide our footsteps,
   so that we may live as a lamp for others,
   to the glory of your name.
Receive our worship,
   and shine in our lives today.

In his name we ask it.
Amen.

26

CONFESSION
FOOTSTEPS OF THE WISE MEN

Lord Jesus Christ,
　this is a day which reminds us
　　of the journey of the wise men –
　　their determination to greet you
　　which inspired them to persevere
　　despite difficulties and disappointments along the way.
　Forgive us that we lack their sense of vision,
　　their willingness to undertake a pilgrimage
　　into the unknown
　　in the confidence that you will lead.
　Forgive us if our response to you has lost its initial sparkle,
　　the flame which once burned so brightly within us
　　now grown cold
　　and our hearts no longer stirred
　　by the prospect of one day seeing you face to face.
　Lord, in your mercy,
　　hear our prayer.

This is a day which reminds us
　　of how you led the magi on their journey,
　　your light always with them –
　　a guiding star,
　　a sign of your presence,
　　a call to follow until they came to the place where the child lay.
　Forgive us that we are so often closed to your guidance,
　　unable or unwilling to see your hand,
　　more concerned with our own way than yours,
　　reluctant to commit ourselves to anything
　　when the final goal is not clear.
　Forgive us for talking of faith as a journey
　　but turning it instead into a comfortable destination.
　Lord, in your mercy,
　　hear our prayer.

This is a day which reminds us of the magi's worship –
    their falling to their knees before you,
    their bowing in homage,
    their mood of joy and exultation, wonder and privilege.
Forgive us for losing such feelings –
    for being casual,
    complacent,
    even blasé when we come into your presence,
    taking it all for granted.
Forgive us for offering our worship out of habit or duty,
    outwardly correct but inwardly empty.
Lord, in your mercy,
    hear our prayer.

This is a day which reminds us of the magi's gifts,
    their presents of gold, frankincense and myrrh,
    each one an expression of love,
    a token of esteem,
    a symbol of all you meant to them.
Forgive us that, though we have received so much,
    we give so little,
    our thoughts more for ourselves than for you,
    our offering made out of routine
    rather than as a sacred act of consecration.
Forgive us that we give what we feel we can afford
    rather than what your great love and goodness deserves.
Lord, in your mercy,
    hear our prayer.

Lord Jesus Christ,
    we come to recommit ourselves to the journey of faith,
    to follow where you would lead,
    to bring you our worship
    and to offer ourselves in joyful service.
Receive us in all our weakness
    and go with us on our way,
    that we may live and work for your kingdom.
Lord, in your mercy,
    hear our prayer.

For we ask it in your name.
Amen.

27

INTERCESSION
SEEKING AND FINDING

Lord Jesus Christ,
    you promised that those who seek will find,
        and in the pilgrimage of the magi
        we find proof of that promise.
So now we bring you our prayers for all in our world,
        known and unknown to us,
        who, in different ways, are searching.
May your light shine upon them:
    a beacon of hope and a lamp to their path.

We pray for those who search for meaning,
    their lives empty,
    devoid of purpose,
    hungry for something or someone to put their trust in.
In the bewildering variety of this world's voices,
    each claiming to offer the answer,
    may your love break through
    and the message of the gospel touch their hearts,
    so that they might find in you
    the one who is the Way, the Truth and the Life.
May your light shine upon them:
    a beacon of hope and a lamp to their path.

We pray for those for whom the journey of life is hard,
    beset by pain, sickness and sorrow,
    or overwhelmed by disaster, deprivation and injustice.
In the trials they face and the burdens they struggle with
    may your love break through
    and the message of the gospel bring strength and comfort,
    help, healing and inspiration.
May your light shine in the darkness:
    a beacon of hope and a lamp to their path.

We pray for those unsure of the way ahead,
    faced by difficult choices and vital decisions,
    troubled by situations in which they can see no way forward
    or doubting their ability to cope
    with the demands the future will bring.
In the uncertainties of this ever-changing world,
    may your love break through
    and the message of the gospel bring a new sense of direction,
    an inner peace,
    and the assurance which you alone can give,
    so that, whatever they may face,
    they will know that nothing will ever separate them
    from your love.
May your light shine upon them:
    a beacon of hope and a lamp to their path.

We pray for those who have gone astray –
    betraying their principles,
    or their loved ones,
    or, above all, you.
In this world of so many subtle yet powerful temptations,
    may your love break through
    and the message of the gospel bring new beginnings,
    so that, however low they might have fallen,
    they will know themselves forgiven,
    accepted and restored.
May your light shine in the darkness:
    a beacon of hope and a lamp to their path.

Lord Jesus Christ,
    hear our prayer
        for all who seek purpose, help, guidance and mercy.
    May they find in you the answer to their prayer
        and the end to their searching.

In your name we ask it.
Amen.

LENT

28

ASH WEDNESDAY
THE RIGHTEOUSNESS OF GOD

Living God,
   you have taught us that we should long to know you better,
      not just to want that
      but to urgently, passionately and wholeheartedly yearn for it,
      striving with all our being
      to understand your will and fulfil your purpose.
   Blessed are those who hunger and thirst after righteousness,
   for they shall be filled.

Teach us the secret of such hunger.
Instead of cluttering our lives with so much that can never satisfy,
   teach us to empty ourselves so that we may be filled by you;
   to desire your kingdom,
   seek your will
   and study your word,
   earnestly,
   eagerly,
   expectantly.
Blessed are those who hunger and thirst after righteousness,
   for they shall be filled.

However much we know of your love,
   however richly you may have blessed us,
   teach us to keep that hunger alive,
   to thirst always for a deepening of our faith,
   a strengthening of our service
   and a greater awareness of your purpose.
Blessed are those who hunger and thirst after righteousness,
   for they shall be filled.

Thanks be to God,
   through Jesus Christ our Lord.
Amen.

29

PRAISE
THE WONDER OF GOD

Loving God,
    we praise you for your coming to us in Christ,
        walking our earth and sharing our humanity.
    For the wonder of your love,
        we praise you.

We praise you for the inspiration you give us through him –
    the knowledge that he experienced temptation,
    just as we do,
    yet refused to compromise,
    staying true to his chosen path despite the awful cost.
For the wonder of your love,
    we praise you.

We praise you for the revelation of your purpose in Jesus,
    everything we see of you throughout his earthly ministry.
We remember how he taught the multitude,
    instructed his disciples
    and interpreted the law;
    how he healed the sick,
    responded to the needy
    and cared for the poor;
    how he confronted injustice,
    challenged oppression
    and overcame evil.
For the wonder of your love,
    we praise you.

We praise you
> for the supreme demonstration of your grace at Calvary –
> the fact that you were willing to identify yourself with us
> not only in life but in death,
> enduring the agony of crucifixion,
> and the awful burden of our sinfulness.

For the wonder of your love,
> **we praise you.**

Loving God,
> we come, at this season,
> > to recall your goodness,
> > to marvel at your grace
> > and to commit ourselves to your service.

For the wonder of your love,
> **we praise you.**

Through Jesus Christ our Lord.
Amen.

30

PRAISE
THE ACCEPTANCE OF GOD

Merciful God,
    we remember today how you reached out
        through the ministry of Christ,
        welcoming those whom society had rejected,
        accepting those whom the world considered unacceptable.
    You have time for us, just as we are:
    Lord, we praise you.

We remember how you called Matthew, the tax-collector,
    how you dined with Zacchaeus,
    how you touched the lepers,
    and how you showed mercy to the woman caught in adultery,
    time and again, breaking the mould,
    offering us, through his faithfulness,
    forgiveness and new life.
You have time for us, just as we are:
    Lord, we praise you.

We remember that you forgave rather than condemned,
    built up rather than pulled down,
    encouraged rather than criticised,
    drew near rather than kept your distance.
You have time for us, just as we are:
    Lord, we praise you.

Merciful God,
    we rejoice that you accept us today,
        not for any actions on our part,
        nor through anything we may one day do,
        but simply by your grace.
    You have time for us, just as we are:
    Lord, we praise you.

We rejoice that you value us
    despite our many weaknesses and our repeated faults,
    your nature always to have mercy,
    your grace inexhaustible.
You have time for us, just as we are:
    Lord, we praise you.

Help us to express our worship
    through receiving the love you so freely offer,
    and celebrating your gift of new life.
You have time for us, just as we are:
    Lord, we praise you.

In the name of Christ.
Amen.

31

PRAISE
THE STRENGTH OF GOD

Sovereign God,
   we praise you today
      for the great wonder at the heart of the gospel –
      your sharing our humanity and enduring our weakness.
   You are sovereign over all,
      yet you became our servant.
   You are the holy one of God,
      yet you were tempted just as we are.
   You are the giver of life,
      yet you endured the darkness of death.
   You are the Lord of lords,
      yet you were crowned with thorns.
   You are enthroned on high,
      yet you consented to be brought low.
   In what the world counted weakness
      you displayed true strength.
   Great is your name,
      and greatly to be praised.

We praise you for your love
      that is able to turn human expectations upside down,
      and we rejoice in everything this means for us today –
      that when we are weak, you are strong,
      when we feel most helpless, you are most powerful,
      when we can do little, you can do much.
   Great is your name,
      and greatly to be praised.

We praise you that your way is not one of coercion but of love,
  your power transforming from within,
  never forcing anyone to comply with your wishes
  but graciously inviting a response.
We thank you that, year after year,
  generation after generation,
  you have worked through ordinary flawed individuals like us,
  to make known your love
  and to bring nearer your kingdom.
Great is your name,
  and greatly to be praised.

Sovereign God,
  Servant God,
    we praise you
    that, despite everything which conspires against you,
    everything which frustrates your purpose,
    your will shall finally triumph,
    nothing able to overcome your goodness,
    or to extinguish your love in Christ.
May we live each day in that conviction,
  bringing honour and glory to you.
Great is your name,
  and greatly to be praised.

Amen.

32

Confession
The challenge of God

Gracious God,
  we thank you for the example you have shown to us in Christ,
    the model we see in him of faithful service.
We thank you for the dedication he showed
    throughout his ministry;
    the fact that he was not prepared to cut corners
    or take the easy way out,
    but rather confronted injustice and evil
    head to head and face to face.
You challenge us to stand up for what is right:
  give us the courage to respond.

Forgive us that we so rarely follow his example.
We turn a blind eye to what we know to be wrong,
    even bending the rules ourselves.
We go along with the crowd
    rather than face being thought different.
We close our eyes and ears to what we would rather not think about.
We make excuses for, and seek to justify, our faults.
We give way to temptation,
    promising next time will be different.
We wash our hands of difficult decisions,
    claiming it is none of our business.
You challenge us to stand up for what is right:
  give us the courage to respond.

Gracious God,
>forgive us those times when we have failed to speak up for right,
>>when we have colluded in wrong,
>>and when we have lost sight of both.
>Renew us through your Spirit,
>>restore us through your love,
>>equip us through your power,
>>and so enable us to live faithfully as your people.
>You challenge us to stand up for what is right:
>>**give us the courage to respond.**

Through Jesus Christ our Lord.
Amen.

33

CONFESSION
THE GRACE OF GOD

Loving God,
  once more we have failed you,
    once more we seek your pardon.
  Through your grace,
    have mercy.

Forgive us that, like your people across the ages,
  we are all too human –
  our spirits willing but our flesh weak,
  our intentions good but our living up to them poor,
  our commitment real but our discipleship all too often false.
Through your grace,
  have mercy.

Forgive us that though you speak to us day by day,
  though you challenge us through your word,
  though your voice is there for all ready to hear it,
  repeatedly we have been slow to listen.
Through your grace,
  have mercy.

Forgive us that though you have tried to lead us back to you,
  disciplining us in love,
  gently correcting our mistakes,
  we have wilfully rejected your guidance.
Through your grace,
  have mercy.

Forgive us that though you have always been faithful,
  never letting us down,
  constant in your care,
  we have been unfaithful in so much.
Through your grace,
  have mercy.

Forgive us that though you are worthy of all praise,
   though you and you alone hold the key to life,
   and though each day you draw near to us,
   many times we have not made time for you.
Through your grace,
   have mercy.

Loving God,
   help us to recognise our faults
     and, with your help, to turn from them,
     so that we may be the people you would have us be.
Through your grace,
   have mercy.

In the name of Christ.
Amen.

34

Confession
The pardon of God

Merciful God,
> we have failed you again in so much,
>> in the things we have done
>> and the things we have not done –
>> our faith weak,
>> our discipleship hesitant,
>> our commitment poor –
>> and yet still you accept us.
> For your unfailing pardon,
>> **receive our thanks.**

We have not worshipped you as we should,
> or served you as you desire,
> or obeyed you as you command,
> and yet still you care.
For your unfailing pardon,
> **receive our thanks.**

We have created you in our own image,
> forsaking you for our own interests,
> losing sight of your kingdom,
> and yet still we have a place in your purpose.
For your unfailing pardon,
> **receive our thanks.**

We have not loved you with heart and soul and mind,
> we have not loved our brothers and sisters in Christ,
> we have not loved our neighbours as ourselves,
> and yet still *you love us.*
For your unfailing pardon,
> **receive our thanks.**

We have failed to take up our cross to follow Christ,
 we have denied your Spirit freedom to move within us,
 we have sinned against you and others
 in thought and word and deed,
 and yet still you call us your children.
For your unfailing pardon,
 receive our thanks.

Merciful God,
 forgive us,
  cleanse us,
  restore and renew us.
Assure us once more of your forgiveness,
 for we are truly sorry,
 and send us out in newness of life,
 to live and work to your glory.
For your unfailing pardon,
 receive our thanks.

In the name of Christ.
Amen.

35

THANKSGIVING
THE MERCY OF GOD

Gracious God,
   we thank you that you are a God
      who sees not the outside but the inside,
      a God who is not taken in by external appearances
      but who looks into the inner depths of our heart and soul.

We thank you for the reassurance which that brings,
      the confidence we can have
      that, though we repeatedly disobey you,
      consistently breaking your commandments
      and failing to live as you have called us to,
      still you know that we earnestly desire to be your people,
      that we long to be better disciples of Christ.
For your unfailing mercy,
   receive our thanks.

We thank you that you see not merely the end product
      but the initial intention,
      not just the final results but the desire that precedes it.
But we recognise also the challenge that truth brings,
      for we know that we can never deceive you
      with outward show.
Though our lives may appear blameless,
      our faith strong,
      our works good
      and our words right,
      you and you alone know the reality in our hearts,
      the truth beneath.
For your unfailing mercy,
   receive our thanks.

Gracious God,
    help us not just to lift up our hands but our hearts,
        not just our voices but our souls.
    Fill us with the power of your Spirit
        and the love of Christ,
        so that we may become more like the people
        you would have us be.
    For your unfailing mercy,
        receive our thanks.

In the name of Jesus we pray.
Amen.

36

THANKSGIVING
THE SERVANT OF GOD

Lord Jesus Christ,
    you entered our world,
        taking on our humanity,
        identifying yourself totally with us.
    For your astonishing love,
        we thank you.

You came to lead us out of darkness into your marvellous light,
        to set us free from everything that separates us
        from one another and from you,
        to bring us life in all its fullness.
    For your astonishing love,
        we thank you.

You came as the Word made flesh,
        as King of kings and Lord of lords,
        as the Prince of Peace,
        as the Son of God.
    For your astonishing love,
        we thank you.

And yet you came taking the form of a servant,
        humbling yourself even to death on a cross,
        offering your life for many,
        taking the way of costly sacrifice.
    For your astonishing love,
        we thank you.

You could have served yourself,
        looked to your own glory,
        but you resisted temptation,
        your thoughts only for us.
    For your astonishing love,
        we thank you.

You give us the privilege of sharing in the work of your kingdom,
offering our service in turn,
giving of ourselves without reserve,
putting our own interests second
to the needs of those around us.
For your astonishing love,
we thank you.

Lord Jesus Christ,
teach us to show our gratitude in all we do,
all we say,
all we think
and all we are.
For your astonishing love,
we thank you.

Amen.

37

THANKSGIVING
THE PRESENCE OF GOD

Loving God,
worthy of all praise and honour,
we come to offer our worship,
to be still and know that you are God.
Open our eyes to your presence.

You are all good, all holy,
merciful and loving,
faithful and true.
Open our eyes to your presence.

We lift up our hearts with joy,
our voices in thanksgiving,
our lives in adoration.
Open our eyes to your presence.

We thank you for this season of Lent,
this time which invites us to pause and take stock,
to reflect on the things in life which really matter.
Open our eyes to your presence.

We thank you for this time and place set apart week by week,
these special moments when we focus on you
and remind ourselves of your living presence.
Open our eyes to your presence.

We thank you that you want to speak to us,
teach us,
and deepen our relationship with you.
Open our eyes to your presence.

Help us to use this time to hear your voice,
discern your will,
and experience your love.
Open our eyes to your presence.

Loving God,
   draw us closer to you,
      so that we may return to our homes,
      our daily lives and the world around us
      with renewed hope, vision, strength and faith.
   Open our eyes to your presence.

Through Jesus Christ our Lord.
Amen.

38

PETITION
THE PEACE OF GOD

Gracious God,
    you have promised to all who love you
        a peace that passes understanding.
    Forgive us that we have failed to make that our own.
    Teach us to be still,
        and to know that you are God.

We rush about, our minds preoccupied by many things,
    filling our days with frantic activity,
    cramming ever more into every moment,
    our lives dominated by a sense of the unforgiving minute.
We strive and hanker after that which is finally unimportant,
    unable to satisfy.
We brood and worry over problems that we cannot change,
    magnifying little things out of all proportion.
Teach us to be still,
    and to know that you are God.

Speak to us through the example of Jesus –
    the way he made time for quietness
    so that he could speak with you,
    the need he recognised for space and silence
    in which to seek your guidance
    and to reflect on your will.
Teach us to be still,
    and to know that you are God.

Gracious God,
    forgive us that for all our busyness
        we so often forget the one thing needful,
        the one thing that really matters –
        the knowledge of your love.
    Help us to live each day,
        each moment,
        with that foremost in our minds,
        and so may we find your peace,
        the rest for our souls that you have promised.
    Teach us to be still
        and to know that you are God.

Through Jesus Christ our Lord.
Amen.

39

PETITION
THE LOVE OF GOD

Gracious God,
    we praise you that you are, above all else, a God of love,
        not of judgement, anger or vengeance,
        but of constant and total love.
    You have given your all for us:
        teach us to give freely in turn.

Though we fail you again and again,
    caring more about ourselves than you,
    and more about ourselves than others,
    still you go on loving us,
    fiercely and wholeheartedly.
You have given your all for us:
    teach us to give freely in turn.

Though we turn away from you,
    wilfully rejecting your guidance
    and repeatedly betraying your trust,
    still you long to take us back,
    to restore a living, loving relationship.
You have given your all for us:
    teach us to give freely in turn.

Though our relationship with you is so often one-sided,
    our commitment in such contrast to your faithfulness,
    our response so feeble beside your grace,
    still you go on blessing us,
    your generosity inexhaustible.
You have given your all for us:
    teach us to give freely in turn.

Though we fail to love others,
>divorcing faith from our daily relationships,
>allowing divisions to come between us,
>and forgetful of our responsibilities towards the wider world,
>still you have time for us,
>patiently seeking to deepen our commitment
>and broaden our horizons.
You have given your all for us:
>**teach us to give freely in turn.**

Gracious God,
>help us so to know you that your love flows through us,
>reaching upwards in worship,
>inwards in fellowship
>and outwards in service,
>to the glory of your name.
You have given your all for us:
>**teach us to give freely in turn.**

In the name of Christ.
Amen.

40

PETITION
THE WILL OF GOD

Loving God,
    there are times when our knowledge of your will is flawed,
        when we need the wisdom, humility and courage
        to accept we are wrong.
    Teach us always to be open to that possibility,
        never so full of our own importance
        that we are blind to our weaknesses.
    But there are times too when, like Jesus in the wilderness,
        we have to hold on to what we know is right,
        despite every pressure to the contrary,
        standing firm against popular opinion,
        even when it risks alienating family or friends.
    Help us to know when those times are,
        and teach us to do your will.

Save us from taking the enticing path of compromise,
    the easy path of capitulation,
    or the cowardly path of leaving decisions to someone else.
Give us strength, in the day of testing,
    to be true to ourselves and true to you.
Help us to know when those times are,
    and teach us to do your will.

In the name of Christ.
Amen.

41

INTERCESSION
THE KINGDOM OF GOD

Lord Jesus Christ,
    we pray, week in, week out, that your kingdom will come
        and your will be done.
    It's easy to say the words,
        far harder to mean them,
        for they are concerned finally not just with you but with us.
    Help us to understand that your kingdom is not just in the future,
        but something that begins within us, here and now,
        and so help us to recognise our role in bringing it nearer,
        through the love we show,
        the care we display
        and the service we offer.
    Your kingdom come, your will be done,
        on earth as it is in heaven.

So now we pray for our world
    and for an end to all that frustrates your purpose.
    We think of those in countries racked by conflict,
        famine, disease and poverty;
        of those who face repression and discrimination,
        persecuted for what they believe or for who they are;
        and of those who are victims of crime, violence and war.
    Your kingdom come, your will be done,
        on earth as it is in heaven.

We pray for the unemployed and homeless,
    the sick and suffering,
    the lonely and unloved,
    the disabled and disadvantaged.
    Your kingdom come, your will be done,
        on earth as it is in heaven.

We pray for those who work
   to build a more just and loving world,
   all who strive to bring help and healing to those in need –
   pastors, preachers, missionaries and evangelists,
   doctors, nurses, psychiatrists, counsellors.
Your kingdom come, your will be done,
   on earth as it is in heaven.

We think, too, of aid agencies,
   pressure groups, charities, churches,
   politicians, police and members of the armed forces –
   these and so many others who, in different ways,
   contribute to the fulfilment of your purpose.
Your kingdom come, your will be done,
   on earth as it is in heaven.

Lord Jesus Christ,
   we look forward to that day when you will rule in splendour,
      when you will establish justice between the nations
      and there will be an end to sorrow,
      suffering, darkness and death.
   Until then,
      help us to commit ourselves to your service
      and to work for your glory,
      so that we may honestly say and truly mean:
Your kingdom come, your will be done,
   on earth as it is in heaven.

In your name we pray.
Amen.

42

INTERCESSION
THE PURPOSE OF GOD

Almighty and everlasting God,
   we do not always know what to ask for in our prayers
      for there is so much that we do not know or understand,
      yet we know that you are active in our world,
      moving in human hearts and in the events of history
      to fulfil your purpose.
So we come now to you,
      and, in quiet faith, we place ourselves and our world
      into your hands,
      asking that your will may be done,
      despite everything that conspires against it.
All things are yours:
   we entrust them into your keeping.

We bring ourselves,
      weak, faithless, hesitant, foolish.
We bring all we are and all we long to be,
      seeking your help and your transforming touch.
All things are yours:
   we entrust them into your keeping.

We bring those who are part of our lives –
      family and friends,
      neighbours and colleagues at work,
      all those whom we meet in the daily round of life.
All things are yours:
   we entrust them into your keeping.

We bring our world –
   the rich and poor,
   powerful and weak,
   well-fed and hungry,
   healthy and sick;
   those who enjoy peace and those who endure war,
   those who revel in freedom and those who fight for justice.
All things are yours:
   we entrust them into your keeping.

Almighty and everlasting God,
   we thank you that you are involved in our lives,
      active in our world,
      concerned about everything you have made.
   We rejoice that you hold all things ultimately in your hands.
   And so we leave them confidently with you,
      asking only this:
      'Your will be done,
      your kingdom come,
      on earth as it is in heaven.'
   All things are yours:
      we entrust them into your keeping.

Through Jesus Christ our Lord.
Amen.

43

INTERCESSION
THE FORGIVENESS OF GOD

Merciful God,
  we pray for those who walk through life with a sense of guilt,
    burdened by past mistakes,
    overwhelmed by a sense of failure,
    troubled by feelings of shame,
    depressed by the knowledge of their own weakness.
  Help them to understand that in you
    they can find true forgiveness
    and a new beginning.
  In your mercy,
    hear us.

We pray for those who commit evil
  with no sense of wrong-doing,
  no concept of sin,
  no hint of remorse,
  no sign of scruples.
Help them to glimpse what is right and good,
  and to be touched by the renewing, transforming grace of Christ.
In your mercy,
  hear us.

We pray for those who have been wronged by others;
  hurt,
  deceived,
  betrayed,
  let down.
Help them to be ready to forgive others
  as you have forgiven them.
In your mercy,
  hear us.

We pray for those whose relationships are being tested –
  with family and friends,
  with those at work or in their place of leisure,
  with other Christians,
  even in their own fellowship.
Help them to understand the cause of division between them
  and to work towards the healing of all such rifts,
  forgiving and seeking forgiveness.
In your mercy,
  hear us.

Merciful God,
  help all those who are burdened by past mistakes
    to discover the forgiveness you so freely offer,
    and to show that mercy themselves.
In your mercy,
  hear us.

  Amen.

HOLY WEEK

44

Palm Sunday praise
The King of Glory

Lord Jesus Christ,
    we greet you today as the Word made flesh,
        before all,
        beyond all,
        within all –
        the one in whom all things have their being,
        yet entering our world of space and time,
        sharing our humanity,
        experiencing the joys and sorrows of flesh and blood,
        living and dying among us
        so that we might share in the joy of your kingdom.
Blessed is the king who comes in the name of the Lord!
Hosanna in the highest heaven!

We greet you as the Messiah,
        the Son of David,
        King of Israel –
        Servant of all,
        Saviour of all,
        anointed for burial,
        crowned with thorns
        and lifted high on a cross –
        your kingdom not of this world.
Blessed is the king who comes in the name of the Lord!
Hosanna in the highest heaven!

We greet you as Lord of the empty tomb –
        the risen Christ,
        victorious over death,
        triumphant over evil,
        the one who has gone before us,
        whose Spirit walks with us now,
        and who will be there to greet us at our journey's end –
        Jesus Christ, the pioneer and perfecter of our faith.
Blessed is the king who comes in the name of the Lord!
Hosanna in the highest heaven!

We greet you as the King of kings and Lord of lords,
    the ascended and exalted Lamb of God,
    ruler of the ends of the earth,
    enthroned in splendour,
    seated at the right hand of the Father,
    worthy of all honour and glory and blessing –
    the King of Glory!
Blessed is the king who comes in the name of the Lord!
Hosanna in the highest heaven!

Lord Jesus Christ,
    we greet you today with joyful worship and reverent praise.
    Hear our prayer
        and accept our homage,
        for we offer it in your name and to your glory.

    Amen.

45

PALM SUNDAY CONFESSION
THE KING OF LOVE

Lord Jesus Christ,
    we claim to be your followers,
        and we declare that you are the Lord and King of our lives,
        but all too often our actions deny our words.
    When you look at our lives,
        the weakness of our faith
        and the frailty of our commitment,
        you must grieve over us
        as surely as you wept for Jerusalem long ago.
    You offer us salvation,
        joy, peace and fulfilment,
        yet we so easily let it slip through our fingers.
    King of Love,
        have mercy upon us.

We thank you that your kingdom is not of this world,
        that you rule not as a dictator but as a servant,
        winning the hearts of your people,
        inspiring devotion through who and what you are.
    If you dealt with us as we deserve,
        then our future would be bleak,
        none of us able to stand before you,
        for day after day we break your commandments,
        betraying your love,
        ignoring your guidance,
        our faith fickle,
        our allegiance poor.
    King of Love,
        have mercy upon us.

Forgive us all the ways we fail you,
   through thought, word and deed.
Forgive our limited understanding of your greatness
   and the narrowness of our vision.
Forgive our inability to grasp the values of your kingdom,
   still less to base our lives upon them.
We want to bring honour to you,
   but so often we do the opposite.
King of Love,
   have mercy upon us.

Lord Jesus,
   we come before your throne,
      throwing ourselves upon your grace,
      and asking you to receive our worship,
      despite its weakness;
      to accept our service,
      despite our many faults.
   Rule in our hearts
      and use us for your glory.
   King of Love,
      have mercy upon us.

In your name we ask it.
Amen.

46

PALM SUNDAY PETITION AND INTERCESSION
THE PRINCE OF PEACE

Lord Jesus Christ,
   you came not as a king mighty in battle,
     but as the Prince of Peace,
     the promised deliverer,
     sent to heal and restore our broken world.
   So now we pray for peace and unity between nations.
   Your kingdom come,
     your will be done.

We thank you for signs of hope in the world today –
     for the desire to make this planet a safer place,
     for initiatives that have been taken
     to reduce nuclear and conventional arms,
     for the breaking down of seemingly insurmountable barriers,
     and for a willingness to engage in genuine dialogue
     rather than empty rhetoric.
Prosper all such efforts,
     and grant that a spirit of trust and co-operation
     may develop among all.
   Your kingdom come,
     your will be done.

We pray for those places where tension continues –
     where there is still hatred,
     division,
     violence
     and slaughter.
We pray for all those caught up in the awfulness of war –
     those maimed and injured,
     those who have lost loved ones,
     those for whom life will never be the same again.
Break down the barriers which keep people apart –
     the prejudice and intolerance,

greed and envy,
injustice and exploitation which continue to scar our world.
May your Spirit of love overcome all that causes people
to take up arms against one another.
Your kingdom come,
your will be done.

Lord Jesus Christ,
Prince of Peace,
come again to our world
and bring the unity that you alone can bring.
May the day come when swords shall be beaten into ploughshares,
and spears turned into pruning hooks;
when nation shall not lift sword against nation,
neither learn war any more;
a day when no one will hurt or destroy
on all your holy mountain.
Your kingdom come,
your will be done.

For your name's sake.
Amen.

47

HOLY MONDAY
A DAUNTING PROSPECT

Lord Jesus Christ,
    we will never know just what you felt
        in that week leading up to the cross,
        but what we do know
        is that you were human just as we are,
        experiencing the same emotions that we feel,
        wrestling with the same pressures and temptations.
    And we have little doubt how we would have acted
        had we been in your shoes,
        facing the awful prospect of suffering and death –
        our love of life so great,
        our fear of death so strong.
    Yet though you were tempted like us,
        and though you longed for the cup of suffering
        to be taken from you,
        you stayed true to your calling,
        faithful to the last.
    When we face trials in turn,
        Lord, deliver us from evil.

We marvel at the constancy of your love,
    at the fact that though, from the beginning of your ministry,
    you knew what it would cost you,
    still you continued on your chosen path,
    refusing to be deflected from your purpose.
You could have used your powers for your own ends,
    succumbed to the attraction of popular acclaim
    and worldly glory,
    and had it been us in your place,
    we would probably have done precisely that,
    our yearning for acceptance so great,
    our fear of rejection so strong.
Yet though you were tempted like us,

and though you longed to see your kingdom
established here on earth,
you stayed true to your calling,
faithful to the last.
When we face trials in turn,
Lord, deliver us from evil.

We rejoice that you refused
to compromise your mission in any way,
your thoughts all for others rather than yourself.
While we would have toned down our message,
avoided controversy,
taken the course of least resistance,
you refused even to countenance such an option,
knowing that to do so
would have been to deprive people of your love,
and to dilute the good news you had come to bring.
You healed the sick even on the Sabbath,
you proclaimed forgiveness of sins,
you dined with those deemed the dregs of society,
condemning hypocrisy and corruption,
and overturning the tables of the money-changers in the temple.
We know we would have taken an easier path,
avoiding confrontation wherever possible,
our instinct for self-preservation so great,
our fear of suffering so strong.
Yet though you were tempted like us,
and though you longed for the cup of suffering
to be taken from you,
you stayed true to your calling,
faithful to the last.
When we face trials in turn,
Lord, deliver us from evil.

Lord Jesus Christ,
we rejoice today at the wonder of your love,
and we pray for strength to walk in your footsteps,
firm in our faith and true to our calling.
Hear our prayer,
for your name's sake.
Amen.

48

HOLY TUESDAY
A PAINFUL PROSPECT

Lord Jesus Christ,
  we think of that week leading up to your cross,
    and of the agony you must have gone through
    during that time,
    even before the thorns were pressed on to your head,
    the lash tore into your back
    and the nails pierced your hands and feet.
  For your unquenchable love,
    Lord, we praise you.

You lived with the knowledge that all this was to come –
  the torment of fear,
  of waiting for the inevitable
  and wondering whether you could endure the pain –
  and you did it for us,
  taking the way of the cross
  so that we might discover the way to life.
For your unquenchable love,
  Lord, we praise you.

Yet it wasn't only the burden of fear you wrestled with
  during that week;
  it was equally, and perhaps more,
  the pain of hurt and disappointment,
  for you knew that Judas would soon betray you,
  Peter deny you,
  and your followers melt away into the darkness,
  leaving you to face your fate alone.
You knew that,
  and you knew equally
  that we, in turn, would repeatedly forsake you,
  yet still you carried on,
  your love refusing to be denied.
For your unquenchable love,
  Lord, we praise you.

You died for those who could not keep watch with you
for even one hour;
for people like us,
our spirits willing but our flesh weak;
but you carried on regardless,
taking the way of sacrifice
so that we might be cleansed from our sin
and find forgiveness.
For your unquenchable love,
Lord, we praise you.

Lord Jesus Christ,
receive our worship,
receive our thanks,
receive what we are with all our faults,
and consecrate us to your service,
for your name's sake.
Amen.

49

HOLY WEDNESDAY
A CHALLENGING PROSPECT

Lord Jesus Christ,
   we want to follow you,
      to walk where you would lead
      and travel the road of faithful discipleship,
      but, though that desire is real,
      sometimes the way is hard and the path uncertain,
      such that we wonder if we can see the journey through.
   We look to you for guidance:
      lead us forward in faith.

Despite all our talk of commitment,
   our service is weak and our faith is poor.
We are afraid of the unknown,
   nervous of anything that involves risk
   and the possibility of sacrifice.
We want to be sure of our ground,
   clear as to what is being asked of us.
We look to you for guidance:
   lead us forward in faith.

Like the disciples before us,
   we seek some guarantee it will all be worth it.
Teach us today, through the example you gave,
   to walk by faith and not by sight.
We look to you for guidance:
   lead us forward in faith.

Remind us that our trust is in things unseen,
    that you hold in store for us things too wonderful
    for words ever to express.
Inspire us with the prospect of your eternal kingdom
    in which there will be no more pain or sorrow,
    no more darkness or death,
    but where we will be one with you and all your people
    for all eternity.
We look to you for guidance:
    lead us forward in faith.

Remind us that, for the joy set before you,
    you endured the cross,
    disregarding its shame,
    and that you sit now at the right hand of the throne of God.
Teach us to trust in you, the pioneer and perfecter of our faith,
    and so let us lay aside everything that holds us back
    and run with perseverance the race that is set before us.
We look to you for guidance:
    lead us forward in faith.

For your name's sake.
Amen.

50

MAUNDY THURSDAY PRAISE
BROKEN FOR US

Lord Jesus Christ,
  we celebrate today the astonishing truth
    that lies at the heart of this week –
    the fact that you endured the humiliation of Gethsemane,
    the agony of the cross
    and the darkness of the tomb,
    not because you had to
    but because you chose to.
  You gave your life so that we might live.
  You were broken so that we might be made whole.
  Receive our praise.

We marvel that, from the beginning of your ministry,
    you knew the fate it would lead to,
    the cost involved,
    and yet you continued undeterred,
    despite ridicule, threats and outright hostility,
    your concern always for others rather than yourself.
  You gave your life so that we might live.
  You were broken so that we might be made whole.
  Receive our praise.

We celebrate your awesome commitment,
    your refusal to be deflected from your chosen path.
  You could have courted public acclaim,
    seized earthly power
    or secured personal gain,
    but instead you chose the way of humility,
    service and self-sacrifice,
    the lonely path of the cross.
  You gave your life so that we might live.
  You were broken so that we might be made whole.
  Receive our praise.

We thank you for your faithfulness to the last,
  conscious of how tempting it must have been
  to save yourself instead of us.
You could have taken a road other than towards Jerusalem,
  walked away from Gethsemane,
  stepped down from the cross,
  but you didn't,
  preferring to put your will second to the will of the Father,
  your immediate future second to our eternal destiny.
You gave your life so that we might live.
You were broken so that we might be made whole.
Receive our praise.

Lord Jesus Christ,
  however often we hear it, we never fail to be amazed
  by the magnitude of your love
  and the awesomeness of your sacrifice.
We deserve so little, yet you gave so much.
We serve you so poorly, yet your grace is so rich.
So we come in thanksgiving and celebration
  to offer you our heartfelt worship,
  and to commit ourselves again to your service.
You gave your life so that we might live.
You were broken so that we might be made whole.
Receive our praise.

For your name's sake.
Amen.

51

MAUNDY THURSDAY CONFESSION
BROKEN BY US

Lord Jesus Christ,
 we are happy to remember that you were broken *for* us,
  less willing to acknowledge that you were broken *by* us;
  yet that is the inescapable truth.
 You took on *our* punishment,
  suffered for *our* sin,
  paid the price for *our* mistakes,
  so that we might receive mercy and discover new life.
 For all the ways we continue to break your body,
  gracious Saviour, forgive us.

You call us to break bread and share wine
 in remembrance of you,
 but, though outwardly we obey,
 inwardly it is a different story,
 our lack of love,
 timid witness,
 stunted vision
 and half-hearted commitment,
 each revealing our forgetfulness of your love.
 For all the ways we continue to break your body,
  gracious Saviour, forgive us.

You call us to live as your people,
 a family testifying to your grace
 through the love we show for one another
 and the unity we share,
 but all too often we demonstrate division,
 mistrust,
 intolerance,
 even hatred.
 For all the ways we continue to break your body,
  gracious Saviour, forgive us.

You call us to minister in your name,
    to express your care for all through word and deed,
    but day after day we let you down.
Through the compassion we fail to show,
    the love we fail to express
    and the justice we fail to fight for;
    through the hungry we fail to feed,
    the sick we fail to visit
    and the needy we fail to clothe;
    through the truths we distort,
    the hurt we cause
    and the selfishness we indulge in,
    we inflict more pain upon you,
    driving the nails once more through your hands and feet,
    hanging you once again upon your cross.
For all the ways we continue to break your body,
    gracious Saviour, forgive us.

Lord Jesus Christ,
    broken *for* us,
        broken *by* us,
        you owe us nothing,
        we owe you everything,
        for you gave your all to set us free,
        and yet still we fail you,
        time after time,
        day after day.
For all the ways we continue to break your body,
    gracious Saviour, forgive us.

Cleanse us,
    renew us
    and restore us
    for your name's sake.
Amen.

52

MAUNDY THURSDAY INTERCESSION
BROKEN FOR ALL

Lord Jesus Christ,
 we remember today that you were broken not only for us,
  or even for many,
  but for all.
 We rejoice that your love isn't for the select few but for everyone –
  young and old,
  rich and poor,
  male and female,
  black and white.
 So then we pray for our world in all its need.
 May your grace bring hope;
  may your love bring healing.

We pray for all who feel broken today –
 shattered by disappointment, tragedy and bereavement;
 overwhelmed by poverty and hunger, disease and deprivation,
 crushed by injustice, oppression, imprisonment and violence –
 all those who have been broken in body, mind and spirit,
 battered by the circumstances and events of life.
May your grace bring hope;
 may your love bring healing.

We pray for those who long for wholeness –
 delivery from physical pain, sickness and disease,
 freedom from fear, anxiety and depression,
 an answer to inner emptiness and spiritual longing,
 the opportunity to be at peace with you, their neighbour
 and themselves.
May your grace bring hope;
 may your love bring healing.

Lord Jesus Christ,
   broken for all,
      reach out now to our broken world
      and teach us to reach out in turn.
   Show us where you would have us serve,
      teach us what you would have us do,
      and use us to fulfil your purposes.
   May your grace bring hope;
      may your love bring healing.

To the glory of your name.
Amen.

53

GOOD FRIDAY ACT OF WITNESS
BENEATH THE CROSS OF JESUS

Loving God,
    we gather around this cross in the name of Christ,
        thanking you again for its astonishing message,
        its power to speak and challenge in so many ways.

    We rejoice in the love it represents,
        the sacrifice so freely offered on our behalf,
        so that we might experience life in all its fullness.

    We celebrate the forgiveness it proclaims,
        an end to all that has gone before
        and a new beginning, the slate wiped clean.

    We praise you for the freedom it brings,
        liberation from everything that destroys love,
        devalues life and denies the future.

    May it be a sign of the faith we share,
        a simple witness to Christ reaching out into this community,
        and a challenge to all to consider his call
        and respond to his love.

Loving God,
    give us courage to take up our cross in turn,
        and to walk the way of Christ.
    May our lives speak of him,
        even as this cross speaks so clearly of you.
    In his name we pray.
    Amen.

54

GOOD FRIDAY PRAISE
A MAN LIKE US

Gracious God,
    we praise you for the astonishing love we recall today,
        the love you showed to all humankind
        through your coming, living and dying among us in Christ.
    We thank you for being willing to endure so much for our sakes –
        to face the mental agony,
        the physical torture
        and the spiritual torment involved in the cross.
    But, above all, we praise you that you did that
        through a person as human as we are,
        experiencing the same temptations,
        torn by the same fears,
        sharing the same joys and sorrows,
        suffering the same pain.
    You became one with us:
        may we become one with you.

We thank you for the assurance this brings –
    the knowledge that you understand
    the trials and tribulations we go through;
    the worries, concerns, doubts and problems
    which confront us each day.
We thank you for the inspiration this brings –
    the example in Christ of humanity at its most selfless,
    courageous,
    compassionate
    and loving.
We thank you for the challenge this brings –
    the call to follow in his footsteps,
    to take up our cross,
    to deny ourselves
    and to offer our service.
You became one with us:
    may we become one with you.

You could have disassociated yourself from our sinfulness,
   yet you identified with us fully.
You could have demanded we pay the price for our folly,
   but you chose rather to pay it yourself.
You could have lectured us about the importance of love,
   but instead you demonstrated what love really means.
You experienced humanity at its worst
   and revealed it at its best,
   opening up a new dimension of life
   for all who will receive you.
You became one with us:
   may we become one with you.

Gracious God,
   you became human,
      flesh and blood like us.
   Accept our praise
      and receive our thanksgiving,
      through Jesus Christ our Lord,
   Amen.

55

GOOD FRIDAY CONFESSION
A MAN OF SORROWS

Lord Jesus Christ,
  you know what it is to feel sorrow,
    for you endured some of the deepest hurt
    anyone could ever face.
  You were betrayed by one of your chosen followers,
    denied by another who you counted as the closest of friends,
    abandoned by those who had followed you
    throughout your ministry,
    and yet still you were willing to give everything for them,
    even life itself.
  For all the ways we add to your sorrow,
    Lord, have mercy.

Forgive us that we prolong your grief each day,
    betraying our convictions,
    denying our faith through the way we live,
    abandoning your way and rejecting your love.
  We are weak and faithless,
    proud, greedy, selfish,
    careless in discipleship
    and poor in our commitment.
  For all the ways we add to your sorrow,
    Lord, have mercy.

You brought life to the world,
    hope, love and light,
    but you endured the heartbreak of seeing it all rejected,
    the world turning its back on your grace
    and spurning your goodness.
  Forgive us that sometimes we do the same,
    keeping you at arm's length,
    resisting your guidance,
    even while we believe we are serving you.
  For all the ways we add to your sorrow,
    Lord, have mercy.

Lord Jesus Christ,
  you endured pain and humiliation,
    an inner turmoil beyond words,
    and you faced that for *us* as much as anyone.
  You were wounded for *our* transgressions,
    crushed for *our* iniquities.
  You bore the punishment which made *us* whole,
    and by *your* bruises *we* are healed.
  We thank you for the awesomeness of your grace,
    and we acknowledge with shame the poverty of our response.
  Forgive us our failure to honour you as you deserve,
    our inability to love as you have loved us.
  For all the ways we add to your sorrow,
    Lord, have mercy.

Hear us,
    cleanse us
    and renew us,
    for in your name we pray.
  Amen.

56

GOOD FRIDAY THANKSGIVING
A MAN APART

Lord Jesus Christ,
    we thank you again today for the wonder of your grace
        and the awesomeness of your sacrifice.
    Though you were human just as we are,
        experiencing the same feelings and sensations as we do,
        you were unlike anyone has been before or since,
        unparalleled in the extent of your love,
        matchless in your selflessness –
        truly, a man apart.
    For your willingness to give and go on giving,
        Lord, we thank you.

You could have served yourself,
    secured wealth, influence, personal glory,
    anything you cared to name.
You could have saved yourself,
    avoided the heartache of Gethsemane,
    the agony of the cross,
    no power able to hold you.
But you didn't,
    resolved instead to stay true to your calling –
    truly, a man apart.
For your willingness to give and go on giving,
    Lord, we thank you.

You chose to suffer and die
    so that we might be set free
    from everything that holds us captive.
You freely surrendered all
    so that we might inherit life
    and enter into the joy of your kingdom.
You made yourself as nothing
    so that we might receive everything –
    truly, you are a man apart.
For your willingness to give and go on giving,
    Lord, we thank you.

Lord Jesus Christ,
    there is no one like you,
        no one to whom you can be compared,
        your greatness beyond measure,
        your love beyond words.
    In you we see human life as it has never been seen elsewhere,
        yet we glimpse also what life could and should be for all.
    Inspire us through your example,
        renew us through your grace,
        and refashion us through your Spirit,
        so that we may reflect a little of your goodness
        and live to your glory.
    Come to us now and help us to be a little more like you –
        truly, a man apart.
    For your willingness to give and go on giving,
        Lord, we thank you.

    Amen.

57

GOOD FRIDAY INTERCESSION
A MAN FOR OTHERS

Lord Jesus Christ,
  we remember today
    how your concern throughout your ministry
    was not for yourself but for others –
    the vulnerable,
    the distressed,
    the sick,
    the despised;
    all those who were marginalised in society –
    downtrodden,
    oppressed,
    rejected.
  You came as the man for others:
    come again to our world today.

We remember how you had a special place in your heart
    for the poor,
    and so we pray for the millions suffering still
    under the yoke of poverty
    with all the attendant misery that involves –
    victims of failed harvests, natural disasters and civil wars,
    crying to us for help,
    begging for food to stave their hunger,
    homes to house their children,
    resources to build a better future,
    an opportunity to start again
    free from the shackles of debt.
  You came as the man for others:
    come again to our world today.

We remember how you suffered at the hands of others,
    and so we pray for all who endure violence and cruelty,
    all who are wounded in body, mind and spirit
    by acts of inhumanity.
We pray for victims of racism and discrimination,
    of verbal and physical bullying,
    of assault and abuse,
    intimidation and torture,
    terrorism and war.
You came as the man for others:
    come again to our world today.

Lord Jesus Christ,
    you lived for others,
        you died for others
        and you rose for all.
Help us to live in turn as your people,
    seeking to serve rather than be served,
    to give rather than to receive.
Teach us to reach out in love
    and so to make real your compassion
    and represent your body here on earth.
You came as the man for others:
    come again to our world today.

We ask it in your name.
Amen.

EASTER

58

PRAISE
LIFE FROM DEATH

Lord Jesus Christ,
  it seemed like the end of everything –
    the hope you had brought gone for ever –
    for you were dead,
    laid in a tomb,
    a stone sealing the entrance.
  Your followers had watched you suffer,
    heard you draw your last breath,
    watched as a spear was thrust into your side
    and sobbed as your body was taken down from the cross,
    limp and lifeless.
  It was over,
    finished,
    no possibility of change.
  Except suddenly the stone was rolled away,
    the tomb was empty,
    you were there speaking words of peace,
    you were alive!
  Risen Lord,
    lead us from death to life.

  For us, too, death can seem the end of everything –
    the end of all our hopes,
    all our striving,
    all our dreams;
    the last enemy which one day each of us must face,
    no matter who we are or what we do.
  Risen Lord,
    lead us from death to life.

  For many the death of someone close to them
    seems the end of everything –
    the joy they had known,

the love they shared,
the life they had built together,
all lost for ever.
The present seems devoid of meaning,
the future empty of hope,
while the past serves only to remind them of their pain.
Risen Lord,
lead us from death to life.

We praise you, that despite appearances,
death is not the end of everything –
for the victory you won was not just for you but for all,
the enemy defeated,
the grave conquered,
the future assured.
You are the resurrection and the life,
the one who leads us not just now but throughout eternity,
nothing in heaven or earth,
in this world or the next,
able to separate us from your constant love.
Risen Lord,
lead us from death to life.

Lord Jesus Christ,
we praise you for the message of Easter,
the assurance that life is not in vain,
that love is not blotted out,
that faith is not futile.
We praise you that death is not the end but a new beginning,
a gateway to heaven,
a door on to untold blessings you hold in store for us.
Receive the worship we offer you this day,
and teach us to live each day
in the light of your Easter triumph.
Risen Lord,
lead us from death to life.

For your name's sake.
Amen.

59

PRAISE
GOOD FROM EVIL

Lord Jesus Christ,
  when you were taken before Herod and Pilate,
    when you suffered in agony on the cross,
    and when your body was sealed in a tomb,
    it looked as though evil had triumphed,
    as though love, goodness and truth had finally been defeated.
  But you rose again,
    love triumphant,
    goodness vindicated,
    truth victorious.
  Living Lord,
    to you be the praise and glory.

Your enemies had done their worst,
    mocking you,
    beating you,
    nailing you to a cross,
    and for three days it seemed that hatred, deceit and violence
    had won the battle.
  But you rose again,
    renewing,
    restoring,
    redeeming.
  Living Lord,
    to you be the praise and glory.

It looked as though hope was groundless,
    faith futile,
    the future empty,
    for your purpose appeared to be destroyed,
    broken beyond redemption.
But you rose again,
    reviving confidence,
    rekindling trust,
    recreating life itself.
Living Lord,
    to you be the praise and glory.

Your friends had failed you when you needed them most –
    betraying you,
    denying you,
    abandoning you,
    and they were consumed by guilt and shame.
But you rose again,
    forgiving,
    accepting,
    affirming.
Living Lord,
    to you be the praise and glory.

Lord Jesus Christ,
    it's hard sometimes not to question,
        not to be perplexed at life's injustices
        and ask if your kingdom can ever truly come.
But you rose again,
    light in our darkness,
    faith in our confusion,
    heaven touching earth.
Living Lord,
    to you be the praise and glory.

For your name's sake.
Amen.

60

PRAISE
STRENGTH FROM WEAKNESS

Lord Jesus Christ,
   we are reminded today
      of how your followers must have felt as Easter dawned –
      women walking sadly to the tomb,
      disciples trudging wearily home along the Emmaus Road,
      Apostles gathered together behind locked doors –
      all of them, to a man or woman, devastated,
      stunned by what had taken place,
      overwhelmed by sorrow and confusion.
   Gracious Lord, sovereign yet servant,
      in weakness you are our strength:
      receive our Easter praise.

We recall how they had looked forward
      to the coming of your kingdom,
      convinced that the day was near,
      refusing to believe, despite your warnings,
      that any harm could befall the Messiah.
We think of their sense of helplessness
      as they saw you taken before Pilate,
      whipped and ridiculed,
      nailed to a cross,
      laid in a tomb.
It looked as though you were powerless to resist,
      as though faith in you had been misguided and trust misplaced,
      for instead of glory they saw only humiliation,
      instead of a crown of victory, a crown of thorns.
Gracious Lord, sovereign yet servant,
      in weakness you are our strength:
      receive our Easter praise.

We praise you that at the empty tomb,
 on the Emmaus Road
 and in that room locked against the world
 you demonstrated that you were not defeated but victorious,
 your purpose not destroyed but gloriously fulfilled.
The events of Good Friday were seen for what they were:
 not a hideous mistake or an unseen catastrophe
 but an integral part of your sovereign plan,
 the ultimate expression of your love
 through which you brought life to all.
Gracious Lord, sovereign yet servant,
 in weakness you are our strength:
 receive our Easter praise.

We recall then, finally, how your followers must have felt
 on the day of resurrection –
 women running back to tell the news,
 disciples returning from Emmaus rejoicing,
 Apostles gazing in wonder as you stood there among them.
We recall how tears of sorrow turned to tears of joy,
 how eyes closed to the truth were opened
 at the breaking of bread,
 how minds clouded by doubt were illuminated by faith.
New purpose, new confidence, new faith
 emerged in lives which had seemed broken;
 your triumph was complete.
Gracious Lord, sovereign yet servant,
 in weakness you are our strength:
 receive our Easter praise.

Lord Jesus Christ,
 crucified yet risen,
  servant of all yet King of kings and Lord of lords,
  hear our prayer
  for your name's sake.
 Amen.

61

CONFESSION
COMMITMENT FROM DENIAL

Lord Jesus Christ,
   we marvel today at the extent of your love
     and the wonder of your grace.
You were betrayed, denied and abandoned,
   yet still, willingly, you went to your death,
   offering your life for the life of the world.
And, after you rose again,
   you appeared first to those who had forsaken you,
   reaching out your hands in acceptance,
   speaking your word of peace.
Time and again we fail you.
Lord, have mercy.
Time and again you welcome us back.
Teach us to walk in faith.

We know that our faith is no better than that of those first disciples,
   our courage no stronger,
   our commitment no more able to withstand adversity.
All too often we betray you through the way we live,
   we deny you through the things we say and do,
   we abandon you,
   preferring the easy and undemanding road
   rather than the way of the cross.
Time and again we fail you.
Lord, have mercy.
Time and again you welcome us back.
Teach us to walk in faith.

Thank you for being ready to forgive and forget,
    to offer us the opportunity to make amends.
You understand our weakness
    and, through your grace,
    you do not simply invite us to start again,
    you give us help and strength to follow you more closely.
When we fall, you pick us up,
    when we lose our way, you show us the way forward.
Always you are there to restore and renew.
Time and again we fail you.
Lord, have mercy.
Time and again you welcome us back.
Teach us to walk in faith.

Lord Jesus Christ,
    we are not worthy to bear your name,
        for we fail you so often in so many ways.
But we come in all our sinfulness,
        confessing our failure,
        acknowledging our faults
        and throwing ourselves once more upon your great mercy.
Above all, we come committing ourselves afresh to your service,
        resolved to live more faithfully as your people,
        to stay true to you as you stay true to us.
Time and again we fail you.
Lord, have mercy.
Time and again you welcome us back.
Teach us to walk in faith.

We ask it for your name's sake.
Amen.

62

CONFESSION
LIGHT FROM DARKNESS

Lord Jesus Christ,
    you call us to walk in the light,
        yet so often we walk instead in darkness.

We know that we should love one another –
    that we should put the needs of others before our own,
    denying ourselves in order to give service –
    but the pull of self-interest is hard to resist.
We know that we should put aside everything
    that destroys relationships –
    everything that comes between us and our neighbour,
    that comes between us and you –
    but old habits are hard to overcome.
We know that we should put faith into action –
    not just talking about love
    but expressing it through deeds,
    not just speaking of your kingdom
    but striving to bring it closer –
    yet so often we fail to practise what we preach.
Instead of shining as a lamp set on a hill
    we hide our light under a bushel.
Light of the world,
    dispel our darkness.

Forgive us those times we have spread darkness rather than light –
   the words that have wounded,
   sown discontent,
   cast judgement
   or spoken falsely;
   the deeds that have caused bitterness,
   created trouble,
   denied love
   or abandoned responsibility.
Forgive everything in our lives which undermines your purpose
   and betrays our calling.
Light of the world,
   dispel our darkness.

We have no claim on your goodness,
   no grounds to ask for mercy,
   and yet we know that you took upon yourself
   the burden of human sinfulness,
   enduring the awfulness of death,
   and you rose again,
   opening the way to life for all,
   nothing finally able to extinguish your light.
We rejoice that, on the day of resurrection,
   a new kingdom dawned,
   a kingdom in which one day there will be no more night,
   nor need of any sunshine,
   for your light will illuminate all.
Shine in our hearts now, we pray,
   and may the brightness of your presence flood our souls.
Light of the world,
   dispel our darkness.

We ask it for your name's sake.
Amen.

63

CONFESSION
TRUTH FROM FALSEHOOD

Lord Jesus Christ,
  you promised that we will know the truth
    and the truth will set us free.
We thank you that we have experienced
    something of the reality of that promise
    through our experience of your love and goodness,
    your light shining in our hearts,
    but we confess that we do not always find truth easy,
    there being a part of us that prefers falsehood,
    hiding behind untruth or half-truths.
We deceive ourselves,
  we deceive others,
    so many facts hard to face and harder still to accept.
Forgive all that is false in our lives
  and lead us into truth.

We are not alone in our folly,
    for across history it has been the same story.
Your enemies brought false witnesses
    to testify against you at your trial,
    and, even after your resurrection,
    the authorities bribed the guards at the tomb
    to lie about what had happened,
    intent on suppressing a truth they could not live with.
But we rejoice in the fact that the truth triumphed despite this,
    even Pilate declaring you innocent before your accusers,
    and we give thanks that the good news of the resurrection
    continues to be preached across the world to this day,
    an eloquent testimony to its life-changing power.
Forgive all that is false in our lives
  and lead us into truth.

We do not presume to judge others
  for we know we are as guilty as any.
We have known the right way to take and opted for the wrong,
  we have understood good and chosen evil,
  we have glimpsed light and walked in darkness.
When honesty has involved sacrifice,
  when integrity has entailed cost,
  we have at best been economical with the truth,
  and at times ignored it completely.
Forgive all that is false in our lives
  and lead us into truth.

Lord Jesus Christ,
  you are the Way, the Truth and the Life;
    you set us free from the need for pretence,
    for you accept us as we are,
    and you give us strength to stand up for what is right.
Teach us to open our lives to you,
  and to know the truth.
May we receive it with joy,
  speak it in love
  and live by it in faith.
Forgive all that is false in our lives
  and lead us into truth.

For your name's sake.
Amen.

64

THANKSGIVING
NEW FROM OLD

Lord Jesus Christ,
   this is a season of new beginnings –
      not just your glorious resurrection from the dead,
      but the resurrection of broken dreams,
      crushed hopes,
      shattered faith –
      and we praise you for it.
Yet it's hard sometimes
      to believe such new beginnings can apply to us,
      that we too can start again.
We look at our own situations –
      the problems which refuse to go away,
      the mistakes we go on making –
      and we see little prospect of change,
      no reason to believe life can be different.
But you have promised that we shall be born again,
      that anyone who trusts in you will become a new creation;
      renewed, remade, refreshed through your grace.
Risen Saviour, conqueror of sin and death,
      raise us to newness of life.

Help us to remember that, for your followers,
      there seemed no reason to hope.
They had seen you die,
      and they each knew that, in their own way,
      they had brought you to it,
      not so much through their forsaking you in your time of need
      as in the human weakness and sin which that represented –
      the self-interest,
      the lack of commitment,
      the willingness to compromise that is so characteristic of us all.
They were racked by remorse,
      tortured by guilt,
      all too aware of the limitations of their faith.

Yet you came to them,
    risen and victorious,
    but the same Jesus who had suffered and died,
    and to those same disciples who had failed you so miserably
    you brought new power,
    new purpose.
Risen Saviour, conqueror of sin and death,
    raise us to newness of life.

Teach us, however often we might fail,
    never to lose sight of that truth.
Save us from losing our sense of all that you are able to do,
    from growing disheartened,
    disenchanted,
    disillusioned,
    resigned to treading the same old ground
    rather than stepping out into new avenues of faith.
However much it may feel we are getting nowhere,
    however often we may find ourselves
    at what seems like a dead end,
    keep us open to the journey of discovery you hold before us,
    and give us faith to walk with you,
    wherever you would lead us,
    confident of your transforming power in our lives.
Risen Saviour, conqueror of sin and death,
    raise us to newness of life.

Lord Jesus Christ,
    this is a time of new beginnings,
    a fresh start,
    a day in which we celebrate the promise of resurrection for all,
    your gift of new life from old,
    and we praise you for it.
Risen Saviour, conqueror of sin and death,
    raise us to newness of life.

Hear our prayer,
    for we offer it in your name.
Amen.

65

THANKSGIVING
FAITH FROM DOUBT

Lord Jesus Christ,
    we thank you again today for the great miracle of Easter
        and for everything it reveals about your awesome love.

We remember how women came to the tomb,
    intending to anoint your body,
    wondering who would roll the stone away;
    only to find the tomb empty,
    your body gone,
    good news there to greet them!
It is still good news for today!
Lord, we thank you.

We remember how the disciples refused to believe,
    dismissing the women's words as nonsense,
    an idle tale,
    a foolish fantasy;
    only suddenly you were there,
    standing among them,
    speaking your word:
    'Do not be afraid.'
It is still good news for today!
Lord, we thank you.

We remember how Mary stood weeping in the garden,
    confused,
    shaken,
    beside herself with grief,
    even mistaking you for a gardener;
    only then you spoke:
    'Mary',
    and tears gave way to laughter.
It is still good news for today!
Lord, we thank you.

We remember how two weary followers
   were walking on the Emmaus Road,
   dismayed,
   disappointed,
   disillusioned,
   their hope that you might be the Messiah in tatters,
   their dreams crushed;
   only, all at once, you were with them,
   and, as you broke bread,
   their eyes were opened so that they realised it was you,
   Christ crucified but risen.
It is still good news for today!
Lord, we thank you.

We remember how Thomas doubted, despite everything,
   adamant he could not accept your resurrection
   until he'd seen you for himself,
   until he'd put his hands in your wounds
   and met you face to face;
   only, once again, you were there,
   speaking the words he longed to hear:
   'Put your finger here and see my hands.
   Reach out and touch' –
   and after doubt there was faith.
It is still good news for today!
Lord, we thank you.

Lord Jesus Christ,
   we remember today how,
   though all questioned,
   all struggled to accept the glorious truth,
   still you came,
   restoring hope to hearts dulled by despair,
   joy to lives bowed down by sorrow.
It is still good news for today!
Lord, we thank you.

Amen.

66

THANKSGIVING
TRIUMPH FROM TRAGEDY

Lord Jesus Christ,
   we thank you for the great message of Easter –
      your awesome triumph over the forces of darkness
      and the power of evil.
We thank you that, in what the world counted defeat,
      you won the greatest of victories;
      that what looked to be a disaster
      proved to be the most glorious of conquests.
In the valley of sorrow and suffering,
      in the shadow of death,
      you have demonstrated that God is present,
      working out his eternal purpose.
For that glorious truth, we thank you.

We thank you that women arriving at the tomb
      found their tears turned to laughter,
      that disciples on the Emmaus Road
      found confusion turned to faith,
      that Apostles trembling behind locked doors
      found despair turned to confidence,
      that your people across the centuries
      have found sorrow turned to joy.
Time and again you have repeated the Easter miracle,
      supremely demonstrating your purpose
      in the face of events which seem to contradict it.
In the valley of sorrow and suffering,
      in the shadow of death,
      you have demonstrated that God is present,
      working out his eternal purpose.
For that glorious truth, we thank you.

We thank you for our own experiences of your resurrection power –
   occasions when we have cried out
   from the depths of our beings,
   called to you from the pit of despair,
   and discovered not only that you can lift us out,
   but that you were there with us in our need,
   holding our heads above the water,
   and using our experience of adversity
   to deepen our faith and broaden our understanding.
In the valley of sorrow and suffering,
   in the shadow of death,
   you have demonstrated that God is present,
   working out his eternal purpose.
For that glorious truth, we thank you.

We thank you for the assurance that nothing in heaven or earth
   can separate us from your love,
   that no situation, however dreadful it may seem,
   is finally beyond your power to redeem,
   and we rejoice that you hold a kingdom in store for us
   where all this world's trials and tragedies will be no more;
   where we shall dwell for ever in the light of your presence.
Take, then, the changes and chances of this life,
   and help us, whatever we may face,
   to trust that your purpose will triumph over all.
In the valley of sorrow and suffering,
   in the shadow of death,
   you have demonstrated that God is present,
   working out his eternal purpose.
For that glorious truth, we thank you.

Amen.

67

PETITION
CONFIDENCE FROM CONFUSION

Lord Jesus Christ,
  it is hard to believe in you sometimes –
    hard to believe in the message you preached,
    the victory of love you proclaimed,
    the way of sacrifice and self-denial you urged us to follow.
  There is so much in life which challenges our faith,
    speaking instead of the way of self,
    of greed and avarice,
    of evil, injustice and exploitation.
  Yet you rose again from the tomb,
    triumphant over the darkness.
  Your love could not be defeated:
    may that truth turn our doubt to faith.

We look at the course of human history,
    and time after time it is the same –
    a catalogue of hatred, violence, evil and oppression;
    a world in which the strongest survive,
    the wicked prosper
    and the innocent are led like lambs to the slaughter.
  Yet you rose again from the tomb,
    triumphant over the darkness.
  Your love could not be defeated:
    may that truth turn our doubt to faith.

We look at the world today,
    and still it is the same story –
    nations racked by division and war,
    an economic order in which the few indulge their every craving
    while the many are deprived of even their most basic needs;
    an international system in which money outweighs principle;
    a world of drugs, rape, vandalism, child abuse;
    all this and so much more which scars the face of society.

Yet you rose again from the tomb,
   triumphant over the darkness.
Your love could not be defeated:
   may that truth turn our doubt to faith.

Give us new heart today through the message of Easter.
Help us to remember
   that your death made no sense to your followers,
   that violence appeared to be triumphant,
   goodness crushed
   and evil victorious;
   everything they had lived for seemingly sealed in the tomb,
   and faith replaced by confusion.
Yet remind us, too, that you rose again,
   and at your coming the clouds were lifted,
   the darkness was dispelled
   and faith began to shoot again.
Your love could not be defeated:
   may that truth turn our doubt to faith.

Lord Jesus Christ,
   it's hard to believe in you sometimes,
      for there are no easy answers to the harsh realities of life,
      no glib explanations as to why suffering is allowed to continue,
      evil go unchecked and good be unrewarded.
   But you have shown us through your resurrection
      that, whatever it may face,
      love will not finally be extinguished,
      and your purpose cannot be denied.
   One day your will shall be done and your kingdom come.
   Your love could not be defeated:
      may that truth turn our doubt to faith.

We ask it in your name.
Amen.

68

PETITION
PEACE FROM TURMOIL

Lord Jesus Christ,
   there are times when life seems a mystery,
      when we can make no sense of anything,
      not even our faith,
      when the events of life confuse and trouble us
      so that our minds are in turmoil
      and our confidence is destroyed.
   Help us to know you are with us at such times.
   Speak again your word of peace,
      and may our souls find rest.

Remind us of the experience of your followers
      on that first Easter day –
      how you came to them in their confusion –
      each still reeling from the shock of your death,
      struggling to come to terms with the suffering you had endured,
      and the apparent triumph of evil over goodness –
      and how you restored their faith,
      rekindling their joy,
      reviving their vision
      and renewing their commitment.
   Speak again your word of peace,
      and may our souls find rest.

We thank you for your promise to be with us always,
      to the end of the age,
      and we rejoice that we experience the fulfilment of those words
      through the living presence of the Holy Spirit.
   Whatever storms may confront us,
      whatever trials we may face,
      we know that you will always be there,
      meeting us in our confusion to quieten our hearts.
   Speak again your word of peace,
      and may our souls find rest.

We thank you that the day will come
   when your victory will be complete
   and your will accomplished –
   a day when the puzzles that confound us will be resolved,
   when the forces that conspire against your kingdom
   will be overcome
   and when harmony will be established among the nations –
   a day when you will speak your word to all.
Speak again your word of peace,
   and may our souls find rest.

Lord Jesus Christ,
   meet with us when life is hard and our faith is weak,
      and grant the assurance that, despite appearances,
      your purpose continues unchanged,
      your strength remains undiminished
      and your love is indestructible.
Speak again your word of peace,
   and may our souls find rest.

We ask it in your name.
Amen.

69

Petition and intercession
Beginnings from endings

Lord Jesus Christ,
  we remember today how you rose again,
    bringing new beginnings out of what had seemed the end,
    a new chapter in the life of your Church
    which is still being written today.
We recall how your resurrection changed life for the disciples,
    calling them to let go of the past and embrace the future –
    their role no longer simply to follow but to lead,
    to go out in your risen power and proclaim the good news.
We know that life must change for us too,
    but sometimes it is harder than we first anticipated,
    moving on a painful business,
    asking more of us than we feel able to give.
Take all that *has* been
  and direct all that *shall* be.

Reach out to all who are finding endings hard to bear.
We think of those reeling from the termination of employment,
    the breakdown of a relationship
    or eviction from their homes.
Take all that *has* been
  and direct all that *shall* be.

We think of those whose children are leaving home,
    family and friends moving away from each other,
    communities facing the upheaval of change.
Take all that *has* been
  and direct all that *shall* be.

We think of those coming to terms with unfulfilled ambitions,
    let down by broken promises,
    or overcome by sudden catastrophe.
Take all that *has* been
  and direct all that *shall* be.

We think of those disabled by disease,
  mourning the loss of loved ones,
  or suffering from terminal illness.
Take all that *has* been
  and direct all that *shall* be.

We think not only of others but also ourselves.
Show us those areas in our lives
  where it is time to draw a line and move on –
  forms of service which are no longer fruitful,
  activities no longer appropriate,
  dreams no longer viable.
Take all that *has* been
  and direct all that *shall* be.

Give us the wisdom we need to understand
  when it is necessary to accept change
  and even to welcome it,
  and give us courage then to stride out in faith,
  confident that you will lead us from the old to the new.
Take all that *has* been
  and direct all that *shall* be.

Lord Jesus Christ,
  remind us again today that endings can lead to new beginnings,
    that from the old, new life can spring,
    and may that confidence touch our lives
    and bring hope to our troubled world.
  Receive our thanks for all that *has* been
    and open our hearts to all that *shall* be.

We ask it in your name.
Amen.

70

INTERCESSION
LOVE FROM HATRED

Lord Jesus Christ,
   we thank you for the victory of love over hatred
      that we celebrate in this season.
   We praise you for staying true to your chosen path,
      despite all the malice thrown against you,
      the repeated taunts to put yourself first,
      and the very real temptation you must have felt to do just that.
   Hear now our prayer for the world you gave your life for –
      a world so racked by enmity and division
      and so desperately in need of love.
   Gracious Lord, wherever hatred seems to rule,
      may love emerge victorious.

We pray for those whose personal relationships
   have degenerated into hatred –
   scarred by petty grievances and arguments,
   undermined by verbal and physical abuse,
   poisoned by coldness and indifference;
   words spoken to wound rather than woo,
   deeds designed to break down rather than build up,
   all feeling and friendship long since forgotten.
Gracious Lord, wherever hatred seems to rule,
   may love emerge victorious.

We pray for society at large
   where hatred masquerades under a variety of guises –
   prejudice, greed, selfishness, intolerance, ignorance –
   so much that denies, divides and destroys,
   creating a sense of 'them' and 'us',
   the acceptable and the unacceptable.
Gracious Lord, wherever hatred seems to rule,
   may love emerge victorious.

We pray for countries racked by inner tensions
    and at odds with their neighbours –
    torn apart by religious extremism,
    by military dictatorships,
    racial hatred,
    civil war
    and abuses of human rights –
    lives wantonly destroyed,
    families broken,
    communities shattered,
    nations decimated.
Gracious Lord, wherever hatred seems to rule,
    may love emerge victorious.

Lord Jesus Christ,
    we pray for our world in all its need –
    a world of so much hatred,
    yet one which you loved so much you were willing to die for it,
    and a world which you will never abandon,
    no matter how often your love is rejected.
Help us and all people to recognise the folly of our ways –
    to understand that violence only breeds more violence,
    vengeance more vengeance,
    bitterness more bitterness
    and hatred more hatred.
Give us the faith and the courage to try another way,
    the way you revealed so powerfully
    through your life and your death –
    the way of love.
Gracious Lord, wherever hatred seems to rule,
    may love emerge victorious.

We ask it in your name and for your glory.
Amen.

71

INTERCESSION
JOY FROM SORROW

Lord Jesus Christ,
  we remember the trauma
    which your suffering and death brought to your followers,
    a grief which went beyond words
    and which seemed beyond healing.
  We recall how Peter wept bitterly
    when he realised he had denied you as you predicted;
    how women sobbed on the way to the cross,
    and as they watched you die;
    how Mary broke down in the garden, overwhelmed with grief –
    each one a symbol of the desolation and despair
    so many felt at your death.
 But we recall also how Peter rejoiced
    as, three times, you repeated your call,
    how your followers celebrated
    as you stood among them, risen and victorious,
    how Mary's heart soared with wonder as you spoke her name.
Gracious Lord, wherever there is sorrow,
  grant your joy.

We pray for those who suffer today –
  all who endure constant pain,
  who wrestle with illness,
  who are victims of violence
  or whose bodies are broken by accident or injury.
Gracious Lord, wherever there is sorrow,
  grant your joy.

We pray for those who feel betrayed today,
  cheated by loved ones,
  deceived by those they trusted,
  hurt by those they counted as friends,
  or let down by society.
Gracious Lord, wherever there is sorrow,
  grant your joy.

We pray for those who grieve today,
   their hearts broken by tragedy and bereavement,
   their lives torn apart –
   many for whom tears are a constant companion,
   laughter and happiness like some distant memory.
Gracious Lord, wherever there is sorrow,
   grant your joy.

Lord Jesus Christ,
   reach out into our world of so much pain,
      heartache and sadness.
   May your light scatter the shadows,
      your love lift the burdens,
      and your grace bring life in all its fullness.
   Gracious Lord, wherever there is sorrow,
      grant your joy.

We ask it in your name.
Amen.

72

INTERCESSORY REFLECTION
HOPE FROM DESPAIR

Lord Jesus Christ,
    in this world where hopes are so often dashed
        and dreams so often broken,
        we remember today the faith in the future
        you brought to so many,
        both through your coming
        and through your resurrection from the dead.
Lord Jesus, where faith has died and dreams have faded,
    may hope flower again.

We remember how Mary and Joseph looked forward
    to the day of your birth,
        how shepherds and magi caught their breath in wonder
        as they knelt before you,
        how the hearts of Anna and Simeon leapt in anticipation,
        and how your disciples and the crowds that flocked to hear you
        gave thanks,
        convinced that you were the Messiah,
        the one God had promised,
        the long-awaited deliverer come to set them free.
Lord Jesus, where faith has died and dreams have faded,
    may hope flower again.

We remember how that vision of the future
    was shattered by events to follow –
        your pain, humiliation, suffering and death –
        hope ebbing away as the lifeblood seeped from your body –
        an end to their dreams,
        an end to everything.
Lord Jesus, where faith has died and dreams have faded,
    may hope flower again.

We remember how the news spread that the tomb was empty,
    the stone rolled away,
    your body gone,
    and how, despite it all,
    your followers could scarcely bring themselves to hope –
    afraid to take the risk of faith
    in case they should face the heartache of losing you once more.
Lord Jesus, where faith has died and dreams have faded,
    may hope flower again.

But we remember finally how you appeared,
    in all your risen glory –
    in the garden,
    in the upstairs room,
    on the Emmaus road,
    by the Sea of Galilee –
    and the dream was born again,
    the smouldering embers of faith rekindled.
Lord Jesus, where faith has died and dreams have faded,
    may hope flower again.

Lord Jesus Christ,
    a world is waiting, hurting, longing,
      searching for hope,
      crying out for meaning,
      hungry for some reason to believe in the future.
Come again in your living power,
    and bring new life to all.
Lord Jesus, where faith has died and dreams have faded,
    may hope flower again.

In your name we pray.
Amen.

ASCENSION

73

PRAISE
THE KING OF KINGS

Lord Jesus Christ,
 we worship you today as the Lord of lords and King of kings.
 We bring your our praise,
  we offer our homage,
  we dedicate our lives to your service.
 Blessing and honour and glory and might are yours, O Lord,
  this day and for evermore!

We acknowledge you as sovereign over life,
  the Lord of creation, through whom all things were made,
  and in whom we live and move and have our being.
 Blessing and honour and glory and might are yours, O Lord,
  this day and for evermore!

We acknowledge you as sovereign over death,
  the risen Lord who triumphed over the grave,
  the resurrection and the life.
Through you the door to eternity has been opened,
  the path to your everlasting kingdom.
 Blessing and honour and glory and might are yours, O Lord,
  this day and for evermore!

We acknowledge you as sovereign over evil,
  the crucified Christ who nailed our sins to the cross,
  who defeated the powers of darkness,
  who conquered hatred with love.
 Blessing and honour and glory and might are yours, O Lord,
  this day and for evermore!

Lord Jesus Christ,
  we acknowledge you as sovereign over all,
    Lord of space and time,
    ruler of the ends of the earth,
    enthroned in splendour at the right hand of the Father.
  Blessing and honour and glory and might are yours, O Lord,
    this day and for evermore!

Amen.

74

CONFESSION
THE LAMB OF GOD

Lord Jesus Christ,
    we have failed you in so much,
        our lives, time and again, a denial of our calling.
    We have failed to love our neighbour,
        been slow to forgive,
        swift to pass judgement
        and careless of the needs of others.
    Yet, through the immensity of your grace
        and the awesomeness of your sacrifice,
        you offer us redemption from all our sins
        and renewal of life.
    Lamb of God,
        to you be power and wealth,
        wisdom and might,
        honour and glory and blessing!

We profess to be your followers,
    but our faith has been weak and our commitment poor.
We claim to be your body,
    but we have allowed petty divisions to come between us.
We talk of building your kingdom,
    but our thoughts are all for this world and its pleasures.
Yet, despite our weakness, still you love us,
    accepting us as we are,
    cleansing us from all our faults
    and offering us a new beginning –
    the opportunity to put the past behind us and start afresh.
Lamb of God,
    to you be power and wealth,
    wisdom and might,
    honour and glory and blessing!

We are unworthy to bear your name
    and undeserving of your goodness –
    so much about us that is wrong,
    so little that is right –
    yet you went to the cross knowing all that,
    taking the punishment that should have been ours,
    bringing us healing through your wounds,
    and on your shoulders carrying the iniquities of us all.
Lamb of God,
    to you be power and wealth,
    wisdom and might,
    honour and glory and blessing!

Lord Jesus Christ,
    through you we have found joy and fulfilment,
        love and peace,
        grace and mercy.
We have been born again to a living hope,
        our sins forgiven,
        our lives renewed,
        our salvation assured.
Lamb of God,
    to you be power and wealth,
    wisdom and might,
    honour and glory and blessing!

Amen.

75

THANKSGIVING
THE SAVIOUR OF ALL

Lord Jesus Christ,
 we thank you for the truth at the heart of this day –
  that you came to save not just a few,
  nor simply your own people,
  but all the world.
You are the King of kings and Lord of lords,
  your love reaching out to the ends of the earth,
  your glory filling the universe!
Mighty Saviour,
 in thanks we worship you.

We thank you that, though you were born in Bethlehem
  and ministered in Galilee,
  though you spent your life in Palestine
  and died in Jerusalem,
  your love has transformed lives
  in every country and continent,
  crossing barriers of culture, colour and creed,
  unable to be contained by either space or time!
Mighty Saviour,
 in thanks we worship you.

We thank you that no one is outside your love,
  whoever they may be,
  whatever they may have done.
You value all,
  have time for all,
  respond to all.
Mighty Saviour,
 in thanks we worship you.

We greet you now as the sovereign Lord –
   the one who reigns in splendour,
   enthroned at the right hand of the Father,
   and the one who, in the fullness of time,
   will reconcile all things to yourself,
   making peace through your blood
   and establishing your eternal kingdom.
Mighty Saviour,
   in thanks we worship you.

Lord Jesus Christ,
   Saviour of all,
      we look forward to that day when every knee shall bow to you,
      and every tongue confess you as Lord and Saviour.
   To you be praise and glory,
      honour and thanksgiving,
      now and always.
   Amen.

76

INTERCESSION
THE SERVANT KING

Lord Jesus Christ,
    Ruler of all,
        Servant of all,
        we pray again for the kingdoms and rulers of this world,
        that those in positions of authority
        may use their power in the service of their people
        and for the good of all.
    Servant King,
        may your love reign supreme.

We pray for those who take counsel together on behalf of nations,
    all those who carry the responsibility of leadership.
Grant them wisdom in all their decisions,
    humility to listen to the point of view of others,
    courage to stand up for what is right,
    and a determination to work for justice and peace.
Servant King,
    may your love reign supreme.

We think of our own country,
    and we pray for the royal family and especially our Queen,
    thanking you for the example she has given,
    the dedication to duty she has shown,
    and the commitment to our nation she has displayed
    throughout her rule.
Grant to her,
    and to her successor when the time comes,
    your guidance, discernment, strength and inspiration.
Servant King,
    may your love reign supreme.

We pray for our government and members of Parliament,
 giving thanks once more for the service they give.
Guide them in their discussions and decisions,
 and give them a proper sense
 of the responsibility entrusted to them.
Help them to work not just for personal or party interest
 but for the good of all.
Servant King,
 may your love reign supreme.

We pray for all who strive to build a fairer society
 and a better world –
 those who campaign against poverty, injustice and exploitation;
 who work for peace and reconciliation;
 who offer healing to body, mind or spirit;
 who serve the needy.
Encourage them in their work,
 support them in adversity,
 provide the resources they need,
 and make known your love through their ministry.
Servant King,
 may your love reign supreme.

Lord Jesus Christ,
 we pray that your kingdom may come,
 despite everything that seems to fight against it;
 a kingdom in which the first are last and the last first,
 in which everything that frustrates your purpose
 and denies your love is defeated,
 and in which all people live together in justice and harmony.
Servant King,
 may your love reign supreme.

We ask it for your name's sake.
Amen.

PENTECOST

PENTECOST

77

PRAISE
THE OMNIPRESENT SPIRIT

Holy Spirit,
    we rejoice that, as you came to the Apostles
        on that day of Pentecost,
        so you keep on coming to us today;
        making yourself known in different ways,
        at different times
        and in different places,
        but always there,
        constantly moving in our lives.
    For your presence at work within us,
        we give you our praise.

You come when we are most aware of our need –
        bringing comfort in times of sorrow,
        courage in times of fear,
        peace in times of trouble
        and hope in times of despair.
    For your presence at work within us,
        we give you our praise.

You come when we forget our need of you –
        challenging,
        searching,
        refining,
        cleansing;
        inspiring us to greater vision and renewed commitment.
    For your presence at work within us,
        we give you our praise.

You come to us in power –
        releasing unimagined potential,
        imparting unexpected gifts,
        cultivating undreamed-of fruits.
    For your presence at work within us,
        we give you our praise.

You come to us in quietness –
    coaxing us to new initiatives,
    nurturing confidence
    and deepening our faith.
For your presence at work within us,
    we give you our praise.

Holy Spirit,
    we welcome you again –
        opening our minds to your guidance,
        our hearts to your love
        and our lives to your purpose.
Breathe upon us,
    fill and enthuse us,
    and send us out in the service of Christ.
For your presence at work within us,
    we give you our praise.

In his name we pray.
Amen.

78

Confession
The unquenchable Spirit

Holy Spirit,
    we remember today how, on the day of your coming,
        there were many who mocked,
        pouring scorn on the disciples' experience,
        claiming they had drunk too much wine,
        or that they were simply out of their minds.
    You come still today:
    forgive us for being closed to your life-giving presence.

We remember how you re-ignited their faith
    and empowered them for service,
    so that they flung open the locked doors
    behind which they had been hiding,
    and went out among the crowds,
    boldly witnessing to their faith
    and declaring their allegiance to Christ.
You come still today:
    forgive us for being closed to your life-giving presence.

We remember how you worked in the life of the early Church,
    prompting,
    guiding,
    cleansing,
    invigorating,
    opening doors to the gospel,
    and raising up men and women ready to make it known
    through word and deed.
You come still today:
    forgive us for being closed to your life-giving presence.

We remember how you have worked in subsequent generations,
    equipping,
    enabling,
    teaching,
    inspiring,
    breathing new life into age-old structures,
    bringing fresh insights into established tradition,
    and firing your people to imaginative ventures
    built on the foundations of the past.
You come still today:
    forgive us for being closed to your life-giving presence.

We remember how you took ordinary, uneducated people,
    and used them in the most extraordinary of ways;
    how you took those who had miserably failed you,
    and gave them courage to endure suffering and death
    for the sake of faith.
We rejoice that you are able to use ordinary people
    like us here and now,
    provided we are ready to see beyond our own limited horizons,
    and to overcome our fears, doubts and prejudices.
You come still today:
    forgive us for being closed to your life-giving presence.

Holy Spirit,
    you are always moving,
        daily seeking to lead us into truth,
        constantly striving to break through the walls we erect against you.
    You want to deepen our faith,
        enrich our experience,
        strengthen our commitment,
        and enlarge our vision,
        yet, time and again, we allow a lack of expectation
        to frustrate your purpose.
    You come still today:
    forgive us for being closed to your life-giving presence.

Hear this and all our prayers through Jesus Christ our Lord.
Amen.

79

PETITION
THE RENEWING SPIRIT

Spirit of God,
    you swept into the lives of the Apostles,
        and, in a moment, everything was different,
        transformed for ever by your renewing power.
    You breathed new vision into them,
        new hope and faith,
        so that the world was suddenly alive again with promise.
    Suddenly, you were there,
        deep within,
        cleansing,
        encouraging,
        empowering,
        inspiring,
        turning their lives inside-out
        so that nothing would ever be the same again.
    Holy Spirit,
        move in us today.

You came to those looking to serve you
        but uncertain of the way forward,
        to those who believed you could use them
        though they didn't know how,
        to those who recognised the future was full of opportunities
        to serve you,
        but who doubted their ability to respond.
    And, suddenly, the future was clear,
        confidence radiating from them
        as you touched their lives with power from on high.
    Holy Spirit,
        move in us today.

You came to those who had followed Jesus throughout his ministry
and who longed to know him better –
those who had witnessed his preaching and teaching,
who had watched him suffer and die,
and, having seen him gloriously raised to life again,
wanted to grasp better what it all meant,
for them and for others.
And, suddenly, you were there,
calling the words of Jesus to mind,
opening their hearts to the truth,
leading them to an ever-deeper understanding
of everything Christ had achieved.
Holy Spirit,
move in us today.

You came to those conscious of their failure and weakness,
all too aware of their limited abilities,
their flawed faith
and their rebellious natures.
And, suddenly, they discovered new life growing within them,
gifts which they scarcely imagined possible,
and fruits which they had never even contemplated.
Holy Spirit,
move in us today.

Spirit of God,
you swept into the lives of the Apostles,
and, in a moment, everything was different.
Move now in us,
so that our service may be enriched,
our faith deepened
and our lives transformed.
Holy Spirit,
move in us today.

Through Jesus Christ our Lord.
Amen.

80

INTERCESSION
THE TRANSFORMING SPIRIT

Holy Spirit,
  coming as wind and fire,
    free and irrepressible,
    we pray today for all who long for change
    and for all who fear it.

We think of the poor and the hungry,
    the homeless and the refugee,
    the sick and the unemployed,
    the downtrodden and the oppressed –
    these, and so many others, who yearn for a new beginning,
    an opportunity to start afresh.
  May their prayers be answered and their dreams realised.
  As you came at Pentecost,
    come again today.

We pray for those who see change as a threat –
    a sweeping-away of everything that is tried and trusted,
    and the imposition of unknown challenges
    and an uncertain future.
  May they rest secure in the knowledge that,
    whatever else may change,
    you will remain constant.
  As you came at Pentecost,
    come again today.

Holy Spirit,
    coming gently as a dove,
        we pray for all who long for peace,
        and all who have lost sight of what peace really means.
    We think of those in homes racked by tensions,
        families split by petty disputes,
        communities scarred by prejudice and intolerance,
        and countries torn apart by war.
    May dialogue triumph over confrontation,
        and unity replace division.
    As you came at Pentecost,
        come again today.

We pray for those who fill their lives with noise or activity,
    afraid of facing themselves in a time of quiet reflection,
    attempting somehow to mask their sense of emptiness;
    and we pray, too, for those who seek fulfilment
    in that which can never finally satisfy –
    wealth, possessions, power, success.
May they discover the secret of true contentment,
    the peace that passes understanding which only you can give.
As you came at Pentecost,
    come again today.

Holy Spirit,
    you changed the lives of the Apostles
        and of countless people through history,
        just as you are changing our lives in turn,
        each renewed through your sovereign power.
    Come now and change our world in all its need,
        so that it may enjoy hope and peace,
        healing and harmony,
        and so that all may come to a saving knowledge
        of Jesus Christ our Lord.
    As you came at Pentecost,
        come again today.

We ask it for his name's sake.
Amen.

TRINITY SUNDAY

81

PRAISE
BRINGING OUR WORSHIP

God of love,
  we rejoice today that you care for each one of us,
    that we matter so much to you
    that you want to share with us your gift of life
    and lead us into a living, loving relationship with you.
  Father, Son and Holy Spirit,
    receive our praise.

God of grace,
  we bless you for expressing your love so wonderfully in Christ,
    through his birth,
    his ministry,
    his death,
    his resurrection
    and his glorious exaltation.
  Father, Son and Holy Spirit,
    receive our praise.

God of power,
  we thank you for continuing to bless us each day
    through your Holy Spirit,
    nurturing our faith,
    renewing our vision,
    guiding our footsteps
    and equipping us for service.
  Father, Son and Holy Spirit,
    receive our praise.

God of all,
  Three in One and One in Three,
    we praise you that you have called us your children,
    your friends, your people,
    and that you are always with us,
    your love surrounding us wherever we may be,
    whatever we may face.
  Receive now our worship,
    offered to you in awe and wonder,
    in joy and thanksgiving.
  Father, Son and Holy Spirit,
    receive our praise.

  Amen.

82

CONFESSION
BRINGING OUR FAULTS

Sovereign God,
   all loving,
      all gracious,
      all powerful,
      you deserve our praise.
Mighty God,
   ever faithful,
      ever near,
      ever active,
      you deserve our worship.
Eternal God
   all goodness,
      all mercy,
      all truth,
      you deserve our thanks.
Father, Son and Holy Spirit,
   hear our prayer.

You are greater than our minds can grasp,
   yet you have revealed your glory.
You are before all, above all, beyond all,
   yet you lived and died among us.
You are at work in every situation and circumstance,
   yet so often we fail to recognise your presence.
For our narrowness of vision,
   our feebleness of faith,
   our spiritual blindness,
   forgive us, O Lord.
Father, Son and Holy Spirit,
   hear our prayer.

You are there watching over us, day after day.
You are here by our sides, until the end of the age.
You are here within, now and always.
For our rejection of your care,
    our forgetfulness of your presence
    and our stifling of your movement,
    forgive us, O Lord.
Father, Son and Holy Spirit,
    hear our prayer.

Accept now our worship, for all its weakness,
    our discipleship, for all its frailty,
    and our service, for all its limitations.
Speak to us this day,
    so that we may experience more of your love,
    reflect more of your goodness
    and live with more of your power,
Father, Son and Holy Spirit,
    hear our prayer.

And to you, the one God,
    be glory, praise and honour,
    today, tomorrow and for evermore.
Amen.

83

PETITION
BRINGING OUR NEED

Loving God,
   we thank you that you are here among us
      as we join to worship you –
      here as a loving Father watching over his children,
      as our Lord yet also our friend in the person of Jesus,
      as an ever-present reality
      through the daily experience of your Holy Spirit.
   Forgive us that we have lost sight sometimes of your living presence,
      and open our eyes afresh to all that you are
      and everything you are doing.
   Meet with us now, in all your glory,
      and help us to meet with you.

Father God,
   we recognise our need of you,
      and we acknowledge our emptiness deep within.
   We have chased after illusory fulfilment,
      turning our backs on where true happiness lies.
   Help us to recognise everything you have given us
      if only we could but see it –
      the wonder of your love,
      the constancy of your care
      and the greatness of your mercy.
   Teach us to put our trust in you,
      and to seek your kingdom and righteousness,
      and so fill us again with hope, joy and peace.
   Meet with us now, in all your glory,
      and help us to meet with you.

Gracious God,
 you have made yourself known to us in Christ,
  demonstrating the immensity of your love
  and the awesome extent of your mercy,
  yet still sometimes our faith grows cold.
 You have offered us a new beginning,
  renewal and redemption through his life-giving sacrifice,
  yet still, time and again, we go astray.
 Draw closer to us through the risen Christ,
  and inspire us with a vision
  of what life can be like through his grace.
 Meet with us now, in all your glory,
  and help us to meet with you.

Living God,
 inspire us now through the living presence of your Holy Spirit,
  so that we may walk boldly into this new day,
  with new faith and purpose.
 Help us to forget ourselves and to look outwards,
  so that we might bring light to those for whom life seems dark.
 Teach us to live this and every day in the warmth of your presence,
  illuminated by your radiance,
  refreshed by your cleansing touch
  and renewed by your power.
 Meet with us now, in all your glory,
  and help us to meet with you.

Loving God,
 Father, Son and Holy Spirit,
  help us to be aware of your presence amongst us –
  to see you, hear you, know you and love you,
  and so may we offer you fitting worship and service.
 Help us to understand you are with us not just here but everywhere,
  not just now but always,
  and so may every part of our lives reflect your grace
  and proclaim your goodness.
 Meet with us now, in all your glory,
  and help us to meet with you.

Through Jesus Christ our Lord.
Amen.

84

Intercession
Bringing Our World

Father God,
  your purpose is for all,
    for you are the Lord of heaven and earth,
    the Creator of humankind,
    Ruler over history.
  You are always at work,
    always involved in our lives,
    calling,
    guiding,
    speaking
    and responding,
    everyone important to you, no matter who they are,
    each having a place in your purpose.
  So, then, we pray for all in our world who feel they are drifting,
    all who search for meaning to their lives,
    a sense of direction,
    a goal to strive for.
  May they find in Jesus Christ
    the Way, the Truth and the Life.
  In faith we lift them before you:
    hear our prayer.

Son of God,
  your love is for all,
    for you lived and died for others,
    reaching out to both rich and poor,
    Jew and Gentile,
    righteous and unrighteous,
    nobody outside your care,
    no one beyond your grace.
  You gave your all,
    enduring death on a cross,
    so that everyone willing to receive you
    may share in the joy of your kingdom.

So we pray for all in our world today who long for love –
> those who yearn for a meaningful relationship,
> and those whose once-precious relationships have ended in tears;
> those who have been abandoned or orphaned as children,
> and those who cannot have children of their own;
> those cut off from family and friends,
> and those who face the trauma of bereavement.

May they discover in you
> a love that will never let them go.

In faith we lift them before you:
> **hear our prayer.**

Spirit of God,
> your peace is for all,
> > for you are at work in every heart,
> > seen or unseen,
> > recognised or unrecognised,
> > striving to break down the barriers
> > which keep us from one another,
> > from ourselves
> > and from you.

We pray, then, for all in our world who hunger for peace –
> all who are tormented by fear,
> torn by doubt,
> troubled by anxieties,
> or tortured by guilt;
> families separated by feuds,
> communities racked by division,
> and nations ravaged by war.

May they find through you
> peace in body, mind and spirit.

In faith we lift them before you:
> **hear our prayer.**

Almighty God,
Father, Son and Holy Spirit,
we bring you our world,
thankful that it is also *your* world,
precious to you and shaped ultimately by your will.
Remake,
redeem,
renew it through your sovereign power.
May all people everywhere come to know your purpose,
experience your love
and receive your peace,
and may each rejoice in the new life you so yearn to give them.
In faith we lift them before you:
hear our prayer.

Amen.

ALL SAINTS' DAY

85

Approach
The steadfast love of God

Almighty God,
    we come together as those you have called into fellowship,
        to be your people
        and to share in the rich inheritance of your saints.
I will sing of your steadfast love, O Lord, for ever;
    I will proclaim your faithfulness to all generations.

We come to worship you,
        not alone,
        but as part of the worldwide family of the Church,
        united with our brothers and sisters in Christ
        across countries and continents,
        centuries and generations,
        bound together by the same Lord and the same faith.
I will sing of your steadfast love, O Lord, for ever;
    I will proclaim your faithfulness to all generations.

We come as part of the great company of your people
        in heaven and on earth,
        following in the footsteps of past generations,
        picking up the torch
        from those who have run the race before us and kept the faith,
        heirs of your age-old promises.
I will sing of your steadfast love, O Lord, for ever;
    I will proclaim your faithfulness to all generations.

We come as those called to build for the future,
        conscious of successive generations that will follow us,
        and mindful of our responsibility to pass on to them
        the message we have received,
        to offer them inspiration and encouragement
        through the example of our commitment.
I will sing of your steadfast love, O Lord, for ever;
    I will proclaim your faithfulness to all generations.

We come then united with all your people of past, present, and future,
   of here, there, and everywhere,
   all those who call upon your name and offer you their service.
I will sing of your steadfast love, O Lord, for ever;
   I will proclaim your faithfulness to all generations.

Remind us of that wider fellowship of which we are a part,
   and may we recognise more fully
   the rich heritage you have given us,
   the great cloud of witnesses to which we belong.
Open our eyes to all we may learn of you,
   through these and one another.
I will sing of your steadfast love, O Lord, for ever;
   I will proclaim your faithfulness to all generations.

Save us from closed and narrow minds,
   forgive us for small and restricted outlooks,
   and restore us with your people
   to the wholeness and fellowship that you desire.
So may we and your Church everywhere
   offer our worship and service,
   in word and deed,
   to the glory of your name.
I will sing of your steadfast love, O Lord, for ever;
   I will proclaim your faithfulness to all generations.

In the name of Christ, we pray.
Amen.

86

PRAISE AND CONFESSION
THE UNDESERVED FAITHFULNESS OF GOD

Sovereign God,
 Lord of history,
  we come to you in reverent praise.

We come to praise you
 for the way you have worked across the centuries –
 the way you have moved in so many lives
 to make known your purpose,
 offer your guidance
 and express your love.
Great is your faithfulness:
 forgive the feebleness of our response.

We praise you for the way you have spoken throughout history –
 to your people, Israel,
 to your Church,
 to countless generations of believers.
Great is your faithfulness:
 forgive the feebleness of our response.

We praise you for the great cloud of witnesses that surround us –
 our fellowship here,
 your Church across the world,
 and all those who have kept the faith
 and run the race before us.
Great is your faithfulness:
 forgive the feebleness of our response.

We praise you for the example we have been given to follow –
 through the disciples and Apostles,
 through the early Church and its life beyond,
 and through the saints of old.
Great is your faithfulness:
 forgive the feebleness of our response.

Forgive us that we sometimes forget all you have done,
  losing sight of the breadth of your purpose
  and the extent of your love.
Great is your faithfulness:
  forgive the feebleness of our response.

Forgive us that we fail to honour the heritage in which we stand,
  our love for you weak,
  our trust hesitant
  and our commitment poor.
Great is your faithfulness:
  forgive the feebleness of our response.

Forgive us that we walk half-heartedly,
  casual in our discipleship,
  careless in our devotion,
  our hearts concerned with what is trivial and unimportant,
  rather than focused single-mindedly
  on the work of your kingdom.
Great is your faithfulness:
  forgive the feebleness of our response.

Sovereign God,
  as we remind ourselves together
    of your activity throughout history,
    as we reflect on your work through your people,
    speak now to our lives,
    that our love may grow,
    our faith be deepened,
    and our resolve to serve you be strengthened.
So may we live always to your praise and glory.
Great is your faithfulness:
  forgive the feebleness of our response.

Through Jesus Christ our Lord.
Amen.

87

THANKSGIVING AND PETITION
THE PEOPLE OF GOD

Eternal God,
    we thank you for your hand at work throughout history,
        bringing order out of chaos,
        shaping the universe
        and creating the world we live in.
But especially today, we thank you for men and women of faith,
        all those who, across the years and in our own lifetime,
        have given us an example to follow.
For the great company of your people,
    and for our place within it,
    Lord, we thank you.

We thank you for the commitment of Abraham –
    his willingness to step out into the unknown,
    to walk in faith,
    to trust in your promise.
For the great company of your people,
    and for our place within it,
    Lord, we thank you.

We thank you for the dedication of Moses –
    the way you used him to lead your people out of slavery,
    guide them through the wilderness
    and bring them to the Promised Land.
For the great company of your people,
    and for our place within it,
    Lord, we thank you.

We thank you for the prophets –
  those who had the vision and courage to speak your word,
  to pronounce your judgement,
  to make known your mercy
  and to proclaim your love.
For the great company of your people,
  and for our place within it,
  Lord, we thank you.

We thank you for the Apostles –
  for their willingness to leave everything and follow Jesus,
  their witness to his death and resurrection,
  their courage in the face of hostility and persecution.
For the great company of your people,
  and for our place within it,
  Lord, we thank you.

We thank you for the great saints of the Church –
  those whose commitment to you has been self-evident,
  whose devotion to you has shone from their lives,
  who have given heart, mind and soul to the service of Christ.
For the great company of your people,
  and for our place within it,
  Lord, we thank you.

We thank you for those who have made known the gospel to us –
  those who have encouraged and instructed us in faith,
  who have been a source of inspiration,
  who have walked with us on our journey of discipleship.
For the great company of your people,
  and for our place within it,
  Lord, we thank you.

We thank you for one another –
  for our share in the inheritance of your people,
  for our unity in the body of Christ,
  for the comfort, strength and support we are able to give
    one to another.
For the great company of your people,
  and for our place within it,
  Lord, we thank you.

And so we pray finally for ourselves –
    that you will help us to continue
    in the footsteps of those before us,
    keeping the faith,
    running the race with perseverance,
    offering to future generations an example in turn.
For the great company of your people,
    and for our place within it,
    Lord, we thank you.

In the name of Christ.
Amen.

88

INTERCESSION
THE CHURCH OF GOD

Sovereign God,
 we have thought of the wider fellowship that we share in Christ,
  the great company of your people in heaven and on earth
  to which we are privileged to belong,
  and so now we pray for those
  who seek, in turn, to follow you today.
 Rock of ages,
  hear our prayer.

We pray for those for whom commitment is costly –
 those who face hostility, discrimination,
 repression and persecution
 for the cause of the gospel.
Give them strength and courage,
 so that they may keep the faith.
Rock of ages,
 hear our prayer.

We pray for those who are finding the journey of discipleship difficult –
 troubled by doubts,
 plagued by temptation,
 or simply slipping back into old ways.
Give them support and reassurance,
 so that they may walk with new confidence.
Rock of ages,
 hear our prayer.

We pray for those expressing their faith in action –
 individuals through personal acts of kindness,
 and agencies like Christian Aid, CAFOD, Tearfund and Shelter,
 together with so many others,
 working, often against the odds,
 to give expression to the love of Christ.
Give them love and compassion,
 so that they may make Christ real for others.
Rock of ages,
 hear our prayer.

We pray for all seeking to communicate their faith –
 ministers, evangelists, missionaries, chaplains,
 but also ordinary, everyday believers like us –
 each telling in their own way what Jesus means to them.
Give them wisdom and inspiration,
 so that they may speak your word with power.
Rock of ages,
 hear our prayer.

Sovereign God,
 we pray for Christians everywhere striving to live out their faith
  in the world of today,
 with all the pressures, challenges and demands
 that confront them.
Give them guidance and encouragement,
 so that they may grow in grace.
 Grant them humility to learn more of you each day
 and the ability to share their experience
 simply and effectively with others,
 making Christ known through word and deed.
Rock of ages,
 hear our prayer.

All this we ask, through Jesus Christ our Lord.
Amen.

PART TWO

LIFE AND FAITH

OLD AND NEW YEAR

89

PRAISE AND THANKSGIVING
THE CONSTANCY OF GOD'S LOVE

Living God,
　　as we come together on this last day of the year,
　　　　we thank and praise you
　　　　for the way you have led us through good and bad,
　　　　joy and sorrow,
　　　　hope and disappointment,
　　　　pleasure and pain.
For the constancy of your love,
　　faithful across the years,
　　receive our grateful praise.

We thank you for the way you have led us as individuals –
　　the experiences we have gone through,
　　challenges we have faced,
　　and victories achieved;
　　the people we have met,
　　places we have visited,
　　and sights we have seen;
　　the inspiration you have offered,
　　guidance provided,
　　and strength given.
For the constancy of your love,
　　faithful across the years,
　　receive our grateful praise.

We thank you for the way you have led us as a church –
   the things learned,
   fun enjoyed,
   and friendship shared;
   the worship offered,
   faith nurtured,
   and service given;
   the plans made,
   ventures attempted,
   and successes achieved.
For the constancy of your love,
   faithful across the years,
   receive our grateful praise.

We praise you that we can come now in confidence,
   knowing from experience
   that you will be with us in the days ahead,
   looking to lead us forward into new experiences of your love,
   and seeking to help us grow in grace,
   your power sufficient for all our needs,
   whatever we may face.
For the constancy of your love,
   faithful across the years,
   receive our grateful praise.

Receive, then, the worship we bring,
   the service we offer
   and the people we are,
   as individuals and as a church together.
We commit all to you,
   rejoicing in your goodness,
   sure of your grace,
   and trusting in your eternal purpose.
For the constancy of your love,
   faithful across the years,
   receive our grateful praise.

Through Jesus Christ our Lord.
Amen.

90

CONFESSION
A NEW BEGINNING

Gracious God,
    as we come together on the threshold of another year,
        we are conscious of the many ways we have failed you
        over the year gone by.
Forgive what we have been,
    and direct what we shall be.

You have given us innumerable blessings,
    and all too often we have failed to appreciate them.
You have offered us daily guidance,
    and repeatedly we have ignored it.
You have provided countless opportunities for service,
    and we have frittered the majority away.
You have granted us new life in Christ,
    and time and again we have turned back to our old foolish ways.
Forgive what we have been,
    and direct what we shall be.

Despite our high hopes and bold pledges,
    our talk of faith and words about commitment,
    we have been weak,
    disobedient,
    self-centred,
    faithless,
    our discipleship a sorry catalogue of what might have been.
Forgive what we have been,
    and direct what we shall be.

We want to serve you, but the flesh is weak;
    want to obey you, but temptation is strong;
    want to trust you, but doubts are many;
    want to do much, but end up doing little.
Forgive what we have been,
    and direct what we shall be.

Gracious God,
    we stand on the threshold of another year –
        a new beginning,
        a fresh chapter.
    May this sense of newness be echoed in our lives,
        as, through your grace, we start again with a clean slate,
        the past put behind us,
        the future beckoning us forward.
    Help us to live each day as your gift,
        nurtured by the love of Christ
        renewed through your Holy Spirit,
        and so may we live to your praise and glory.
    Forgive what we have been,
        and direct what we shall be.

Through Jesus Christ our Lord.
Amen.

91

PETITION
GRASPING THE FUTURE

Loving God,
  at the turn of another year,
    and the start of another chapter in the life of this church,
    we come to you,
    seeking your guidance
    and committing ourselves once again to your service.
  Take what we are,
    and direct what we shall be.

We come to share with you and one another,
    to offer our thanks and confession,
    to bring you our hopes and fears for the future,
    and to learn more of your purpose for our lives.
  Take what we are,
    and direct what we shall be.

Help us to make the most of the days ahead –
    to use them to the full,
    enjoying each one,
    celebrating your many blessings,
    and bringing honour to you through the way we live.
  Take what we are,
    and direct what we shall be.

Help us to make proper time for ourselves –
    time to work
    rest,
    play
    and reflect.
  Take what we are,
    and direct what we shall be.

Help us to make time for our loved ones –
   to give them the love,
   support
   and care they deserve.
Take what we are,
   and direct what we shall be.

Help us to make time for others –
   to listen,
   encourage,
   serve
   and share.
Take what we are,
   and direct what we shall be.

Help us to make time for you –
   to read your word,
   offer our prayers,
   seek your will
   and respond to your calling.
Take what we are,
   and direct what we shall be.

Loving God,
   we come at the start of another year.
Speak to us now,
   and help us to hear your voice.
Lead us,
   and help us to see your hand.
Teach us,
   and help us to know your will.
Send us out,
   and help us to walk by faith,
   in the knowledge that, as you have been with us
   in the years gone by,
   so you will continue to guide and bless us
   in the days ahead.
Through Christ our Lord.
Amen.

92

Intercession
Those for whom the future seems bleak

Gracious God,
    as we come to you at this time of new beginnings,
        we are reminded of those
        who feel the future holds no promise,
        those who struggle with burdens
        to which they can see no solution.
Reach out in love,
    and grant a new beginning.

We pray for those facing pressures of home –
    relationships strained between husband and wife,
    parent and child,
    brother and sister –
    patience stretched to breaking point.
Reach out in love,
    and grant a new beginning.

We pray for those facing pressures of work –
    overwhelmed by responsibilities,
    caught up in office politics,
    troubled by job insecurity,
    or simply bored and unhappy in what they do.
Reach out in love,
    and grant a new beginning.

We pray for those facing pressures of money –
    struggling to make ends meet,
    crippled by debt,
    frustrated by poor pay,
    or uncertain whether and when their next pay cheque will arrive.
Reach out in love,
    and grant a new beginning.

We pray for those facing pressures of health –
  waiting perhaps for a diagnosis,
  crushed by depression,
  wrestling with infirmity as the years go by,
  or living with the knowledge of terminal illness.
Reach out in love,
  and grant a new beginning.

We pray for those facing pressures of faith –
  racked by doubts,
  troubled by questions,
  feeling themselves cut off from your love,
  enduring the dark night of the soul.
Reach out in love,
  and grant a new beginning.

Gracious God,
  may your love, compassion, strength and support
    reach out to all who are hurting,
    and may you bring to them a sense of hope –
    the conviction that, however bleak it may seem,
    you hold the future in your hands,
    now, and for all eternity.
Reach out in love,
  and grant a new beginning.

Through Jesus Christ our Lord.
Amen.

REDEDICATION SERVICE

93

PRAISE
GOD'S GRACIOUS CALL

Sovereign God,
  we praise you today for your great goodness –
    your love which has redeemed us in Christ,
    which has welcomed us as your people,
    and which watches over us throughout eternity.
  For calling us into your family,
    Lord, we worship you.

We have no claim on your goodness,
    no right to your love,
    for day after day we fail you,
    yet still you rejoice in our praises
    and value the service we offer.
  Despite our disobedience, we know that you are always with us,
    inviting us to receive your forgiveness and start again,
    your patience never exhausted,
    your call never withdrawn.
  For calling us into your family,
    Lord, we worship you.

We have no claim to be called your people,
    for we live so much for ourselves and so little for you,
    yet still you count us as your family,
    your children,
    each one of us precious in your sight.
  Despite our faults, we know that you are always with us,
    inviting us to show your love in word and deed
    to embody your kingdom
    and to reveal your gracious purpose for all.
  For calling us into your family,
    Lord, we worship you.

We have no claim on your faithfulness,
    for we are feeble and foolish,
    constantly wandering from your side,
    swept now this way, now that,
    yet still your love continues undiminished,
    your arms ready to support us
    and your hand leading us forward.
Despite our fickleness, we know that you are always with us,
    inviting us to step out in faith,
    confident that, however often *we* may fail *you*,
    you will never fail *us*.
For calling us into your family,
    Lord, we worship you.

Sovereign God,
    we come to praise you for your great goodness,
      and, in grateful response,
      to rededicate our lives to your service.
Take what we are, in all our weakness,
    and use us to your glory.
For calling us into your family,
    Lord, we worship you.

In the name of Christ.
Amen.

94

CONFESSION
FLAWED DISCIPLESHIP

Loving God,
    time and again across the years
        we have committed ourselves to your service,
        and time and again we have let you down,
        failing to honour our promise,
        breaking faith and straying from your side.
Our words have said one thing,
    our lives another.
Forgive us our weakness,
    and help us to start again.

We have confessed Christ as our Lord
    and pledged ourselves to follow him,
    but when our allegiance has been tested,
    our loyalty put on the line,
    repeatedly we have been found wanting,
    more concerned with our own interests
    and what others may think of us
    than with serving Jesus.
Our words have said one thing,
    our lives another.
Forgive us our weakness,
    and help us to start again.

We have committed ourselves to one another
    and to the work of this fellowship of which we are a part,
    but when personalities have clashed and opinions differed,
    we have been swift to take sides,
    quick to take offence,
    and all too ready to condemn.
Our words have said one thing,
    our lives another.
Forgive us our weakness,
    and help us to start again.

We have spoken of sharing in the ministry of the Church,
    of proclaiming our faith and working for your kingdom,
    but when commitment has involved cost,
    when service has meant putting ourselves out,
    our good intentions have all too rapidly evaporated,
    proving to be little more than fine-sounding ideas.
Our words have said one thing,
    our lives another.
Forgive us our weakness
    and help us to start again.

Loving God,
    we truly want to serve you better,
    and so we come now
    to consecrate our lives to you once again,
    but we know that we will fail you
    as we have failed so often before,
    our faith flawed and our love imperfect.
Have mercy upon us,
    and, by your grace, help us
    to walk more closely with you in the days ahead
    than we have in the days gone by.
Our words have said one thing,
    our lives another.
Forgive us our weakness,
    and help us to start again.

Through Jesus Christ our Lord.
Amen.

95

PETITION
PAST, PRESENT AND FUTURE

Loving God,
    we have come together,
        shared together,
        and worshipped together,
        remembering the past and anticipating the future.
    Take what we are,
        and direct what we shall be.

We thank you for everything that has been achieved here –
    the work and witness of those who have gone before us,
    the faith that sustained them,
    the vision that inspired them –
    and we thank you for the part you call us to play
    in this church's continuing story.
Take what we are,
    and direct what we shall be.

We thank you for the fellowship we share in Christ –
    the support and encouragement,
    strength and inspiration,
    fun and friendship,
    which come through being a part of this family.
Bind us more closely together,
    and unite us in the work of your kingdom.
Take what we are,
    and direct what we shall be.

We thank you for the possibilities that stretch before us,
    the avenues of service waiting to be explored,
    the lives waiting to be touched by the message of the gospel,
    and the gifts you have given us
    so that we might grasp those opportunities.
Take what we are,
    and direct what we shall be.

We pray, then, for one another –
    members and congregation,
    those serving in positions of leadership,
    and those who work behind the scenes,
    all who, in any way, are part of this fellowship.
Deepen our commitment to you,
    to one another
    and to the world beyond.
Take what we are,
    and direct what we shall be.

Loving God,
    we come to commit ourselves afresh to Jesus Christ,
        and to his service within this church.
Give us faith and courage,
    a spirit of adventure
    and a willingness to follow where you would lead.
Take what we are,
    and direct what we shall be.

For we ask it in the name of Jesus Christ our Lord.
Amen.

96

INTERCESSION
DISCERNING GOD'S CALL

Loving God,
   at this time of rededication
     we pray for ourselves and for others.

We pray for those who feel they have failed you –
   burdened by a sense of guilt,
   ashamed of their faithlessness,
   and convinced that their mistakes can never be forgiven.
Assure them of your mercy,
   your constant willingness to help us start again.
Lord, in your mercy,
   hear our prayer.

We pray for those who have lost their faith –
   those who once professed faith in Christ,
   but who have drifted away,
   losing their first flush of enthusiasm,
   and abandoning the commitment they once made.
Stir their hearts,
   and rekindle faith within them.
Lord, in your mercy,
   hear our prayer.

We pray for those unsure of what you would have them do;
   certain that you have called them,
   yet unclear as to the way you would use their gifts,
   or which avenue of service you want them to pursue.
Speak your word,
   and help them to hear your voice.
Lord, in your mercy,
   hear our prayer.

We pray for one another here today –
    the future stretching before us,
    rich in promise,
    full of possibilities for worship, fellowship and service.
Help us to respond in faith,
    and to make the most of all the opportunities life brings us.
Lord, in your mercy,
    hear our prayer.

Loving God,
    may those who do not know you hear your call,
        those who knew you once come to know you again.
        and those who long to know you better receive your guidance.
Come now, and draw us closer to you,
    to the glory of your name.
Lord, in your mercy,
    hear our prayer.

Through Jesus Christ our Lord.
Amen.

WEEK OF PRAYER
FOR CHRISTIAN UNITY

97

PRAISE
CHURCHES TOGETHER

Loving God,
   we have come together in this place sharing the same faith,
     yet we are all different;
     no two of us the same,
     each one of us unique.
   Though we are many, you have made us one:
     together, we praise you.

We have different backgrounds and lifestyles,
     different temperaments and characters,
     different interests and ambitions,
     different feelings and experiences,
     and yet we are bound by the same goal
     and united by the same Lord.
   Though we are many, you have made us one:
     together, we praise you.

We praise you for the individuality that sets us apart,
     for everything in our lives that is special to us –
     the memories that are our own,
     the experiences that have shaped us,
     the people who have influenced our development.
   Though we are many, you have made us one:
     together, we praise you.

We praise you that you come to us in individual ways,
     meeting particular needs
     and calling us to contrasting avenues of service;
     that we come to know you through all kinds of paths,
     at different ages
     and through different traditions;
     that you meet us where we are,
     our faith not something learned by rote

or inherited by birth,
but our own,
each of us having a story to tell –
a story of life;
a story of faith.
Though we are many, you have made us one:
together, we praise you.

We praise you for the community that binds us together,
the fellowship we share in Christ,
the mission he has given us,
the love he has put in our hearts,
the hope we have in common.
Whatever may divide us,
it is as nothing compared to everything that unites us in him.
Though we are many, you have made us one:
together, we praise you.

We praise you for everything we are able to share together –
the rich heritage of the Church,
the inspiration of examples of faith,
the insights of different traditions,
the challenge of diverse experiences.
Though we are many, you have made us one:
together, we praise you.

Loving God,
help us to learn from one another,
never closing our minds to the diversity of your Church.
Help us to grow in faith day by day,
knowing your love and goodness for ourselves.
And help us to share what you have done for us,
and to listen to all you have done for others,
so that our faith may be deepened and our service enriched
as we continue along our individual pathway of faith
and on our pilgrimage together.
Though we are many, you have made us one:
together, we praise you.

Through Jesus Christ our Lord.
Amen.

98

CONFESSION
CHURCHES APART

Living God,
  we thank you for this opportunity to meet together,
    to recognise the wider fellowship of which we are a part,
    to celebrate the faith that we share,
    to consider ways in which we may work for your kingdom,
    and to reflect a little upon what we *are* doing
    and what we *can* do in your service.
You have called us to be one in Christ:
  forgive us the things that divide us.

We confess that though we speak of being 'churches together',
    in reality we are churches apart,
    each pursuing our own agendas
    and concerned with our own people,
    competing rather than complementing,
    duplicating our efforts rather than combining them.
You have called us to be one in Christ:
  forgive us the things that divide us.

We confess that though we talk of unity,
    it is more apparent than real,
    services together like this all too rare,
    suspicion of one another all too common,
    our understanding of the different traditions we represent small,
    and our concern for each other's welfare negligible.
You have called us to be one in Christ:
  forgive us the things that divide us.

We confess that, though we make grand statements
    concerning the kingdom of God
    and about our vision for the future,
    the truth is that our horizons are small,
    our thoughts more often than not turned in upon ourselves
    and our own fellowship,
    and our service extending little further
    than attending worship each Sunday,
    and offering personal devotion when time permits.
You have called us to be one in Christ:
    forgive us the things that divide us.

Open our hearts and minds to one another and to all your people.
Fill us with fresh vision and purpose,
    guide us in our individual witness and in our work together,
    and so may our lives be a living witness to your love
    and a testimony to your renewing grace.
You have called us to be one in Christ:
    forgive us the things that divide us.

In his name we pray.
Amen.

99

PETITION
UNITY IN DIVERSITY

Loving Father,
    once more we come together as a family of your people.
    We come as unique individuals,
        from contrasting backgrounds,
        and with various moods and expectations,
        but bound to each other in Christ.
    Though we are many,
        make us one.

We come with diverse experiences of your love,
    a multiplicity of insights to share,
    and a range of hopes for the future,
    but called together by the same Lord.
Though we are many,
    make us one.

We come with a mixture of gifts,
    an assortment of demands on our time,
    and an array of opportunities for service,
    but sharing a common faith and baptism.
Though we are many,
    make us one.

Loving Father,
    we come to you today rejoicing in our unity and diversity,
    celebrating the variety of talents, personalities
    and experiences you have given us,
    and thanking you for the love of Christ
    which holds them all together.
Take all that we are and fashion us into your people,
    dedicated to your service
    and working for your kingdom.
Though we are many,
    make us one.

Through Jesus Christ our Lord.
Amen.

100

INTERCESSION
HEALING THE WOUNDS

Lord Jesus Christ
    we pray today for your Church,
        conscious of the issues that still divide us,
        our failure to enjoy the oneness you desire.
    Wherever your body is broken today,
        make us one, Lord.

We pray for Christians who feel threatened
    by contrasting patterns of worship,
    diverging expressions of faith,
    and conflicting theological positions;
    who reject those they do not agree with as unsound,
    rather than risk engaging in genuine dialogue.
Give them openness to other points of view.
Wherever your body is broken today,
    make us one, Lord.

We pray for fellowships that have been torn in two,
    split by controversies over doctrine and churchmanship,
    divided over issues of faith and worship,
    or undermined by petty disputes.
Instil in them a spirit of healing and reconciliation.
Wherever your body is broken today,
    make us one, Lord.

We pray for denominations involved in moves towards greater unity,
    striving to overcome years of separation
        but finding themselves tied down by procedure and practicalities,
    frustrated by bureaucracy and tradition.
Grant wisdom and insight, so that obstacles may be overcome.
Wherever your body is broken today,
    make us one, Lord.

Lord Jesus Christ,
   reach out to your Church
      and work in hearts everywhere,
      to break down barriers,
      to overcome prejudice,
      and to bring people together
      in genuine love and understanding.
   Wherever your body is broken today,
      make us one, Lord.

In your name we ask it.
Amen.

LEPROSY SUNDAY

101

THANKSGIVING
FOR THE WORK OF LEPRA
AND THE LEPROSY MISSION

Loving God,
  we thank you today for the work of Lepra and the Leprosy Mission –
    for all who work in places where leprosy is still present,
    striving to help people understand the disease,
    treating those suffering from it,
    helping to rehabilitate those whose bodies have been disfigured
    and mutilated as an indirect result of their condition.
  Gracious God,
    hear our prayer.

We thank you for those who work in our own country –
    bringing the plight of sufferers to our attention,
    raising funds to provide relief,
    sharing news of what has been achieved
    and a vision of what can yet be done.
  Gracious God,
    hear our prayer.

We thank you for the progress that has been made
    in combating leprosy over recent years –
    the many who have been helped,
    the suffering that has been prevented
    and the countless thousands who can look forward
    to a brighter future.
  Gracious God,
    hear our prayer.

Loving God,
   we thank you for the health we are lucky enough to enjoy,
      and we express our gratitude today
      through our worship,
      our giving
      and our prayers.
   Receive all,
      and use them to reach out in the name of Christ,
      and to offer his healing renewing touch.
   Gracious God,
      hear our prayer.

For his sake we ask it.
Amen.

102

INTERCESSION
HEALING AND HEALERS

Gracious God,
    we have been reminded today
        of the work of the Leprosy Mission
        and of all that has been achieved through its efforts.
    So now we pray for its continuing ministry in the days ahead.
    Lord, in your mercy,
        hear our prayer.

We pray for those out in the field
    as they seek to make real the love of Christ,
    whether through the provision of practical support,
    though caring and medical treatment,
    through education,
    or through breaking down the barriers of fear and prejudice
    so long associated with this disease.
Give them the strength,
    the vision
    and the resources they need.
Lord, in your mercy,
    hear our prayer.

We pray for those scarred in body or mind through leprosy –
    maimed and mutilated as a result of their loss of sensation,
    rejected and despised by those who do not understand the disease,
    and viewed with revulsion by those shocked at its ravages.
Give them comfort,
    love,
    support
    and renewal.
Lord, in your mercy,
    hear our prayer.

We pray for countries where leprosy is still a threat
  and where people are still suffering.
Grant that they may find the resources they need
  not just to contain the disease
  but to wipe it out.
Lord, in your mercy,
  hear our prayer.

We pray for those who raise funds for relief,
  or who promote the work of the Leprosy Mission –
  all who seek to challenge, instruct, enthuse and inspire people
  to respond in love,
  and to offer from their plenty,
  so that others might receive the precious gift of health.
Give them the words to speak,
  the courage to speak them
  and the ability to communicate effectively.
Lord, in your mercy,
  hear our prayer.

Gracious God,
  we believe you desire wholeness for all.
  Reach out, then, in love,
    and grant your healing touch.
  Reach out in power,
    and stir our hearts,
    so that we may express our faith in action,
    offering what we can in support of your healing ministry.
  Lord, in your mercy,
    hear our prayer.

Through Jesus Christ our Lord.
Amen.

EDUCATION SUNDAY

103

Thanksgiving and Petition
The privilege of learning
and the task of teaching

Sovereign God,
    we thank you for those involved in the vital task of education,
        all who strive to impart understanding,
        to enthuse people with a thirst for knowledge,
        and to prepare them for the challenges and opportunities of life.
    You have given us a world of infinite riches:
    thank you for all who help us explore it.

We thank you for those who taught us as children,
        opening up new areas of discovery,
        communicating fresh insights,
        and giving us the tools we needed
        to progress further in our studies.
You have given us a world of infinite riches:
thank you for all who help us explore it.

We thank you for those who teach today,
        in playgroups, schools, colleges and universities,
        in evening classes and distance learning courses,
        in areas of special need and adult education,
        in church and Sunday school.
You have given us a world of infinite riches:
thank you for all who help us explore it.

We thank you for the dedication of teachers and lecturers,
        the skill of researchers,
        the patience of examiners,
        the integrity of school inspectors,
        and the industry of secretarial and support staff
        in all places of learning.
You have given us a world of infinite riches:
thank you for all who help us explore it.

We thank you for the access everyone in this country has
    to free education as children,
    and for the opportunity throughout life
    to learn new skills and assimilate knowledge
    which will serve for a lifetime.
Teach all to make the most of the opportunities given to them,
    and help us as a society to safeguard this precious heritage
    for future generations,
    so that others may enjoy, in turn,
    the privilege we have experienced.
You have given us a world of infinite riches:
    thank you for all who help us explore it.

Through Jesus Christ our Lord.
Amen.

104

INTERCESSION
THE DEMANDS OF TEACHING AND LEARNING

Loving God,
   we pray today for those involved
     in the difficult and often unappreciated task of education.
   We pray for teachers with all the pressures they face –
     expectations from parents,
     demands from governments and politicians,
     a growing burden of administration,
     and mounting problems of discipline,
     sometimes involving even a threat to their own safety.
   Grant your wisdom to guide,
     and your hand to bless.

We pray for schools and colleges
     in an increasingly competitive world –
     struggling to balance budgets,
     short of staff and resources,
     disheartened by performances in league tables,
     some even facing the prospect of closure through lack of numbers.
   Grant your wisdom to guide,
     and your hand to bless.

We pray for staff who feel unable to cope
     with the demands made upon them –
     worn down by stress,
     confused by change,
     frustrated by bureaucracy,
     exhausted by unruly pupils.
   Grant your wisdom to guide,
     and your hand to bless.

We pray also for students who feel similarly overwhelmed,
    though by different pressures –
    crushed by a weight of expectations,
    broken by bullying,
    wrestling with learning difficulties,
    fearful of examinations.
Grant your wisdom to guide,
    and your hand to bless.

And we pray finally for governors,
    local education authorities,
    politicians and planners,
    as they seek to respond to changing circumstances,
    juggling with the practical, financial and electoral issues involved.
Grant your wisdom to guide,
    and your hand to bless.

Loving God,
    we pray for all involved in the task of education,
        whether it be those at the forefront of delivery,
        those behind the scenes,
        or students and scholars directly involved
        in the pursuit of knowledge.
    Reach out in love,
        and grant to each your guidance, wisdom, strength and support.
    Grant your wisdom to guide,
        and your hand to bless.

Through Jesus Christ our Lord.
Amen.

MOTHERING SUNDAY

105

PRAISE
A MOTHER'S LOVE

Gracious God,
   on this special day of thanksgiving,
      we catch a glimpse,
      through a mother's love for her child,
      of your love for us;
      the care, dedication and devotion you show to all your children
      which makes you as much 'our Mother' as 'our Father'.
   For the intensity of your love,
      Lord, we praise you.

As a mother nurtures her children,
      instructing,
      feeding,
      clothing,
      guiding,
      so you nurture us,
      carefully leading us towards maturity.
   For the intensity of your love,
      Lord, we praise you.

As a mother tends her children,
      comforting in times of distress,
      reassuring in times of uncertainty,
      encouraging in times of challenge,
      nursing in times of sickness,
      so you tend us,
      always there to lift us up
      and set us on our feet again when we fall.
   For the intensity of your love,
      Lord, we praise you.

As a mother protects her children,
 watching over them day by day,
 alert to danger,
 keeping them from harm,
 and ready if necessary to sacrifice herself for their sakes,
 so you protect us,
 your arms constantly encircling us,
 your hand delivering us from evil.
For the intensity of your love,
 Lord, we praise you.

Gracious God,
 Mother and Father of us all,
  we rejoice today in the wonder of your love
  and the constancy of your care.
Gratefully we respond,
 in joyful worship
 and heartfelt thanksgiving.
For the intensity of your love,
 Lord, we praise you.

In the name of Christ, your only Son.
Amen.

106

CONFESSION
APPRECIATING MOTHERS

Gracious God,
    we are reminded today
        of how easily we take a mother's love for granted,
        failing to express our thanks for the care we receive,
        slow to demonstrate our appreciation
        for the patient nurture given over so many years.
    For forgetting to show our gratitude,
        Lord, forgive us.

We are reminded equally of how easily we take *your* love for granted,
    failing to thank you for the blessings you shower upon us,
    the care with which you daily surround us,
    and the joy with which you fill our lives.
For forgetting to show our gratitude,
    Lord, forgive us.

We have assumed that words do not need saying,
    that our thankfulness can be taken as read.
We have believed love comes easily,
    failing to recognise what it can sometimes cost.
We have imagined because no thanks is asked
    that no thanks is necessary.
For forgetting to show our gratitude,
    Lord, forgive us.

Gracious God,
help us to understand the joy we can bring
    through saying thank you,
    not just today but every day,
    not just to our mothers but to everyone,
    and not just to everyone but to you.
And help us, through the act of thanksgiving,
    to recognise how much we have to be thankful for.
For forgetting to show our gratitude,
    Lord, forgive us.

In the name of Christ we ask it.
Amen.

107

THANKSGIVING
QUALITIES OF MOTHERS

Loving God,
 we thank you for mothers –
  for all they mean or have meant to us,
  for the love they have shown,
  and the care they have given.
 Creator of all,
  receive our thanks.

We thank you for the dedication of mothers –
  the sacrifices they make,
  the support they offer,
  the comfort they bring,
  and the guidance they provide.
 Creator of all,
  receive our thanks.

We thank you for the qualities of mothers –
  their patience,
  kindness,
  concern
  and understanding.
 Creator of all,
  receive our thanks.

We thank you for the role of mothers,
  the part they play in our lives,
  our homes,
  our society
  and our world.
 Creator of all,
  receive our thanks.

We thank you for the joy of mothers –
    the pleasure,
    enrichment,
    laughter and fulfilment,
    which raising children brings.
Creator of all,
    receive our thanks.

We thank you for time spent with mothers –
    the learning,
    playing,
    caring and sharing,
    which are part of family life.
Creator of all,
    receive our thanks.

Loving God,
    we thank you for this day of saying thank you,
        this opportunity to say what we so often mean to say
        but so rarely do.
For mothers and motherhood,
    for children and families,
    we bring you this day our grateful praise.
Creator of all,
    receive our thanks.

Through Jesus Christ our Lord.
Amen.

108

INTERCESSION
THE RESPONSIBILITIES OF MOTHERS
AND THOSE DENIED THE JOY OF MOTHERHOOD

Gracious God,
   on this Mothering Sunday we bring your our prayers
     for all entrusted with the responsibility of motherhood.
   Loving Lord,
     hear our prayer.

We pray for mothers the world over,
   recognising both the joys and demands they experience –
   the privilege and pressures,
   hopes and fears,
   pleasure and pain that motherhood entails.
Equip them with the love, wisdom and strength they need.
Loving Lord,
   hear our prayer.

We pray for single mothers,
   bearing the responsibility of parenthood alone,
   struggling sometimes to make ends meet,
   and stigmatised by certain sections of society.
Grant them the emotional, physical and financial resources they need.
Loving Lord,
   hear our prayer.

We pray for mothers who have experienced heartbreak –
   their children stillborn or seriously disabled,
   injured, maimed or killed through accident or assault,
   struck down by debilitating disease or terminal illness.
Comfort them in their sorrow.
Loving Lord,
   hear our prayer.

We pray for those denied the joy of motherhood –
    enduring the trauma of infertility,
    prevented on health grounds from risking a pregnancy,
    or unable to establish a relationship
    into which children can be born.
Help them to come to terms with their pain.
Loving Lord,
    hear our prayer.

We pray for those who foster or adopt children,
    those who long to do so but who are denied the opportunity,
    and those who for various reasons
    have given up their children
    and who are haunted by the image of what might have been.
Grant them your strength and support.
Loving Lord,
    hear our prayer.

We pray finally for those who long to discover their natural mothers,
    those who have become estranged from them,
    and those whose mothers have died –
    all for whom Mothering Sunday brings pain rather than pleasure,
    hurt rather than happiness.
May your love enfold them always.
Loving Lord,
    hear our prayer.

Gracious God,
    we pray for mothers and children everywhere.
    May your blessing be upon them,
        your hand guide them,
        and your love enrich them all.
Loving Lord,
    hear our prayer.

Through Jesus Christ our Lord.
Amen.

CHRISTIAN AID WEEK

109

PRAISE
THE KINGDOM OF CHRIST

Lord Jesus Christ,
  we remember that you came to turn the world upside down –
    to scatter the proud in the imagination of their hearts;
    to bring down the powerful from their thrones,
    and to lift up the lowly;
    to fill the hungry with good things,
    and to send the rich away empty.
For the dawn of your kingdom,
  and all who work towards its fulfilment,
  we praise you.

We remember that you came to bring good news to the poor;
    to proclaim release for the captives
    and recovery of sight to the blind;
    to let the oppressed go free,
    and to proclaim the year of the Lord's favour.
For the dawn of your kingdom,
  and all who work towards its fulfilment,
  we praise you.

We remember that you came to bring healing to the sick
    and strength to the weak,
    hope to the despairing
    and comfort to the broken-hearted,
    joy to the sorrowful
    and succour to the suffering.
For the dawn of your kingdom,
  and all who work towards its fulfilment,
  we praise you.

We remember that you came to judge with righteousness,
and to decide with equity for the meek of the earth;
to bring love where there is hatred,
peace where there is war,
and life where there is death.
For the dawn of your kingdom,
and all who work towards its fulfilment,
we praise you.

Lord Jesus Christ,
we remember, too, that you come again, day by day,
in the hungry and thirsty,
the stranger and the sick,
the naked and the imprisoned,
your voice calling out for food and water,
for acceptance and compassion,
for clothing and concern.
We thank you for all who respond to your call,
striving to build a better world.
Inspire us through their service,
and teach us to respond in turn.
For the dawn of your kingdom,
and all who work towards its fulfilment,
we praise you.

Amen.

110

CONFESSION
SHOWING WE CARE

Living God,
we are reminded today of the needs of the poor,
and we are genuinely troubled by their plight,
our consciences stirred,
our anger kindled,
and our sympathy evoked.
And yet, we confess,
all too often we have forgotten such needs,
our eyes closed to the pain, deprivation, injustice
and exploitation so many experience.
For turning our back on those in need,
Lord, forgive us.

We speak today of change,
of campaigning for a fairer world.
We pray today for justice,
a fresh start for the poor.
We give today our money,
to support the work of Christian Aid
in everything it is trying to achieve.
But tomorrow we will forget –
the cry of the hungry,
the despair of the sick
and the anger of the poor
put out of our minds
until someone once again reminds us of their suffering.
For turning our back on those in need,
Lord, forgive us.

We are good at expressing concern,
  fine-sounding words coming easily to us,
  but when it comes to action,
  especially if it involves cost,
  it is a different story:
  our own interests put before those of others,
  our response small, if it is there at all.
For turning our back on those in need,
  Lord, forgive us.

Living God,
  have mercy on our greed and selfishness,
  our complacency in the face of the world's evils,
  and our share in a world
  which not only perpetuates the divide between rich and poor
  but which actively pursues policies that widen the gap.
Stir our consciences,
  kindle our anger,
  and evoke our sympathy
  not just today but every day,
  and give us the resolve, through our giving and living,
  to help make a difference.
For turning our back on the needy,
  Lord, forgive us.

In the name of Christ.
Amen.

111

PETITION
WORKING FOR CHANGE

Gracious God,
  as we come to you on this Christian Aid Sunday,
    we are conscious that we are the lucky ones –
    with food in our bellies and a roof over our heads,
    with ample supplies of water and medicine,
    with access to education and technology –
    our lives brimming over with good things.
  You have given us so much:
    teach us to give generously in turn.

We pray for the millions less fortunate than us –
    those for whom hunger is a daily reality,
    a proper home a luxury,
    fresh water, medical care and education a dream,
    and the lifestyles we enjoy here in the West
    a source of wonder and bewilderment.
  You have given us so much:
    teach us to give generously in turn.

We know we cannot change the world alone,
    yet we know also that, with your help, nothing is impossible.
  Teach us, then, to give sacrificially,
    to live more simply,
    and to work for change.
  Teach us to remember those in need,
    in our prayers and in our actions,
    and so, together, help us to make a difference.
  You have given us so much:
    teach us to give generously in turn.

Sovereign God,
    forgive us that it takes a day like Christian Aid Sunday
        to turn our thoughts to the poor.
    Teach us to live for others throughout our lives,
        to practise what we preach,
        and to work towards the fulfilment of our prayers
        through the things we do
        and the people we are.
    You have given us so much:
        teach us to give generously in turn.

In the name of Christ.
Amen.

112

INTERCESSION
THOSE IN NEED AND THOSE WHO WORK FOR JUSTICE

Lord of all,
  we pray for those in need throughout the world,
    remembering that, in their cry, you are calling out for help,
    and that, in responding to them, we respond to you.
  Your kingdom come,
    on earth as it is in heaven.

We pray for those who have no food –
    those for whom hunger is an ever-present experience,
    who do not know where the next meal is coming from,
    who each day face the prospect of starvation.
  Your kingdom come,
    on earth as it is in heaven.

We pray for those deprived of the resources we take for granted –
    fresh water,
    clothing,
    housing,
    education
    and medical care –
    countless millions who have so little
    whilst the few of us have so much.
  Your kingdom come,
    on earth as it is in heaven.

We pray for those like Christian Aid who work for change –
    organising and transporting relief supplies,
    offering resources and opportunities for self-help,
    striving to overcome exploitation and oppression,
    campaigning for peace and justice for all.
  Your kingdom come,
    on earth as it is in heaven.

Use these,
  and all your people,
  to show something of your love and compassion.
Reach out,
  wherever there is hunger, poverty, homelessness and disease,
  and stir the hearts of individuals and nations
  to live more simply,
  so that others may simply live.
Your kingdom come,
  on earth as it is in heaven.

In the name of Christ we ask it.
Amen.

FATHER'S DAY

113

PRAISE
A FATHER'S LOVE

Sovereign God,
   Creator of the heavens and the earth,
      Ruler over space and time,
      we praise you that we can respond to you as a Father;
      that we can approach you,
      not in a spirit of subservience or fear,
      but as your children,
      assured of your love and secure in your purpose.
   Father of all,
      we worship you.

We praise you that you care for us
      as much as any father cares for his child
      and far more besides –
      your hand always there to guide and discipline,
      to provide and protect,
      to comfort and encourage,
      to nurture and cherish.
   Father of all,
      we worship you.

We praise you that your love is inexhaustible –
      that, however often we fail you,
      however many times we may stray from your side,
      you seek us out,
      striving to restore the relationship we have broken,
      always ready to forgive and forget.
   Father of all,
      we worship you.

We praise you that we are made in your image,
   capable of understanding good and evil,
   able to appreciate treasure in heaven
   as well as the many riches of this world,
   and able also to respond to your love in Christ
   and so inherit your kingdom.
Father of all,
   we worship you.

Sovereign God,
   we come to you on this Father's Day,
      giving thanks for everything that fathers mean to us,
      but rejoicing above all in your fatherly care for all.
   With grateful hearts, we bring you praise,
      and commit ourselves again to your service.
Father of all,
   we worship you.

Through Jesus Christ our Lord.
Amen.

114

CONFESSION
GOD'S WILFUL CHILDREN

Gracious God,
    we call you 'our Father',
        but we rarely live as your children ought to live.
We are stubborn, wilful and disobedient,
        repeatedly rejecting your guidance,
        time and again betraying your love.
Father,
    forgive us.

We speak of being called into your family,
        but we are often a family divided,
        allowing petty disputes,
        anger, bitterness, envy and resentment,
        to come between us.
Father,
    forgive us.

We claim to be made in your image,
        but there is very little of you to be seen in us.
We find it hard to love,
        difficult to forgive
        and almost impossible to let go of self.
Father,
    forgive us.

We tell ourselves that our relationship with you is a close one,
        that through Christ we can call you 'Abba, Father',
        but the truth is that we stray far from your side, day after day,
        oblivious to your presence
        and unconcerned about the gulf this creates between us.
Father,
    forgive us.

Gracious God,
  forgive us everything that holds us back from knowing you,
    that prevents us enjoying the special relationship
    you long to share with us.
  Help us to respond joyfully and spontaneously to your love,
    and, in childlike trust,
    to receive the blessings you so long to give us.
  Come to us now,
    and draw us closer to yourself.

Through Jesus Christ our Lord.
Amen.

115

THANKSGIVING
FATHERS AND FATHERHOOD

Gracious God,
   we thank you today for fathers and for all that they do,
     their role sometimes taken for granted
     and yet meaning so much.
Father of mercies,
   receive our thanksgiving.

We thank you for our own fathers –
     for all they have meant to us,
     everything they have contributed to our lives,
     and we acknowledge, with gratitude,
     the support they have offered;
     the care they have shown,
     the instruction they have given,
     and the love they have shared.
Father of mercies,
   receive our thanksgiving.

We thank you for the privilege of fatherhood –
     the wonder of sharing in the creation of a new life,
     the thrill of seeing a child mature into adulthood,
     the awe-inspiring responsibility of nurturing, guiding,
     enabling and encouraging,
     and the sheer joy of giving and receiving love,
     building a relationship that will endure for a lifetime and beyond.
Father of mercies,
   receive our thanksgiving.

Gracious God,
   we thank you for fathers
      and, above all, we thank you for your fatherhood,
      your creation of all,
      your constant nurture,
      your unfailing love which delights to call us your children
      and which is always looking to draw us more deeply
      into the family of your people.
   Father of mercies,
      receive our thanksgiving.

In the name of Christ.
Amen.

116

INTERCESSION
THE RESPONSIBILITY OF FATHERHOOD

Father God,
    we pray today for those entrusted with the responsibility of fatherhood,
        all who have the duty and privilege of raising children,
        fashioning their lives,
            offering a stable and loving environment in which they can grow,
            leading them along the exciting yet demanding path to adulthood.
    Grant them love, insight and devotion.
    Father of all,
        hear our prayer.

We pray for fathers whose marriage
        or relationship with their partner has broken down;
        separated from their children or seeing them only occasionally,
        many having responsibilities for another family,
        and we pray also for stepfathers
        who will fill the role that once was theirs.
    Grant them commitment, dedication and sensitivity.
    Father of all,
        hear our prayer.

We pray for fathers with no sense of responsibility,
        failing to make time for their children,
        careless in offering support and guidance,
        casual in providing discipline,
        essentially washing their hands of their role as parents.
    Grant them forgiveness, understanding
        and the opportunity to make amends.
    Father of all,
        hear our prayer.

We pray for children of broken homes,
 deprived of a father figure
 or knowing first one, then another,
 rarely able to establish a meaningful and lasting relationship.
Grant them stability, support
 and the knowledge that they are still loved.
Father of all,
 hear our prayer.

We pray for children abused by their fathers,
 emotionally scarred for life,
 struggling to come to terms with their experience,
 haunted by an image of fear rather than love.
Grant them healing, peace and courage to face the future.
Father of all,
 hear our prayer.

Finally, we pray for those who have lost their fathers,
 whether as children or as adults,
 for some their father little more than a name,
 for others, a heart-wrenching memory,
 but each carrying a sense of loss.
Grant your strength, your comfort and your hope.
Father of all,
 hear our prayer.

Father God,
 we lift before you today fathers and their children.
 Enfold them in your love,
 and surround them with your fatherly care,
 today and every day.
Father of all,
 hear our prayer.

Through your Son, Jesus Christ our Lord.
Amen.

HARVEST FESTIVAL

117

PRAISE
THE PROVISION OF GOD

Lord of life,
    we gather this day to praise you,
        to acknowledge you as Creator of heaven and earth,
        to thank you for your faithful provision,
        and to celebrate the constant cycle of the seasons,
        of day and night,
        seed-time and harvest.
    Richly you have blessed us.
    Gladly we praise you!

Day by day,
    year by year,
    we see your hand at work,
    we marvel at the beauty of your design,
    and we rejoice in all you have given.
    Richly you have blessed us.
    Gladly we praise you!

We praise you for this vast and awesome universe
    in which you have placed us,
    this world in which we live,
    and this country in which we have been born –
    so many reasons to count our blessings,
    so much to thank you for.
    Richly you have blessed us.
    Gladly we praise you!

We thank you for the harvest which surrounds us today,
    for the many places from which it has come,
    for the toil which has made it possible,
    and for your hand which ultimately lies behind it.
    Richly you have blessed us.
    Gladly we praise you!

Lord of life,
 we recognise again your goodness,
  we remember once more how fortunate we are,
  and we celebrate the bountiful provision of your creation.
 Gladly we come,
  with thankful hearts and joyful worship.
 Richly you have blessed us.
 Gladly we praise you!

In the name of Christ.
Amen.

118

CONFESSION
OUR CARELESS STEWARDSHIP

Gracious God,
  we have so much to thank you for,
    your creation so rich
    and the resources you have given us so many,
    and yet we all too rarely show our gratitude.
We take your blessings for granted,
    complaining about what we haven't got
    instead of rejoicing in what we have.
For the poverty of our response to your great goodness,
    Lord, forgive us.

We are not only ungrateful but irresponsible,
    squandering what you have given,
    frittering away the earth's treasures
    with no thought of tomorrow.
We are part of a world which wantonly pollutes
    and knowingly wastes,
    and we have done little if anything about it,
    preferring a life of comfort
    to the sacrifice a stand of principle would entail.
For the poverty of our response to your great goodness,
    Lord, forgive us.

We are not only irresponsible but selfish,
    our thoughts more often than not
    concerned simply with our own satisfaction
    and the pleasure of the moment.
We forget the needs of those around us,
    we ignore the cry of the poor across the world,
    and we ride roughshod over the claims of future generations
    to their rightful stake in your creation.
We are part of a world in which the few have plenty
    and the rest make do with crumbs from the table;

a world in which the well-being of the future
is sacrificed to the whims of the present;
and once more we have remained silent,
telling ourselves that there is nothing we can do
and so ducking the issue.
For the poverty of our response to your great goodness,
Lord, forgive us.

Gracious God,
we are reminded today
that thanksgiving must be more than simply words,
that it involves the stewardship of your gifts
and the generosity of our giving,
commitment both to you and to others.
Help us, as we celebrate another harvest,
to recognise that challenge and to act upon it.
For the poverty of our response to your great goodness,
Lord, forgive us.

In the name of Christ.
Amen.

119

Thanksgiving and petition
The riches of creation

Loving God,
we bring you this day our thanksgiving
for everything you have given us.
You have blessed us in so much:
teach us to use all your gifts wisely.

We thank you for the infinite beauty of our world,
for the complexity of the universe,
for the wonder of creation that can never be exhausted.
You have blessed us in so much:
teach us to use all your gifts wisely.

We thank you for the constant miracle of day and night,
summer and winter,
springtime and harvest,
the regular cycle of life that we know and depend on.
You have blessed us in so much:
teach us to use all your gifts wisely.

We thank you for the rich resources of this planet,
and for all those who labour in different ways
to make them accessible to us.
You have blessed us in so much:
teach us to use all your gifts wisely.

We thank you for minds with which to understand,
enquire and learn,
for senses with which to see, hear, smell, taste and touch,
and for health to enjoy, savour and celebrate.
You have blessed us in so much:
teach us to use all your gifts wisely.

Forgive us that sometimes we lose our sense of thankfulness,
    becoming complacent and over-familiar
    with the richness of creation.
Forgive us for taking your many gifts for granted,
    forgetting them,
    squandering them,
    even abusing them.
You have blessed us in so much:
    teach us to use all your gifts wisely.

Loving God,
    give us a new sense of joy and gladness,
        hearts that are truly thankful.
Help us to recognise again the awesome riches of creation,
        and to rejoice in the blessings which you shower upon us.
You have blessed us in so much:
    teach us to use all your gifts wisely.

Through Jesus Christ our Lord.
Amen.

120

INTERCESSION
ALL WHO REAP GOD'S HARVEST

Creator God,
 we pray for those to whom we owe our harvest,
  all whose labour and dedication enables us
  to share in the bounty of this world's resources.
 Gracious Lord,
  hear our prayer.

We pray for farmers at this time of difficulty for so many –
 a time of so much change and so many complex issues,
 one crisis and controversy following upon another,
 with a corresponding sense of mistrust and anxiety
 among consumers.
Grant your help in overcoming adversity.
Gracious Lord,
 hear our prayer.

We pray for farmers in other lands –
 denied the resources they need to cultivate their land,
 overwhelmed by drought, flood or other catastrophe,
 oppressed by exploitative regimes
 or economic systems loaded against them –
 both they and their people unable to enjoy
 the due fruits of their labours.
Grant them hope, help and justice.
Gracious Lord,
 hear our prayer.

We pray for those who bring in the harvest of earth and sea –
 minerals, oil, gas, fish –
 a harvest often involving danger to life and limb.
Grant them skill, courage and protection.
Gracious Lord,
 hear our prayer.

We pray for those who make possible the harvest of technology –
scientists, technicians, computer programmers and engineers –
their skills opening up new worlds and untold horizons,
capable of so much good yet so much evil.
Grant them wisdom, ingenuity and a due sense of responsibility.
Gracious Lord,
hear our prayer.

We pray for those who help to reap the harvest of minds –
teachers, students, researchers and scholars –
each striving to expand our knowledge
and enlarge our understanding.
Give them patience, dedication and integrity.
Gracious Lord,
hear our prayer.

Creator God,
hear our prayer for all who make available
the innumerable and diverse riches of your creation.
Equip, inspire and guide them in their work,
so that they may steward your gifts wisely to the good of all.
Gracious Lord,
hear our prayer.

In the name of Jesus Christ our Saviour.
Amen.

ONE WORLD WEEK

121

PRAISE
THE LORD OF ALL

Almighty God,
  Lord of all that is,
    all that has been
    and all that shall be,
    we worship you.
  You are sovereign over heaven and earth:
    gladly, we adore you.

Loving God,
  Lord of all people,
    all nations,
    all cultures,
    we praise you.
  You are sovereign over heaven and earth:
    gladly, we adore you.

Living God,
  Lord of the world,
    the Church,
    and our lives,
    we come to remind ourselves of the breadth of your love,
    the extent of your purpose,
    and the scope of your kingdom.
  You are sovereign over heaven and earth:
    gladly, we adore you.

306 LIFE AND FAITH

Sovereign God,
    open our minds and hearts to all you have done,
        all you are doing
        and all you shall yet do.
    Teach us more of the fellowship we share
        with your people across the world,
        and inspire us through their experience of your grace
        and their expression of discipleship.
    So may we give you the honour and glory that is rightfully yours,
        this and every day.
    You are sovereign over heaven and earth:
        gladly, we adore you.

In the name of Christ.
Amen.

122

CONFESSION
A DIVIDED WORLD

Sovereign God,
   we talk of being 'one world'
      but we know, in reality, that we are not.
   Though we try to push the truth out of our minds,
      we know that we are two worlds –
      a world of rich and a world of poor,
      well-fed and hungry,
      healthy and sick,
      powerful and powerless –
      two worlds between which the divide grows ever greater,
      the contrast ever more shocking.
We are accomplices to the crime:
   Lord, forgive us.

We confess that what is true of the world as a whole
   is true of the rich world we live in,
      our society riven in two between the haves and the have-nots,
      the wealthy and the poor,
      the well-to-do and the underprivileged –
      two societies between which the divide grows ever greater,
      the contrast ever more stark.
We are accomplices to the crime:
   Lord, forgive us.

We confess that, though we speak of pursuing justice
   and seeking change,
      few of us are actually willing to make sacrifices,
      to have less so that others may have more.
We close our eyes to challenges we would rather not face,
   ignoring injustice so long as it does not touch us.
We are accomplices to the crime:
   Lord, forgive us.

Sovereign God,
  help us not just to speak of 'one world',
    nor even simply to pray for it.
  Teach us to work towards the fulfilment of that vision,
    through Jesus Christ our Lord.
  Amen.

123

PETITION
STEWARDS OF CREATION

Creator God,
    sovereign over all,
        we pray today for the world you have given to us.
    We hold it in trust:
        teach us to be wise stewards of creation.

Forgive us the folly of our modern lifestyles,
        the fact that, even though we have repeatedly been warned
        of its costly consequences,
        we are reluctant to change.
Forgive us that, even as we speak,
        some part of the natural world is being destroyed
        and its climate and environment changed,
        perhaps for ever.
We hold it in trust:
        teach us to be wise stewards of creation.

Forgive the short-sightedness and greed
        that has led to this situation,
        the living for today with no thought of tomorrow,
        and the obsession with material possessions
        at the cost of spiritual values.
Forgive the massive divide between rich and poor
        which it has served to create,
        and which makes any prospect
        of resolving the issues involved so remote.
We hold it in trust:
        teach us to be wise stewards of creation.

Grant true wisdom and courage to leaders of nations
in response to this growing crisis.
Stir the hearts of all people everywhere to live more responsibly,
and teach all who profess the name of Christ
to lead by example.
Inspire a deeper understanding of what it means to be one world,
and so may we pass on to our children,
and our children's children,
a world fit to inherit.
We hold it in trust:
teach us to be wise stewards of creation.

Creator God,
hear our prayer,
through Jesus Christ our Lord.
Amen.

124

INTERCESSION
BREAKING DOWN THE BARRIERS

Sovereign God,
  Lord of all,
    we pray once more for our troubled and divided world,
    so full of tension,
    so full of need.
  We pray for our world,
    recognising that it is *your* world also,
    and your world *first*.
  Lord, in your mercy,
    hear our prayer.

We pray for those who strive to bring liberty –
    a world free from religious and political persecution,
    from racial bigotry and ethnic cleansing,
    from dictatorship and oppression.
  Strengthen their resolve,
    and may the evil that holds people captive be destroyed.
  Lord, in your mercy,
    hear our prayer.

We pray for those who strive to bring justice –
    a world free from exploitation and corruption,
    prejudice and discrimination,
    debt and dependence.
  Prosper them in their work,
    and may the rights of all be respected.
  Lord, in your mercy,
    hear our prayer.

We pray for those who strive to bring peace –
   the breaking-down of barriers between nations,
   the challenging of long-held prejudices,
   and the promotion of dialogue and reconciliation.
Encourage them in their efforts,
   and may the fears and suspicions that divide us be overcome.
Lord, in your mercy,
   hear our prayer.

We pray for those who strive to bring answerability –
   an awareness of our common humanity,
   of our responsibility towards the environment,
   and the consequences of actions.
Speak through their voice,
   and so may your creation be passed on intact
   to future generations.
Lord, in your mercy,
   hear our prayer.

Sovereign God,
   come again to our broken world
      and grant your healing.
Bring peace where there is war,
   and love where there is hatred;
   reconciliation where there is division,
   and co-operation where there is conflict;
   good where there is evil,
   and wisdom where there is folly.
Instil in all a willingness
   to engage in dialogue rather than dispute,
   in discussion rather than destruction,
   and so may your world become
   the *one world* you long for it to be.
Lord, in your mercy,
   hear our prayer.

Amen.

REMEMBRANCE SUNDAY

125

REFLECTION (1)
I WAS THERE

Why remember events that happened many years ago? Why perpetuate
memories of a conflict long since past? Many today understandably raise
such questions and had we enjoyed unbroken global peace since the two
World Wars their arguments would carry much force. Only, of course,
the reality is that conflict continues to be all too common. Central America,
the Falklands, Bosnia, Northern Ireland and the Middle East, to name but
a few, have all given stark reminders of the tensions which continue to
scar our world. There are no easy answers to such divisions, and history
has taught us that peace, if secured at all, is a fragile thing, hard won and
easily broken. Yet the cost of war reminds us of the need to establish
global justice and to break down the barriers that continue to exact such
a heavy toll. We owe it not just to the countless human victims of war
but, above all, to God – the greatest victim of all.

I was there –
   there in the trenches among the rats and lice,
   struggling in the mud
   as the machine guns spewed out their hail of bullets,
   lying in agony beside the rows of corpses,
   all around me the bodies of my friends,
   limb torn from limb,
   wounds gaping,
   bodies shattered beyond recognition –
   and my heart bled with them.

I was there in the city as the bombs cascaded from the sky,
   there among the screams and sobs,
   beating back the flames,
   pulling away the rubble,
   searching frantically with the mother
   for the little one she would never see again –
   and, like her, my heart went cold with horror.

I was there in the prison camp,
    beaten, starved, tortured,
    watching helplessly as one by one my loved ones were led away,
    as the smoke rose above the ovens,
    as the carts trundled from the gas chamber, laden with death –
    and my heart groaned in despair.

I was there as the missile struck and the world disintegrated,
    as the deadly cloud rose high above the devastation,
    as we retched in agony,
    as we coughed up blood,
    as we sat hopelessly in the cancer ward,
    knowing the end was near –
    and my heart cried in anger.

Yes, I was there,
    the one who died on a cross to put an end to death and misery,
    dying again,
    and again,
    and if you think it broke your heart,
    remember this: it broke mine too.
You can't change what's been,
    but you can what's yet to be,
    and, believe me, you would if you'd seen what I've seen.

I was there,
    and I'm begging you,
    please,
    please,
    PLEASE,
    don't let it happen again!

126

REFLECTION (2)
IT WAS MARCH

Every night, in the town of Ypres in Belgium, a crowd gathers at 8 o'clock beneath the Menin Gate to observe the ceremony of the Last Post. It is a simple yet profoundly moving tribute to all those who gave their lives during the First World War. The location could hardly be more fitting, the beautiful town of Ypres having been reduced to rubble during that conflict but lovingly restored afterwards, stone for stone. More powerful still, on the Menin Gate are inscribed the names of the thousands of soldiers killed in the Ypres-Salient and with no known grave. There can surely be few more graphic reminders of the awful cost of war. The following poem, offered as an introduction before observing two minutes' silence, seeks to bring home that cost and to prompt reflection on our responsibility today to work for peace. It was written during my time with Toc H, a national movement committed to breaking down barriers of prejudice and discrimination in society, and it encapsulates the principles at the heart of that movement: building bravely, loving widely, thinking fairly and witnessing humbly.

It was March when we visited Ypres,
    just a few weeks short of the spring,
    the flowers were starting to open,
    the birds beginning to sing.
Outside, in fertile lowlands,
    the grass grew lush and green,
    no sign now of the carnage
    which once these fields had seen.
And in the busy centre,
    a constant hum of sound,
    as a milling throng of people
    pursued their daily round.
Few hints here of the horrors
    that racked this charming place,
    mock medieval splendour
    and pleasant open space.

But as the sunlight faded
   and night began to fall,
   a little crowd assembled
   beside the city wall.
In different moods they stood there,
   some laughing, some in tears,
   some talking of the weather,
   some hiding inner fears.
But all at once fell silent
   as the clock came round to eight,
   and a poignant tribute sounded
   beneath the Menin Gate.
Another sad reminder,
   another fond farewell;
   a proud and thankful blessing,
   a heart-rending death knell.

And as the bugles faded
   till their sound was heard no more,
   we saw then all too clearly
   the dreadful face of war.
Instead of names around us
   there were young men in their prime,
   a tragic generation
   cut down before their time.
Our hearts were there beside them,
   we stood knee-deep in mud,
   and shared the awful horror
   of fields dyed red with blood.
We heard their cries of anguish,
   we felt their searing pain,
   and we understood more clearly
   this must never be again.

Yet the battle is not over,
   though the war may long be past,
   the fighting may have halted
   but the cause is only masked.
Unless we come together,
   until we learn to share,
   until we love more widely
   and think in ways more fair;
   until we build so bravely
   that all we say and do
   gives our hope of breaking barriers
   some hope of coming true,
   then the Last Post may be sounded
   in the future just the same,
   but the thousands who it heralds
   will all have died in vain.

127

PRAISE AND THANKSGIVING
THE PRICE OF FREEDOM

Sovereign God,
we praise you today for the freedom we enjoy
as a nation and as individuals –
freedom of speech and expression,
freedom from war and oppression –
a freedom secured at such enormous human cost.
For all we owe to so many,
receive our thanks.

We praise you for those who made such freedom possible,
the countless thousands who sacrificed life and limb
in two World Wars
and in subsequent conflicts,
leaving homes and loved ones, often to return no more.
For all we owe to so many,
receive our thanks.

We praise you for all who have fought against tyranny,
hatred and evil,
prepared to sacrifice everything
rather than allow such forces to hold sway;
and we salute their courage shown in the face of danger,
their dedication to duty,
their determination to battle on against all odds.
For all we owe to so many,
receive our thanks.

We praise you for the peace we enjoy today –
a peace which we need to treasure constantly,
nurture carefully
and safeguard always,
recognising the price at which it was won.
For all we owe to so many,
receive our thanks.

We praise you for those today who fight
for international freedom and justice –
members of UN peace-keeping forces in places of continuing tension,
striving to maintain democracy,
to keep rival factions apart,
to protect innocent civilians,
and to pave the way for a lasting end to hostilities.
For all we owe to so many,
receive our thanks.

Sovereign God,
we praise you today for the freedom we enjoy,
and we pray that the day will come
when there will be no more war,
when the nations of our world will live in harmony,
and when you will rule over all.
Until that time, help us to learn the lessons of the past,
to remember its sacrifices,
and to work as far as we are able for peace.
For all we owe to so many,
receive our thanks.

Through Jesus Christ our Lord.
Amen.

128

CONFESSION
LIVING AS PEACEMAKERS

Loving God,
    we are reminded today of how easy it is to speak of peace,
        and how difficult it is to pursue it;
            how straightforward it sounds to talk of breaking down barriers,
        yet how demanding it is actually to live as peacemakers.
    Yet we are reminded also that this is what you want from us –
        to live in such a way that we heal wounds rather than create them,
        that we unite rather than divide,
        that we reconcile rather than separate.
    For our share in the world's continuing pain,
        Lord, forgive us.

We confess the things within us which make for conflict –
    pride,
    greed,
    envy,
    intolerance,
    our nursing of petty grievances,
    our unwillingness to forgive,
    our preoccupation with self and our lack of time for others –
    so much that we are as guilty of as any other.
    For our share in the world's continuing pain,
        Lord, forgive us.

Rescue us from all that keeps us apart,
    and put a new spirit within us –
    a spirit of love and openness,
    acceptance and understanding,
    healing and reconciliation.
May the peace we pray for begin here and now in our hearts,
    and so may we be instruments of your peace,
    bringing healing to our broken world,
    and harmony between nations.
For our share in the world's continuing pain,
    Lord, forgive us.

In the name of Christ.
Amen.

129

INTERCESSION
VICTIMS OF WAR AND KEEPERS OF PEACE

Lord of all,
   hear us now as we pray for the victims of war
      and for peace in our world.

   We pray for those across the world who bear the scars of conflict –
      the injured, maimed and mentally distressed,
      those who have lost their limbs, their reason or their loved ones
      through the horrors of war.
   Lord, in your mercy,
      hear our prayer.

   We pray for those left homeless or as refugees,
      those who have lost their livelihoods and security,
      and those who still live in daily fear for their lives.
   Lord, in your mercy,
      hear our prayer.

   We pray for children who have been orphaned,
      parents who mourn their children,
      husbands and wives who have lost their partners –
      countless families whose lives will never be the same again.
   Lord, in your mercy,
      hear our prayer.

   We pray for those in the armed forces,
      charged with keeping the peace in countries across the world –
      their work involving months away from family and friends,
      and often danger to themselves.
   Lord, in your mercy,
      hear our prayer.

We pray for world leaders and rulers,
politicians and diplomats –
those whose decisions and negotiations
affect the lives of so many,
and in whose hands peace ultimately lies.
Lord, in your mercy,
hear our prayer.

Lord of all,
give wisdom to all who work for peace,
so that a more secure future may be ensured for all.
Give courage to those who strive for justice,
so that the causes of conflict may be overcome.
Give strength to those who seek to break down barriers,
that divisions over race, colour, creed and culture may be ended.
Grant that wherever war, or the threat of war,
continues to haunt lives,
a way of reconciliation may be found,
and harmony established between people and nations.
Lord, in your mercy,
hear our prayer.

In the name of Christ.
Amen.

SONGS OF PRAISE/
MUSIC SERVICE

130

PRAISE
A LIFE OF PRAISE

Gracious God,
   we are here to worship you –
      to lift up our voices in grateful praise,
      to make music together;
      a joyful noise,
      a new song of thanksgiving.
   I will sing to the Lord as long as I live.
   I will sing praise to my God while I have my being.

We do not lift up our voices only, but also our hearts –
      celebrating your great goodness,
      rejoicing in your awesome love,
      exulting in your unfailing grace.
   I will sing to the Lord as long as I live.
   I will sing praise to my God while I have my being.

We lift up our minds –
      focusing our thoughts upon you,
      on your will,
      your word,
      your kingdom.
   I will sing to the Lord as long as I live.
   I will sing praise to my God while I have my being.

We lift up our eyes –
      marvelling at the breadth of your purpose,
      the wonder of your creation,
      the awesomeness of your love.
   I will sing to the Lord as long as I live.
   I will sing praise to my God while I have my being.

We lift up our lives –
offering not just our music and song,
but everything we are,
all we say and think and do,
asking that you will take us
and consecrate us to your service,
transforming our lives through your renewing power.

Gracious God,
we are here to worship you –
to lift up our voices in grateful praise,
to make music together;
a joyful noise,
a new song of thanksgiving.
Accept what we offer for the reason that we offer it –
to give you the glory that is rightfully yours,
in heaven and on earth,
now and for evermore.
I will sing to the Lord as long as I live.
I will sing praise to my God while I have my being.

Thanks be to God,
through Jesus Christ our Lord.
Amen.

131

CONFESSION
SUPERFICIAL WORSHIP

Loving God,
    we are here to celebrate the gift of music,
        to offer you our songs as an expression of our praise,
        and we thank you for this special way
        of offering you worship.
    Yet we know that, like all good things, this gift can be misused,
        the medium obscuring the meaning behind it,
        the act more important than the intention,
        so that you have to say to us,
        as you said to your people centuries ago:
        'Take away from me the noise of your songs;
        I will not listen to the melody of your harps.'
When our worship says one thing and our lives another,
    Lord, forgive us.

We know that words alone aren't important
    unless they are backed up through our actions.
Forgive us the ways we fail to do that –
    our failure to pursue justice and to live righteously,
    to live in such a way that your love is seen through us
    and the dawn of your kingdom brought a little closer.
When our worship says one thing and our lives another,
    Lord, forgive us.

We know that the words that we sing and the love we proclaim
    should be so much a part of us
    that they inspire our every thought and action;
    that our worship should reflect
    the way you have touched our lives
    and express the commitment we joyfully offer back to you.
When our worship says one thing and our lives another,
    Lord, forgive us.

Forgive us that our singing has too often been shallow –
    the facts of our lives in stark contrast to the theory.
We have forgotten our neighbours and forgotten you,
    dancing to a very different tune
    from that which we trumpet in our worship.
We have had little sense of your presence in our lives
    and still less of our responsibility to others,
    our worship offered as part of our routine
    rather than as a living testimony to our love and devotion.
When our worship says one thing and our lives another,
    Lord, forgive us.

Loving God,
    save us from approaching worship out of habit,
    and equally from treating it as simply having a good time.
Save us from singing with no thought as to the words we use,
    or from offering praises with no substance underneath.
Speak to us through everything we share in today,
    and so, in turn, may we dedicate our lives to your service
    and give glory to you through the people we are.
When our worship says one thing and our lives another,
    Lord, forgive us.

Through Jesus Christ our Lord.
Amen.

132

THANKSGIVING AND PETITION
THANK YOU FOR THE MUSIC

Loving God,
  we thank you for the gift of music –
    for the way it is able to move and thrill,
    enthral and inspire us,
    stirring our emotions and expressing our feelings
    in a way that transcends words.
  My heart exults,
    and with my song I will give thanks.

We thank you for the way that music and song enrich our worship –
    their ability to capture our imagination
    and speak of your presence,
    their power to articulate our faith
    and encapsulate our response,
    their capacity to sum up our praise
    and declare our allegiance to Christ.
  My heart exults,
    and with my song I will give thanks.

We thank you for the great wealth of hymns, songs and choruses
    you have given us –
    some that have stood the test of time,
    others which are vibrantly new,
    some able to comfort and encourage,
    others serving to disturb and challenge,
    yet each in different ways speaking of your goodness
    and declaring your love.
  My heart exults,
    and with my song I will give thanks.

Help us to sing and make music,
    not just for the joy of doing so, special though that may be,
    but in a spirit of worship,
    consecrating our words and melodies to you,
    offering all, thoughtfully and prayerfully,
    as an expression of our devotion,
    a token of our gratitude,
    and a symbol of our commitment.
My heart exults,
    and with my song I will give thanks.

Loving God,
    may the songs of our lips
        and the music of our hearts,
        be acceptable in your sight,
        today and every day.
My heart exults,
    and with my song I will give thanks.

In the name of Christ.
Amen.

133

INTERCESSION
THOSE WHOSE SONG IS ONE OF PAIN

Living God,
    we have sung your praises,
        offering to you our worship in joyful celebration,
        but we know that there are some
        who have very different feelings at this time.
    We remember how your people long ago
        cried out by the waters of Babylon:
        'How can we sing the Lord's song in a strange land?' –
        their lives overwhelmed by sudden catastrophe,
        their hopes for the future crushed,
        their faith in your purpose shaken.
    So now we pray for those today
        who are facing sorrow and suffering,
        all for whom life seems a burden rather than a blessing.
    Reach out in love,
        and put a song of joy into their hearts.

We pray for those whose song is one of despair –
    the poor and weak,
    the oppressed and exploited,
    the hungry and homeless –
    all those denied the opportunity to help themselves,
    condemned to a lifetime of making do as best they can.
Reach out in love,
    and put a song of joy into their hearts.

We pray for those whose song is one of fear –
    those in lands torn by war,
    in communities racked by violence,
    in homes and relationships broken by abuse;
    victims of racial discrimination and sexual harassment,
    or religious intolerance and political persecution –
    all whose safety is daily in doubt.
Reach out in love,
    and put a song of joy into their hearts.

We pray for those whose song is one of grief –
  all who have lost loved ones,
  or seen them broken by accident or sickness,
  or whose relationships have ended in separation;
  those who have been betrayed or otherwise let down,
  who have been hurt by words or deeds,
  whose hopes and dreams have come to nothing.
Reach out in love,
  and put a song of joy into their hearts.

We pray for those whose song is one of pain –
  the sick and the suffering,
  wrestling with chronic disease,
  coming to terms with disabling injury,
  battling against terminal illness.
Reach out in love,
  and put a song of joy into their hearts.

We pray for those whose song is one of confusion –
  overwhelmed by the complexities of life,
  unsure of their ability to cope
  with its demands and responsibilities,
  uncertain as to the right way forward.
Reach out in love,
  and put a song of joy into their hearts.

Living God,
  we look forward to that day
    when every tongue will sing your praises,
    and all will rejoice in the light of your presence.
  Until that time,
    may everyone for whom life is hard
    know your hand upon them,
    and find in you the strength and the hope they need
    to walk safely through the valley of tears
    and the shadow of suffering,
    confident that night shall give way to dawn.
Reach out in love,
  and put a song of joy into their hearts.

Through Jesus Christ our Lord.
Amen.

CHURCH ANNIVERSARY

134

PRAISE
THE UNCHANGING GOD

Sovereign God,
  Lord of past, present and future,
    Lord of all,
    we come together, as we have so often come across the years,
    to thank and praise you.

We come rejoicing that, in all the uncertainties of life,
    we find in you one who is unchanging,
    a rock on which we can base our lives,
    a shield to protect us along the way,
    a light to guide our footsteps,
    and a love that fills our hearts with joy.
You have been our dwelling-place in all generations.
From everlasting to everlasting you are God.

We come to praise you for all the ways you have blessed us,
    as individuals and as a church –
    for the times of fellowship we have shared,
    the faith that has been nurtured,
    the support given and received,
    and the friendships established.
You have been our dwelling-place in all generations.
From everlasting to everlasting you are God.

We praise you for the experiences we have gone through together –
    the hopes realised,
    disappointments overcome,
    lessons learned,
    service offered.
You have been our dwelling-place in all generations.
From everlasting to everlasting you are God.

Forgive us that we are slow sometimes to remember your goodness,
  and swift to forget your many blessings.
We lose sight of the resources you put at our disposal,
  dwelling on *our fears* rather than *your strength,*
  our problems rather than *your promises,*
  our lives rather than *your kingdom.*
We become wrapped up in what is unimportant,
  putting our trust in what finally cannot satisfy,
  and our energy into what ultimately is secondary to our calling.
Our love, faith and commitment ebb and flow as each day passes,
  yet still you have been true to us,
  rich in mercy and grace.
You have been our dwelling-place in all generations.
From everlasting to everlasting you are God.

Receive our thanks that you are so different from us –
  faithful,
  constant,
  unchanging,
  always willing to show mercy,
  forever reaching out in love.
Receive our praise that you have been able to work through our lives,
  despite as well as because of us.
You have been our dwelling-place in all generations.
From everlasting to everlasting you are God.

Sovereign God,
  go with us now in the days ahead.
  Help us to recognise that, though all else may fail,
    you will not,
    and may that knowledge shape our life together.
  Help us to build on all that has gone before,
    so that we may follow you more faithfully,
    love you more truly,
    and see more clearly what you would have us do.
You have been our dwelling-place in all generations.
From everlasting to everlasting you are God.

To you be praise and glory,
  now and for evermore.
  through Jesus Christ our Lord.
Amen.

135

CONFESSION
THE FAITHFULNESS OF GOD

Sovereign God,
    as we think today of your great faithfulness,
        the constancy of your love,
        and the dependability of your grace,
        so we are made conscious of our faithlessness,
        our inconstancy,
        our fickle, undependable faith.
For our failure to live as your people,
    Lord, forgive us.

We have so much that should inspire us,
    so many reasons to put our trust in you,
    for you have sustained and guided this church across the years,
    speaking your word,
    calling fresh generations to faith,
    and opening up new avenues of service;
    yet still our faith is weak and our vision small,
    our life together often frustrating your kingdom
    rather than bringing it closer.
For our failure to live as your people,
    Lord, forgive us.

We have so much to celebrate, as a church and as individuals –
    the faith we share in common,
    the opportunity to meet together,
    the diversity of gifts within our fellowship,
    the sheer joy of life;
    yet all too often we have failed to rejoice,
    brooding instead on our problems,
    dwelling on past mistakes,
    consumed by our frustrations.
For our failure to live as your people,
    Lord, forgive us.

We have so much to share together –
  our hopes and dreams,
  joys and blessings,
  insights and observations,
  each of us having differing experiences of your love
  and contrasting journeys of faith;
  yet we have been careless in making time for fellowship,
  and when we have come together
  we have allowed petty divisions to come between us,
  clashes of opinion and personality
  overshadowing our unity in Christ.
For our failure to live as your people,
  Lord, forgive us.

Sovereign God,
  we come today reminded of your faithfulness to us,
    shown, not because of any virtue on our part,
    but out of your sheer grace.
  By that same grace, we ask, help us to draw closer to you,
    and to grow to maturity in Christ,
    and so, in the days ahead, may we learn to be faithful in turn.
For our failure to live as your people,
  Lord, forgive us.

In Jesus' name.
Amen.

136

PETITION
VISION FOR OUR CHURCH

Living God,
we thank you for the fellowship of your Church,
and, above all today, we thank you for the fellowship
to which we belong.
We praise you for all we experience here –
the fellowship we share,
the worship we offer,
the activities we are involved in.
Take everything we are,
everything we have been,
and help us to recognise everything you would have us be.

We thank you for those who had the vision to begin work here,
those whose dreams continued and sustained what they started,
and those who are part of this fellowship now.
Help us to build on all that has been accomplished,
and to grasp the opportunity you give us to help shape the future.
Take everything we are,
everything we have been,
and help us to recognise everything you would have us be.

Save us from ever growing complacent,
from becoming a people with no vision,
content simply to keep our doors open.
Save us from becoming closed to all that is new and different,
from turning in on ourselves,
or from being divided in our goals.
Take everything we are,
everything we have been,
and help us to recognise everything you would have us be.

Give us a vision of the way you can use us,
    the way you can deepen our fellowship,
    the way you can speak to us.
Help us to dream of what our church can become,
    of what your Church can be,
    and help us to work towards that dream's fulfilment.
Take everything we are,
    everything we have been,
    and help us to recognise everything you would have us be.

In the name of Jesus Christ our Lord.
Amen.

137

INTERCESSION
THE CHURCH'S MISSION

Loving God,
we have given you thanks for our church here,
remembering all we have shared together,
and looking forward to everything the future still holds.
Hear now our prayer for your people in every place.
Grant your blessing upon their life and witness,
and upon all you have called to service.
Build up your Church
and so bring closer your kingdom.

We pray for those involved in mission,
either at home or overseas –
evangelists,
preachers,
chaplains,
missionaries,
all those who seek to proclaim the gospel
and make known the love of Christ.
Build up your Church
and so bring closer your kingdom.

We pray for those who exercise roles of leadership,
whether it be over individual fellowships,
dioceses,
districts,
associations,
denominations,
or ecumenical groupings.
Build up your Church
and so bring closer your kingdom.

We pray for those who witness to you in their daily life and work,
 expressing their faith in all kinds of occupations and vocations,
 fleshing out the gospel,
 putting it into practice,
 exploring what it means
 in concrete and sometimes difficult situations.
Build up your Church
 and so bring closer your kingdom.

We pray for those who work for Christian unity,
 striving to draw your divided Church together,
 breaking down barriers,
 and building bridges of trust, respect, and co-operation.
Build up your Church
 and so bring closer your kingdom.

Loving God,
 guide your people,
 strengthen, equip and inspire each one for service,
 and so may we, with them, joyfully serve you,
 sensitively proclaim you,
 and faithfully express your love for all.
Build up your Church
 and so bring closer your kingdom.

Through Jesus Christ our Lord.
Amen.

CHURCH MEETINGS

138

Opening reflection
Meeting together

We come,
   we talk,
   we hear,
   but do we listen?

We come,
   we reflect,
   we consider,
   but do we learn?

We come,
   we exchange greetings,
   we share time,
   but do we meet?

Lord,
   it's easy to talk of fellowship,
   but hard to take the step of trust;
   easy to give *our* opinion,
   but hard to receive those of others;
   easy to open our mouths,
   but hard to open our souls.
Come among us now,
   and, through your Spirit, draw us more deeply into your love
   and closer to one another.
Break down everything that prevents dialogue and denies fellowship,
   and so, instead of simply coming to another meeting,
   help us to meet together.
Amen.

139

PETITION
WORKING FOR THE KINGDOM

Loving God,
    we meet together once more to seek your will
        and to commit ourselves afresh to the service of Christ.
    We come to worship you,
        to speak with you,
        to learn from you,
        so that we may be equipped to serve you better.
    You have called us together:
    send us out to work for your kingdom.

Be present with us now in this time together.
May it be an occasion of learning
    about one another and about you,
    of deepening friendships and strengthening faith,
    of encouragement and inspiration,
    and of renewal in our life together as a church.
You have called us together:
send us out to work for your kingdom.

Help us to recognise the variety of gifts you have given us,
    the many different skills and abilities represented here,
    and help us to understand
    how these can most effectively be used,
    both here and in the wider world.
You have called us together:
send us out to work for your kingdom.

Help us to be open to you through being open to one another,
    to love you through loving one another,
    to serve you through serving one another.
May the sincerity and warmth of our fellowship
    be a living testimony to the transforming power of Christ,
    and may it spill over into all our daily relationships.
You have called us together:
send us out to work for your kingdom.

Help us to recognise the wider family of which we are a part,
    the churches of our town and country,
    churches in other lands,
    and the Church universal.
Open our minds to all that we can give and receive,
    to everything we can learn
    from those who have gone before us,
    and to our own responsibilities
    as part of the great company of your people.
You have called us together:
    send us out to work for your kingdom.

Help us, finally, to respond to the needs of others,
    remembering that your love is not just for the Church
    but for the world.
Show us where you would have us serve you,
    and give us the vision to hear and respond –
    to put our words into action,
    to show our faith through our deeds,
    to proclaim the gospel through demonstrating your care for all.
You have called us together:
    send us out to work for your kingdom.

Through Jesus Christ our Lord.
Amen.

140

CLOSING PRAYER
PUTTING IT INTO PRACTICE

Living God,
  we have spent time together today,
    we have shared words, news and ideas,
    and we thank you for all this has meant to us,
    everything we have given and received through being here.
  But we know that you do not call us simply to words or ideas
    but, above all, to action,
    to express our convictions through deeds,
    our faith through works.
  Guide us, then, as we return to the daily tasks of life,
    and help us to make real there what we have discussed here.
  Teach us to practise what we preach,
    to turn our dreams into reality,
    and so may we share in building a fairer society
    and a better world,
    to the glory of your name.
  Amen.

141

ANNUAL GENERAL MEETING
LIFE TOGETHER

Loving God,
   we thank you for the fellowship of the Church –
      for the privilege of belonging to your people
      and sharing in the ministry of the Body of Christ.
   Unite us in love,
      and send us out in faith.

We thank you for the fellowship of our church here –
      for the friendship, encouragement, support and inspiration
      we gain from it,
      and for the ties that bind us together in Christ.
Unite us in love,
      and send us out in faith.

We thank you for one another –
      for the various gifts you have given us as a family
      and for the quirks and characteristics
      which make us what we are.
Unite us in love,
      and send us out in faith.

We thank you for the history of this church –
      all those who have run the race before us
      and to whom we owe our being here now.
Unite us in love,
      and send us out in faith.

We thank you for those whose work among us we recognise today –
      all who have offered spiritual guidance, nurture and inspiration,
      and all who have offered a practical ministry,
      sometimes unseen, unnoticed.
Unite us in love,
      and send us out in faith.

We thank you for the possibilities you set before us –
  new avenues of service inviting our response,
  and new opportunities for witness waiting to be grasped.
Unite us in love,
  and send us out in faith.

We thank you for those who will take up office
  as a result of this meeting –
  using their talents, their time and their energy
  both here among us and, above all, in the cause of Christ.
Unite us in love,
  and send us out in faith.

Loving God,
  we thank you for the fellowship of the Church –
    for the privilege of belonging to your people –
    and we ask you to help us honour that calling
    through all we are and do.
Unite us in love
  and send us out in faith.

Through Jesus Christ our Lord.
Amen.

CHURCH MEMBERSHIP

142

PRAISE, THANKSGIVING AND PETITION
THE FELLOWSHIP OF THE CHURCH

Loving God,
  we praise you for having called us your children,
    your people,
    your Church.
  We thank you for setting us apart to be the Body of Christ
    his friends,
    his disciples.
  Once we were strangers from you and one another,
    but now we are a holy nation,
    a royal priesthood,
    chosen by and precious to you.
  Unite us in love,
    and equip us for service.

We praise you for bringing us here together,
  and for breaking down the barriers which keep us apart.
We thank you for the friendship we find in this fellowship,
  for the faith that we share,
  the love that binds us together,
  the support we are able to give and receive,
  and the gifts which are present among us.
Unite us in love,
  and equip us for service.

We praise you for the wider Church of which we are a part,
  for Christians of different countries and cultures,
  each working out their faith
  in a multitude of places and situations.
We thank you for all that we can learn from them,
  for the examples they give of courage and perseverance,
  vision and commitment,
  mission and service,
  fellowship and worship.
Unite us in love,
  and equip us for service.

Open our hearts and minds
    to all that we can share in your family.
Speak to us
    through one another here and the faith of others across the world.
Challenge us
    through the insights of our brothers and sisters in Christ.
Guide, encourage and inspire us
    through their discipleship.
Teach us to look and listen,
    to learn as well as teach,
    to receive as well as give,
    to recognise the awesome riches you have given us
    in the fellowship of your people,
    and so help us to play our part in being your Church
    and working for your kingdom,
    here on earth.
Unite us in love,
    and equip us for service.

Through Jesus Christ our Lord.
Amen.

143

THANKSGIVING AND PETITION
THE MEANING OF FELLOWSHIP

Father God,
    as part of your people in every place and time,
        your children,
        your family,
        we join in worship.
Unite us in faith,
    and send us out in love.

You have called us to Christian fellowship,
        to life together,
        to be your people,
        the Body of Christ,
        united in him.
Unite us in faith,
    and send us out in love.

We thank you for the trust you have put in us,
        the privilege of working for your kingdom,
        and the honour of bearing the name of Christ.
We praise you for the grace you have shown us through him,
        and for the love which binds us together as his Church.
We rejoice that as friends of Jesus
        we have become friends of you and one another.
Unite us in faith,
    and send us out in love.

Teach us through this time of worship and fellowship
 more of what it means to be your people.
Unite us in heart and mind,
 word and deed,
 faith and love,
 work and witness,
 so that our life together will speak of you and your goodness.
Unite us in faith
 and send us out in love.

Through Jesus Christ our Lord.
Amen.

144

THANKSGIVING AND PETITION
LIVING IN FELLOWSHIP

Lord Jesus Christ,
    we thank you that you always have room in your heart for us;
        help us to make room in our lives for one another.
    Save us from ever being so occupied with our own affairs,
        so wrapped up in our own small world,
        that we have no time for the fellowship
        to which you have called us.
    Though we are many,
        make us one.

Teach us to open our hearts to one another,
    sharing joys and sorrows,
    offering support and encouragement to any in need among us,
    remembering each other in prayer
    and, through word and deed, expressing the love
    that binds us together in Christ.
Though we are many,
    make us one.

Teach us to live in harmony,
    recognising that we are part of your Body,
    called to represent you here on earth,
    and so save us from selfish attitudes,
    unforgiving hearts,
    and closed minds.
Though we are many,
    make us one.

Teach us to use our gifts, whatever they may be, for the good of all,
    to look for opportunities to offer service,
    to be open to ways in which we can use our gifts,
    and so to contribute fully to our life together.
Though we are many,
    make us one.

Teach us to work together,
>   not pursuing our own ends
>   but striving, as a team, towards a common goal,
>   united in the service of others
>   and the cause of your kingdom.
Though we are many,
>   **make us one.**

Lord,
>   you have called us to be one people,
>   bound together in genuine love and concern for one another,
>   so that others might see something of you
>   in the fellowship we share,
>   and through that catch a glimpse of your purpose for all.
>   Help us to recognise today
>   what it means to be members of your Church,
>   and, by your grace, help us to live up to that high calling,
>   to the glory of your name.
Though we are many,
>   **make us one.**

Amen.

145

INTERCESSION
THE CHURCH'S LIFE AND WITNESS

Lord God our Father,
  we thank you for the family to which you have called us,
    for our fellowship here,
    the denomination of which we are part,
    and the great company of the Church, past, present and future.
  For all your people,
    hear our prayer.

We pray for one another,
    those of our fellowship who have moved away,
    those who are confined to their homes through age and infirmity,
    those who are unwell,
    those who have become disillusioned
    and those who have lost their faith.
  For all your people,
    hear our prayer.

We pray for the churches of our town,
    striving through word and deed
    to make known the love of Christ in this community.
  We think especially of those in positions of leadership and oversight,
    asking that you will give them
    the faith and wisdom that they need,
    and we pray also for those in their charge,
    that they will respond gladly to opportunities for service,
    making vision become reality.
  For all your people,
    hear our prayer.

We pray for the wider family of the Church,
   all those seeking to work out their faith
   in their own particular situations.
We think especially of those who are persecuted for their beliefs,
   all for whom commitment to Christ is dangerous and costly.
Grant them courage in adversity,
   and help them to stand up for their convictions against all the odds.
For all your people,
   hear our prayer.

We pray for the unity of the Church,
   for the breaking-down of barriers
   and a further growing together,
   and we pray also for the witness of your people everywhere,
   that through their life and service
   your love will be made known,
   your word proclaimed,
   and your kingdom brought closer.
For all your people,
   hear our prayer.

Through Jesus Christ our Lord.
Amen.

MISSION AND OUTREACH

146

PRAISE
WITNESSES TO CHRIST

Sovereign God,
    we thank you for all those
        with the courage to speak out in your name,
        to declare their faith
        and testify to the new life you have given them in Christ.
    For their faithful witness,
        receive our praise.

We thank you for the Apostles and members of the early Church,
    sent out as your witnesses in a hostile world,
    enduring hostility, ridicule and persecution,
    yet, despite it all, proclaiming the gospel with power.
For their faithful witness,
    receive our praise.

We thank you for those
    who have acted as missionaries since that time,
    giving up their security and livelihood,
    often endangering health and life itself for the sake of Christ,
    such was their determination to make your name known.
For their faithful witness,
    receive our praise.

We thank you for those who proclaim the gospel today,
    not just overseas but here in this country,
    evangelists, preachers and teachers,
    each, through different ministries, calling people to faith,
    sharing the message of your love.
For their faithful witness,
    receive our praise.

We praise you for Christians in places
    where they face persecution,
    their commitment proving costly,
    their faith tested to the limit,
    yet none the less working to lead others
    to a saving knowledge of Christ.
For their faithful witness,
    receive our praise.

We praise you for ordinary Christians like us,
    speaking of your love,
    testifying to the difference you have made to their lives,
    talking freely of Christ to those around them.
For their faithful witness,
    receive our praise.

Gracious God,
    give to all who speak for you
        the words to say and the opportunity to say them,
        and inspire us through their example,
        so that we, in turn, may share what you have done for us,
        and, through word and deed, be ambassadors for Christ.
    In his name we ask it.
    Amen.

147

Confession
Failure to Witness

Lord Jesus Christ,
    we want to witness to your love,
        to share with others what you have done for us,
        and to reflect something of your love
        through the people we are.
We want to be a light to those around us,
        proclaiming your saving love through word and deed.
But we do not always know how, or where, or when.
For our failure to make you known,
    Lord, have mercy.

We mean to speak out,
    but, when the moment comes,
    we are nervous and tongue-tied,
    uncertain as to what to say,
    afraid of doing more harm than good,
    our clumsy efforts leading people away from you
    rather than towards a consideration of your claims.
For our failure to make you known,
    Lord, have mercy.

We are afraid of promising much but delivering little,
    of offering enthusiastic but empty witness
    that owes more to us than you,
    and so we back away,
    biting our tongues,
    telling ourselves that next time will be different.
For our failure to make you known,
    Lord, have mercy.

We are sometimes lacking in faith,
    sceptical that anyone will want to listen,
    and unable to believe they could really change even if they did,
    and so we keep quiet,
    convinced that to do otherwise
    would be to waste our time and theirs.
For our failure to make you known,
    Lord, have mercy.

Lord Jesus Christ,
    teach us that it is not the cleverness of our words
        that has the power to change lives,
        but the message of your love
        and the wonder of your grace.
Teach us that you can use our witness
        beyond our wildest expectations
        when it is offered from the heart,
        a spontaneous and genuine expression of all you mean to us.
Teach us to trust in you,
        confident that you will give us the words to say
        when we need them,
        and give us faith to leave the rest to you,
        even though we may never personally see the results.
Save us from making excuses
        or from evading your challenge,
        and so help us, openly and honestly, to speak for you
        and live to your glory.
For our failure to make you known,
    Lord, have mercy.

In your name we pray.
Amen.

148

PETITION
A TIME AND A PLACE

Lord Jesus Christ,
    you call us to go out and proclaim the gospel,
        to make disciples of all nations,
        to demonstrate the reality of your love
        through word and deed.
We want to honour that calling,
    but we are aware of the danger
    of doing more harm than good through our witness,
    of putting people off rather than drawing them to faith.
So now we pray once more for your guidance in mission.
You have given us good news:
    teach us how to share it.

Inspire and enable us to speak for you
    when the opportunity arises,
    not to fail in our responsibilities
    or rely on others to do what we should do ourselves,
    but to tell gladly and honestly what you mean to us
    and what you have done in our lives.
You have given us good news:
    teach us how to share it.

Show us those times when it is right to speak out,
    when the soil is ready
    to receive the seed of your word and bear harvest.
But teach us also when it is necessary to let go,
    to recognise that we have done our best
    and must leave things in your hands.
You have given us good news:
    teach us how to share it.

Save us from making excuses to evade the call to witness,
>   but save us also from pushing people against their will,
>   forcing our faith upon those for whom it is not welcome.
Teach us when it is time to speak and time to remain silent,
>   time to encourage and time to hold back,
>   time to try again and time to move on.
You have given us good news:
>   **teach us how to share it.**

And teach us also that words are never enough,
>   that it is the quality of our caring,
>   the sincerity of our love
>   and the genuineness of our actions
>   which will finally speak the loudest.
Grant that, like you,
>   what we say will be matched by what we do,
>   and what we believe be shown in who we are.
You have given us good news:
>   **teach us how to share it.**

Lord Jesus Christ,
>   you have touched our lives,
>   you have brought us joy,
>   you have given us life in all its fullness,
>   and we want to share with others
>   the blessing we have received.
Inspire us through your love,
>   equip us through your Spirit,
>   and send us out to make you known.
You have given us good news:
>   **teach us how to share it.**

In your name we pray.
Amen.

149

INTERCESSION
A BEATITUDE PEOPLE

Lord Jesus Christ,
 we pray once more for your Church
  and for its ministry to the world.
May it be a source of love, hope and comfort,
  compassion, challenge and inspiration.
Lord, in your mercy,
 hear our prayer.

May your followers in every place find the faith and courage,
  vision and commitment,
  to live as beatitude people,
  poor and humble in spirit,
  merciful in attitude,
  pure in heart,
  hungry for peace and thirsty for righteousness,
  and so, as individuals and together,
  may your Church testify to your redeeming love
  and renewing power,
  speaking through word and deed of your care for all,
  your desire for justice,
  and your willingness to show mercy.
Lord, in your mercy,
 hear our prayer.

Reach out through all you specially call to proclaim your name –
  those gifted as evangelists,
  those working abroad as missionaries
  or here in our own country,
  each seeking to share their faith
  and to make your love known.
But reach out also through everyday believers such as us,
  ordinary Christians telling others
  about their experience of your goodness
  and about the difference you have made to their lives.
Lord, in your mercy,
 hear our prayer.

Grant to all your people the inspiration of your Holy Spirit,
    and the light of Christ in their hearts.
Help them to recognise the opportunities you provide,
    to respond to your guidance
    and so faithfully to proclaim the good news.
Lord, in your mercy,
    hear our prayer.

For we ask it in your name.
Amen.

INFANT BAPTISM / DEDICATION

150

PRAISE
THE GIVER OF LIFE

Sovereign God,
   giver of life,
      creator of all that is and has been,
      sustainer of the universe,
      we praise you.
Hear our prayer.

Living God,
   giver of joy,
      of the blessings we receive each day
      and of the love we share together,
      we praise you.
Hear our prayer.

Gracious God,
   giver of mercy,
      always forgiving,
      constantly bringing renewal and restoration,
      we praise you.
Hear our prayer.

Faithful God,
   giver of guidance,
      forever by our side,
      instructing,
      leading,
      challenging,
      equipping,
      we praise you.
Hear our prayer.

Generous God,
  giver of all our needs,
    providing,
    nurturing,
    nourishing,
    fulfilling,
    we praise you.
  Hear our prayer.

Creator God,
  we come this day,
    rejoicing in the new life you have given,
    filled with joy,
    trusting in your mercy,
    and assured of your gracious guidance.
  We come in celebration
    to give thanks
    and to commit ourselves and this child to you,
    as, together, we praise you.
  Hear our prayer.

  Through Jesus Christ our Lord.
  Amen.

151

THANKSGIVING
THE GIFT OF LIFE

(For *AB* insert the full name of the candidate;
for *A* insert the Christian name only)

Loving God,
 we thank you for the gift of life and for the miracle of birth,
  the wonder of a new-born child,
  fashioned by your hand,
  lovingly created,
  and bringing such joy to so many.
 We come in worship.
 Hear our prayer.

We thank you for the life of *AB*,
 for all that stretches before *him/her* –
 the possibilities, joys and discoveries you hold in store,
 the enrichment *he/she* will bring through *his/her* presence,
 and the times we will share with *him/her*
 over the years to come.
 We come in worship.
 Hear our prayer.

We thank you for the love that surrounds *A* –
 the care of *his/her* parents,
 the support of family and friends,
 the prayers of this fellowship,
 and your own everlasting arms.
 We come in worship.
 Hear our prayer.

We thank you for the happiness we share this day –
 the joy *A*'s birth has brought,
 the hope it has kindled,
 and the thanksgiving it has evoked.
 We come in worship.
 Hear our prayer.

We thank you for your gift of eternal life –
    a life which begins here and now,
    bringing peace, love and fulfilment,
    yet which promises greater joys to come.
We come in worship.
Hear our prayer.

Loving God,
    this is a day of thanksgiving, celebration and dedication,
        a day to honour you
        and to acknowledge your goodness.
    Gladly we consecrate *A* to you
        and joyfully we commit ourselves in the same faith.
We come in worship.
Hear our prayer.

Through Jesus Christ our Lord.
Amen.

152

PETITION AND INTERCESSION
GOD'S HELP AND GUIDANCE

(For *AB* insert the full name of the candidate;
for *A* insert the Christian name only)

Gracious God,
  we pray for *AB* in whatever the future may hold for *him/her*.
  May your hand be there to lead,
    and your love be there to bless.

Grant help to *A* in times of learning,
    so that *he/she* may grow in wisdom and understanding,
    in knowledge, skill and ability,
    and in experience and character,
    equipped to make the most of life's possibilities.
  May your hand be there to lead,
    and your love be there to bless.

Grant *A* your strength in times of testing –
    the ability to overcome difficulties,
    withstand trials,
    and conquer temptation,
    staying true to *his/her* convictions
    and emerging stronger out of adversity.
  May your hand be there to lead,
    and your love be there to bless.

Grant your guidance in times of uncertainty –
    discernment as to the right way forward,
    patience in coming to a decision,
    and confidence that a door will open,
    your will ultimately becoming apparent.
  May your hand be there to lead,
    and your love be there to bless.

Grant your peace in times of turmoil –
    the knowledge that, whatever may happen, you are there,
    nothing ever able to separate us from your love,
    and so may *A* be able
    to meet changing circumstances of life with equanimity,
    assured of your ultimate purpose.
May your hand be there to lead,
    and your love be there to bless.

    Grant your blessing in times of opportunity,
    so that *A* may discover lasting love,
    enduring joy,
    and fulfilment in work, faith and life.
May your hand be there to lead,
    and your love be there to bless.

Gracious God,
    we ask you to put your hand upon *A*,
    to watch over *him/her*,
    to direct *his/her* footsteps
    and to make known your love,
    so that *he/she* may respond freely to you
    in *his/her* own time and way.
May your hand be there to lead,
    and your love be there to bless.

In the name of Christ we ask it.
Amen.

153

BLESSING

(For *AB* insert the full name of the candidate)

AB,
   the Lord watch over you, this and every day,
   the Lord guide your footsteps and keep you from evil,
   the Lord grant you health and strength, joy and fulfilment,
   your whole life long.
The Lord be a blessing to you,
   leading you in the way of peace, wisdom, love and humility,
   so that you in turn may be a blessing to others.
The Lord fill you with light
   and enfold you in love,
   now and for evermore.
Through Jesus Christ our Lord.
Amen.

BELIEVERS' BAPTISM/
CONFIRMATION

154

PRAISE
THE PURPOSE OF GOD

(For *AB* insert the full name of the candidate;
for *A* insert the Christian name only)

Sovereign God,
    we praise you for all the ways you work in our lives –
        the fact that you love us before we ever know it,
        call us before we realise you are able to use us,
        and guide us before we even begin to respond.
    For welcoming us into your family,
        joyfully we worship you.

We praise you that you call us,
    not because we deserve it,
    nor because we are in any way specially qualified to serve you,
    but solely by your grace,
    reaching out in love day after day
    until you have drawn us to yourself.
For welcoming us into your family,
    joyfully we worship you.

We praise you that you can use every one of us –
    that we are all special in your sight,
    able to receive the gifts of your Spirit
    and contribute to the work of your kingdom.
For welcoming us into your family,
    joyfully we worship you.

We praise you that you have led *AB* to this point of decision,
    this moment when *he/she* wants to respond to your love
    and, of *his/her* own free will,
    commit *himself/herself* to the service of Christ
    and to his work within this church.
For welcoming us into your family,
    joyfully we worship you.

We praise you for everything that has led up to this moment –
   the reflection,
   sharing,
   friendship
   and nurture
   that have brought *A* to identify *himself/herself*
   with this fellowship
   and to confess Jesus Christ as *his/her* Lord and Saviour.
For welcoming us into your family,
   joyfully we worship you.

Sovereign God,
   we praise you for *A*,
      for everything *he/she* means to us,
      for everything *he/she* means to you,
      for everything we mean to each other.
   Unite us in faith,
      and bind us together in love,
      so that the promises made now
      may be honoured in the days ahead,
      to the glory of your name.
   For welcoming us into your family,
      joyfully we worship you.

Through Jesus Christ our Lord.
Amen.

155

CONFESSION
THE PARDON OF GOD

Gracious God,
  if we say we have no sin, we deceive ourselves,
    and the truth is not in us.
  If we confess our sins,
    you, who are faithful and just,
    will forgive our sins
    and cleanse us from all unrighteousness.
  We thank you for that promise,
    and we come now in faith,
    acknowledging our sinfulness,
    and seeking your pardon.
  Lord, in your mercy,
    hear our prayer.

We may possibly deceive ourselves,
  but we know we can never deceive you,
  for you see us as we really are,
  with all our faults and weaknesses,
  our unworthy actions and ugly thoughts;
  and so we come with shame,
  acknowledging our dependence on your grace,
  and seeking your pardon.
Lord, in your mercy,
  hear our prayer.

We have no claim on your goodness,
  for, despite our best intentions,
  our promises of commitment and pledges of loyalty,
  we let you down time and again,
  our words saying one thing,
  our lives another;
  and so we come with sorrow,
  acknowledging our need of help,
  and seeking your pardon.
Lord, in your mercy,
  hear our prayer.

We want to serve you,
    we mean to follow the way of Christ,
    but our hearts are fickle and our faith is flawed,
    the spirit willing but the flesh weak;
    and so we come in humility,
    acknowledging our faithlessness,
    and seeking your pardon.
Lord, in your mercy,
    hear our prayer.

Gracious God,
    we thank you that you are a God slow to anger
        and abounding in steadfast love,
        a God who is swift to pardon
        and delighting to forgive.
We praise you that you treat us not according to our deserts
        but according to your grace,
        always ready to put the past behind us
        and to help us to start again.
You invite us to wash and be clean,
        to confess our sins and to receive your forgiveness;
        and so we come now with joy,
        acknowledging your grace
        and assured of your pardon!
Lord, in your mercy,
    hear our prayer.

Through Jesus Christ our Lord.
Amen.

156

PETITION AND INTERCESSION
THE CALL OF GOD

(For *A* insert the Christian name of the candidate)

Living God,
   we thank you for your call,
      your gracious invitation to respond to your love
      that goes on reaching out to us
      until we have turned to you
      and accepted the gift of new life you so long to give us.
   Gracious Lord,
      hear us.

We thank you for the way *A* has responded to that call,
      publicly committing *his/her* life today to the service of Christ,
      and we pray now for everything the future holds for *him/her*.
Grant your guidance, strength and inspiration,
      keep *his/her* faith strong
      and *his/her* love for you burning bright,
      and may your blessing enrich *his/her* life.
Gracious Lord,
      hear us.

We pray for all those who have committed their lives to you,
      declaring Jesus Christ as their Lord and Saviour.
Equip them for service,
      unite them in love,
      empower them through your Spirit,
      and bless them with peace.
Gracious Lord,
      hear us.

We pray for those who resist your call,
    afraid of what commitment might entail.
Conquer their doubts,
    overcome their hesitation,
    and may they discover the blessing they have been missing.
Gracious Lord,
    hear us.

We pray for those who are unmoved by your call,
    untouched by the message of the gospel.
Speak your word,
    stir their hearts,
    and touch their lives with your blessing.
Gracious Lord,
    hear us.

We pray for those who have responded to your call
    and then gone back,
    the faith they once professed grown cold.
Rekindle the flame,
    restore their vision
    and may your blessing thrill them once more.
Gracious Lord,
    hear us.

Living God,
    may your word reach out with power,
        creating, sustaining and renewing faith.
May your call touch our lives, today and always,
    and may we respond with heartfelt devotion
    and faithful service,
    to the glory of your name.
Gracious Lord,
    hear us.

Through Jesus Christ our Lord.
Amen.

157

BLESSING

May the word of God guide your footsteps,
  the power of God equip you for service,
  the grace of God constantly renew you
  and the love of God surround you always.
May your vision be clear,
  your commitment strong,
  and your faith constant.
May peace flood your soul
  and light shine from your heart.
May Christ be your constant companion
  on the path of discipleship,
  until your journey is over
  and you meet with God face to face,
  secure in the joy of his everlasting kingdom.
The Lord bless and keep you,
  now and for evermore.
Amen.

CHRISTIAN MARRIAGE

158

APPROACH
THE GIFT OF LOVE

(For *A* and *C* insert the Christian names of the bride and groom)

Gracious God,
    we are here to celebrate,
        to rejoice and give thanks.
We come, not just to enjoy a special occasion,
        but to seek your blessing upon a continuing journey,
        a lifetime of exploration and discovery
        in which we pray that your love
        will grow, flourish and blossom.
Meet with us now.
Be with us always.

We are here to witness an act of commitment,
        a mutual pledging of vows,
        a consecration of two lives woven into one relationship.
Meet with us now.
Be with us always.

We are here to praise you for the gift of love,
        to thank you for the joy *A* and *C* have found in each other,
        and to commit the future into your hands.
Meet with us now.
Be with us always.

Gracious God,
    draw near to us in this service,
        draw near to *A* and *C*,
        and may your sovereign love enfold us all,
        this day and for evermore.
Meet with us now.
Be with us always.

Through Jesus Christ our Lord.
Amen.

159

PRAISE
A SPECIAL DAY

(For *A* and *C* insert the Christian names of the bride and groom)

Sovereign God,
    this is a day of love –
        a time of joining together,
        exchanging vows,
        uniting two lives as one.
    For all that this day means,
        receive our praise.

This is a day of joy –
        an occasion of celebration,
        laughter,
        and thanksgiving.
    For all that this day means,
        receive our praise.

This is a day for reminiscing –
        for remembering everything *A* and *C* have meant
        to their loved ones over the years,
        for looking back to the times we have shared with them,
        and for recalling how their love for each other has grown
        since they first met.
    For all that this day means,
        receive our praise.

This is a day for anticipation –
        for looking forward to everything the future holds,
        for sharing in *A* and *C*'s excitement as they plan ahead,
        and for rejoicing in this new chapter in their lives.
    For all that this day means,
        receive our praise.

This is a day for worship –
    for recognising your presence here among us,
    acknowledging your goodness
    and asking your blessing on *A* and *C*
    in the years ahead.
For all that this day means,
    receive our praise.

Sovereign God,
    we thank you for this special day –
        put your hand upon it.
    We thank you for this special couple –
        put your hand on them.
    We thank you for the opportunity
        to share in this happy occasion –
        put your hand on us.
Come now,
    and make this time everything we want it to be,
    and everything you can make it become.
For all that this day means,
    receive our praise.

Through Jesus Christ our Lord.
Amen.

160

THANKSGIVING
A CONTINUING JOURNEY

(For *A* and *C* insert the Christian names of the bride and groom)

Gracious God,
    we thank you for *A* and *C*,
        for all they mean to each other,
        and all they mean to us.
Loving Lord,
    gratefully we worship you.

We thank you for the way you have brought *A* and *C* together,
    the times they have shared,
    and the love that has grown between them.
And we praise you that they have reached this point
    of committing themselves to each other in marriage,
    pledging before you and this congregation
    their desire to share their lives together,
    for better, for worse,
    for richer, for poorer,
    in sickness and in health,
    till they are parted by death.
Loving Lord,
    gratefully we worship you.

We thank you for the joy that *A* and *B* feel at this moment,
    and the joy we share with them;
    the sense of promise and excitement
    which has touched all our lives today,
    and which we pray will continue for *A* and *C*
    in the years ahead.
Loving Lord,
    gratefully we worship you.

We thank you for everything that has led up to this day –
    the moment *A* and *C* first met,
    the way they have grown together,
    the planning and preparation behind this service
    and the reception to come,
    the buying of gifts and sending of cards –
    everything that helps to make this day so special.
And, above all, we thank you for your guiding hand
    which makes not just this day possible, but every day,
    and which is always outstretched in love,
    looking to draw us to your side.
Loving Lord,
    gratefully we worship you.

Gracious God,
    we come today with grateful hearts,
        to celebrate,
        to rejoice,
    and to seek your blessing on the journey
    which *A* and *C* are stepping out into today.
Go with them both,
    and with us all,
    now and for evermore.
Loving Lord,
    gratefully we worship you.

In the name of Christ.
Amen.

161

RENEWAL OF WEDDING VOWS
AN ENDURING PARTNERSHIP

(This prayer is for those celebrating a special anniversary and
wishing to commit themselves to each other once again as
an act of thanksgiving. For *A* and *C* insert the Christian
names of the couple renewing their vows.)

Gracious God,
    we praise you for your gift of love –
        that most precious of gifts which endures beyond all others,
        bearing all things,
        believing all things
        and hoping all things.
    We rejoice that it is a love such as this
        which we come to celebrate today.
    Receive our thanks,
        and accept our worship.

We thank you for the joy that comes
    from two lives truly being shared,
    from two people becoming one,
    each complementing and enriching the other,
    each helping love to grow.
Receive our thanks,
    and accept our worship.

We recall before you everything *A* and *C* have shared
    across the years –
    the joys and sorrows,
    hopes and fears,
    triumphs and disappointments,
    pleasure and pain –
    and we thank you that they have shared those times together,
    offering mutual support, strength and encouragement.
Receive our thanks,
    and accept our worship.

We celebrate everything their love has meant to others –
    the inspiration it has given,
    happiness it has contributed to,
    security it has provided,
    and example it has offered to family and friends alike.
Receive our thanks,
    and accept our worship.

We acknowledge your love which has been a constant thread
    throughout their relationship –
    your presence which has always been with them,
    your hand upon them today,
    and the assurance that you will continue to bless them
    in the years ahead,
    whatever life may bring.
Receive our thanks,
    and accept our worship.

So now we bring you this day of celebration
    and this act of recommitment,
    acknowledging with gratitude the good times enjoyed,
    and looking forward with expectation to the joys yet to come.
Receive our thanks,
    and accept our worship.

Through Jesus Christ our Lord.
Amen.

162

REMAKING OF WEDDING VOWS
STARTING AGAIN

(This prayer is for those who have experienced difficulties in
their marriage and who wish to remake their vows as a symbol
of their desire to start again. For *A* and *C* insert the Christian
names of the couple remaking their vows.)

Living God,
   you tell us that love is patient and kind,
      not envious or boastful, arrogant or rude.
You say that love is not irritable or resentful,
      insisting on its own way and rejoicing in wrongdoing,
      but, instead, it rejoices in the truth,
      bearing all things,
      believing all things,
      hoping all things,
      enduring all things.
We confess that our love isn't always like that,
      all too often falling far short of such an ideal.
It is sometimes shaken,
      and, on occasions, tested to breaking point.
Yet we come today acknowledging our weakness
      and asking for another chance to love as you love us.
Receive what we are,
   and direct what we shall be.

We come with *A* and *C* today,
      acknowledging mistakes that have been made,
      errors of judgement and lack of thought –
      the words that shouldn't have been spoken
      and those that should but never were;
      the deeds that shouldn't have been contemplated
      and those we failed even to consider –
      and we ask your forgiveness for them all.
Receive what we are,
   and direct what we shall be.

Give to *A* and *C* the ability to start afresh –
 to put the past behind them,
 learning its lessons yet allowing its wounds to heal –
 and help each of us in turn to learn likewise,
 open to others' point of view,
 ready to forgive and forget,
 always looking to see the best rather than the worst.
Receive what we are
 and direct what we shall be.

Living God,
 we believe you are a God who makes all things new,
 constantly restoring and recreating,
 and so we come to share in this act of rededication,
 this renewal of vows and affirming of commitment.
Move within *A* and *C*,
 work within us,
 and fill each one of us with your love,
 in body, mind and spirit.
Receive what we are,
 and direct what we shall be.

Through Jesus Christ our Lord.
Amen.

163

BLESSING

(For *A* and *C* insert the Christian names of the bride and groom)

A and *C*,
   may the grace of God always surround you,
   enriching your lives and nurturing your love,
   seasoning your words and shaping your actions,
   uniting you in times of trial,
   supporting you in moments of sorrow,
   and bringing you lasting joy and enduring fulfilment.
May the Lord be with you,
   his hands below,
   his arms around,
   and his Spirit within you,
   and may he lead you this and every day,
   as you travel together along life's chequered path.
In the name of Christ.
Amen.

CHRISTIAN BURIAL

164

Words of approach

We have come together in the presence of God,
 and in the name of Christ.
We come with sorrow,
 but also with hope;
 to express loss,
 but also to give thanks;
 to recognise death,
 but also to celebrate life;
 to look back at all that has been,
 but also to look forward to all that is yet to be.
Come then in faith, for God is here –
 the God who has promised that, in life or in death,
 he is with us,
 the God who gives all who truly believe
 the assurance of his eternal blessing.

165

THANKSGIVING
A LOVED ONE AND ALL THEY HAVE MEANT

(For *AB* insert the full name of the deceased;
for *A* insert Christian name only)

Gracious God,
    we entrust *AB* into your everlasting care,
        and, as we do so, we thank you again
        for all *he/she* has meant to us,
        for the person *he/she* has been,
        for the service *he/she* has offered
        and for the contribution *he/she* has made to our lives.
    Gratefully we come:
        lovingly we give thanks.

We thank you for everything *A* has meant to *his/her* family,
    to colleagues and friends,
    to us here today,
    and we thank you for all *he/she* continues to mean to you
    as well as to us.
Gratefully we come:
    lovingly we give thanks.

We thank you for *A*'s achievements
    which we can look back on with pride,
    the challenges faced,
    the obstacles overcome,
    the successes won,
    the potential fulfilled.
Gratefully we come:
    lovingly we give thanks.

We thank you for the experiences we have been through together,
    the love and friendship we have shared,
    the qualities and characteristics which made *A* special to us.
Gratefully we come:
    lovingly we give thanks.

We thank you for *A*'s faith*,
>   *his/her* commitment to Christ,
>   faithful discipleship
>   and personal experience of your love.
> Gratefully we come:
> >   **lovingly we give thanks.**

We thank you for all we owe to *A*,
>   for the innumerable ways in which *he/she* enriched our lives,
>   and for the memories we will always have
>   as a lasting tribute and enduring legacy.
> Gratefully we come:
> >   **lovingly we give thanks.**

Gracious God,
>   we come in hope and confidence,
> >   trusting in your promise,
> >   and assured of your gracious purpose,
> >   and in that faith we entrust both *A* and ourselves
> >   into your gracious keeping,
> >   now and for all eternity.
> Gratefully we come:
> >   **lovingly we give thanks.**

Through Jesus Christ our Lord.
Amen.

* Omit this stanza of the prayer if the deceased professed no Christian faith

166

PRAISE
CHRIST'S VICTORY OVER DEATH

(For *A* insert the Christian name of the deceased)

Loving God,
    we praise you that on this day of mourning,
        and at this time of pain,
        we can come still with hope in our hearts
        and thanksgiving on our lips,
        for we know that what seems like the end
        with you is a new beginning.
Christ has died.
Christ has risen.
Thanks be to God!

We praise you that in Jesus
    you experienced not just our life but our death –
    that you endured the darkness of Gethsemane,
    the agony of the cross,
    and the finality of the tomb;
    and you emerged victorious,
    triumphant over everything that would keep us from you,
    conquering death itself.
Christ has died.
Christ has risen.
Thanks be to God!

We thank you that where the world saw only defeat,
    you brought victory;
    that in despair and sorrow, you brought joy;
    that in darkness and doubt, you brought light;
    that nothing is able to overshadow your love,
    no power able to withstand your purpose.
Christ has died.
Christ has risen.
Thanks be to God!

Loving God,
 we praise you that we can come today
  not to close a book but to end a chapter,
  not to say goodbye
  but rather to bid a friend farewell for now.
 In that confidence we entrust *A* into your eternal care,
  knowing that the love which surrounds *him/her*
  surrounds us all,
  now and for evermore.
 Christ has died.
 Christ has risen.
 Thanks be to God!

 Amen.

167

INTERCESSION
MOURNING FAMILY AND FRIENDS

(For *A* insert the Christian name of the deceased)

Loving God,
    as we wrestle now with our grief,
        we are reminded of all who have lost loved ones,
        whose lives have been touched by tragedy,
        and who are overwhelmed by sorrow.
    Lord, in your mercy,
        hear our prayer.

We pray for them in their shock, hurt and bewilderment.
We lift before you their sense of desolation and despair,
        their feelings of numbness and emptiness,
        their aching hearts which see just a blank void
        where so much joy used to be.
    Lord, in your mercy,
        hear our prayer.

We pray for each one of us here today
        and especially for those closest to *A*;
        for *(enter names as appropriate)*.
Reach out and encircle them in your loving arms.
Grant them the comfort you have promised to all who mourn,
        your peace that passes understanding,
        your light that reaches into the darkest places of life
        and beyond into the darkness of death.
    Lord, in your mercy,
        hear our prayer.

Loving God,
   may the hope of the gospel,
      the experience of your love,
      and the support of family and friends
      bring the help that is needed at this time;
      the strength to endure sorrow in all its intensity
      and to face death in all its apparent finality,
      yet ultimately to look forward in faith,
      knowing that, in Christ, nothing can finally separate us
      from you or from those we love.
   Lord, in your mercy,
      hear our prayer.

We ask it for his name's sake.
Amen.

168

COMMITTAL

(For *A* insert the Christian name of the deceased)

Gracious God,
  we commit our friend,
    our loved one,
    into your everlasting care,
    with sorrowful hearts,
    thankful hearts,
    and confident hearts.

  Receive *A* into your glorious kingdom,
    your peace that passes understanding,
    your joy that knows no bounds,
    your love that is all in all;
    and grant us your guidance and strength,
    until we too are with Christ,
    with *A*,
    and with all your people,
    rejoicing in your gracious presence,
    through Jesus Christ our Lord.

  Amen.

169

DEDICATION OF A PLAQUE, GRAVESTONE, OR OTHER MEMORIAL

(For *AB* insert the full name of the deceased;
for *A* insert Christian name only)

Loving God,
  we dedicate this *plaque/stone/memorial** to *AB*
    in the name of Christ,
    as a symbol of our remembering,
    a sign of our thanksgiving,
    a token of our recognition,
    and an expression of our love.

We look back with gratitude for all *A* has meant to us,
    for everything we have shared together,
    for *his/her* love as a *husband/wife,*
    parent, brother/sister, friend,
    for all the things which made *him/her*
    such a special part of our lives.

We look forward in confidence,
    in faith,
    and in expectation
    to our reunion with *A,*
    with all your people,
    and with Christ himself,
    in your everlasting kingdom;
    that time when there will be no more pain,
    and no more tears,
    an end to suffering, sin and death.

* Insert name of item to be dedicated as appropriate

And so we pray for your continued comfort in the present,
   your strength and support,
   your peace and guidance,
   your help to laugh and love once more.
May we honour *A*'s name by honouring you
   and living each day to your praise and glory,
   through Jesus Christ our Lord.

Amen.

PART THREE

ORDINARY SUNDAYS

PRAYERS OF APPROACH

170

BRINGING OUR WORSHIP

Sovereign God,
  we have come to worship you –
    to declare your faithfulness,
    to acknowledge your majesty,
    and to marvel at your love.
  Lord of heaven and earth,
    receive our praise.

We are here to rejoice –
    to bring our thanks,
    to express our wonder,
    and to celebrate your goodness.
  Lord of heaven and earth,
    receive our praise.

We are here to seek mercy –
    to confess our mistakes,
    to recognise our weaknesses,
    and to ask for your pardon.
  Lord of heaven and earth,
    receive our praise.

We are here to pray –
    for ourselves,
    our world
    and one another
  Lord of heaven and earth,
    receive our praise.

We come to receive –
    hungry to hear you,
    thirsting to know you better,
    longing to be filled.
  Lord of heaven and earth,
    receive our praise.

We come to give –
>   to offer our money,
>   our time
>   and our love in the service of Christ.
> Lord of heaven and earth,
>   **receive our praise.**

We come to listen –
>   to the message of Scripture,
>   to the words of Christ,
>   and to the inner prompting of your Holy Spirit.
> Lord of heaven and earth,
>   **receive our praise.**

We come to speak –
>   to sing your praises,
>   to declare our faith
>   and to make known the gospel.
> Lord of heaven and earth,
>   **receive our praise.**

Sovereign God,
>   accept this time of worship,
>   and help us through it to draw nearer to you.
> Open our hearts to the love of Christ,
>   our lives to the movement of your Spirit,
>   our minds to all that you are and continue to do,
>   and so may we worship you
>   not just in these few moments that we have set aside,
>   but in every moment of our lives,
>   to the glory of your name.
> Lord of heaven and earth,
>   **receive our praise.**

Through Jesus Christ our Lord.
Amen.

171

COMING IN FAITH

Living God,
    you have spoken to your people across the centuries,
        you identified yourself with humankind in Jesus Christ,
        you dwell within us through your Holy Spirit,
        making your presence come alive.
    Accept now the worship we offer,
    and use us for your kingdom.

Loving God,
    having come to us, you call us to come to you,
        promising that *in* Christ we shall find rest for our souls,
        that *through* Christ our spiritual hunger shall be satisfied,
        and that *from* Christ we shall receive life in all its fullness.
    Accept now the worship we offer,
    and use us for your kingdom.

Gracious God,
    we come in response to your call,
        to offer our worship,
        our thanks,
        our confession,
        our lives.
    Accept now the worship we offer,
    and use us for your kingdom.

Sovereign God,
    we come,
        seeking your guidance,
        your strength,
        your renewal
        and your will.
Accept now the worship we offer,
    and use us for your kingdom.

Lord of all,
    help us to come to you not just as an outward gesture,
        a matter of routine or duty,
        but in heart and mind and soul.
    Help us to make space in our hectic lives
        to be still in your presence,
        and so may *we* live in you and *you* in us.
    Accept now the worship we offer,
        and use us for your kingdom.

We ask it through Jesus Christ our Lord.
Amen.

172

BRINGING OURSELVES

Almighty God,
  creator and ruler of all,
    all good,
    all loving,
    all merciful,
    we worship you.

We come to acknowledge your greatness,
  to celebrate your love,
  to thank you for your mercy,
  and to rejoice in your unchanging purpose.
For who and what you are,
  we worship you.

We come to focus our minds upon you,
  not that we might turn aside from the world
  or forget its need,
  but so that we might return to our daily lives
  with a greater vision of your purpose,
  a deeper sense of your presence around us,
  and a firmer resolve to serve you
  in the place where you have put us.
For who and what you are,
  we worship you.

Awaken us afresh to the wonder of your presence,
  the mystery of your person
  and the extent of your will.
Inspire us with a new sense of your majesty and authority,
  so that we may worship you,
  not just with our lips,
  but with heart and mind and soul.
For who and what you are,
  we worship you.

Meet with us now,
  and help us to live each day in the light of your presence.
Give to us a constant awareness of your greatness and your love,
  so that whatever confronts us,
  whatever challenge we face,
  whatever situation we find ourselves in,
  we may be equipped to meet it in your name,
  and to offer lives of true discipleship pleasing in your sight.
For who and what you are,
  we worship you.

Through Jesus Christ our Lord.
Amen.

173

BRINGING OUR LIVES

Loving Lord,
  we offer you our praise,
    acknowledging you as our God,
    ruler of all,
    the giver of life,
    the beginning and end of all things.
  Take what we bring,
    and use it for your glory.

We offer our hymns, prayers and readings,
    our words and thoughts,
    our money, our lives and our fellowship.
  Take what we bring,
    and use it for your glory.

We offer you the week ahead –
    our work and leisure,
    commitments and responsibilities,
    plans and programme.
  Take what we bring,
    and use it for your glory.

We offer you our lives –
    our hopes and fears,
    gifts and interests,
    time and energy.
  Take what we bring,
    and use it for your glory.

Sovereign God
  may our every act and every day be lived in your power,
    through your love,
    to your praise and glory.
  Take what we bring,
    and use it for your glory.

In the name of Christ.
Amen.

174

BRINGING OUR ALL

Lord of all,
in reverence and humility,
awe and wonder,
we come to worship you.
Meet with us now,
be with us always.

We step aside from the busy routine of our lives –
a few moments away from our daily activities
and humdrum concerns;
an opportunity to bring them
quietly and prayerfully before you,
and to place them in your hands.
Meet with us now,
be with us always.

We bring ourselves –
our strengths and weaknesses,
our faith and doubts,
our hopes and fears.
Meet with us now,
be with us always.

We bring our families, our friends and neighbours –
those we love,
those we know,
and those we simply pass in the street.
Meet with us now,
be with us always.

We bring our community, our town, our country
and our world –
places near and far,
integral to our lives
or far removed from our experience.
Meet with us now,
be with us always.

In quiet confidence we entrust all into your care,
    knowing that your love is more powerful
    and your power more loving
    than we can ever know or imagine.
Meet with us now,
    be with us always.

Lord of all,
    we come to worship you,
        bringing ourselves,
        bringing our loved ones,
        bringing our all.
    Meet with us now,
        be with us always.

Amen.

175

OFFERING OUR WORSHIP

Almighty God,
    we join together to worship you,
        knowing that you are here,
        concerned about each one of us,
        waiting to speak your word,
        ready to forgive, bless and lead us.
    We come in faith:
        meet with us now.

So now we bring you our songs and our reading of your word,
    our thinking and listening,
    our praying and praising.
We bring the fellowship we share,
    the discipleship we offer,
    the world we belong to,
    and the lives you have given us.
We come in faith:
    meet with us now.

Open our eyes and our hearts to your presence,
    and teach us, through all that we do this day,
    to be your children,
    your disciples,
    your Church,
    your people.
We come in faith:
    meet with us now.

Through Jesus Christ our Lord.
Amen.

176

A LIFE OF WORSHIP

Great and wonderful God,
 we come into your presence with joy and wonder,
  celebrating your goodness,
  acknowledging your love.
Receive our worship now,
 and help us to serve you always.

We come conscious of our sinfulness,
 but rejoicing in your mercy,
 all too aware of our unworthiness,
 yet celebrating your awesome forgiveness.
Receive our worship now,
 and help us to serve you always.

We come seeking to worship you
 not just for these few moments,
 or in this place,
 or in one small part of our lives,
 but in all our actions, words and deeds,
 through the people we are and the lives we lead.
Receive our worship now,
 and help us to serve you always.

For all the ways we have failed to live as your people,
 forgive us.
Lead us closer to you and teach us your will,
 so that what we say with our lips
 we may truly practise in our lives,
 to the glory of your name.
Receive our worship now,
 and help us to serve you always.

Through Jesus Christ our Lord.
Amen.

177

USING OUR TIME IN WORSHIP

Loving God,
   we thank you for this opportunity
      to bring you our worship.
   Help us to use it.

Help us, through this time together,
   to recognise that you are here,
   to realise how many blessings we have received,
   and to understand how much you love us.
Lord, in your mercy,
   hear our prayer.

Teach us to listen to your voice and to follow where you lead,
   to love one another and to live as your family,
   to be the people you would have us be.
Lord, in your mercy,
   hear our prayer.

Accept our praise for everything you are,
   our gratitude for everything you have given,
   and our sorrow for everything we have done wrong.
Lord, in your mercy,
   hear our prayer.

Give to us a sense of your presence in all things,
   the assurance of your forgiveness,
   and strength to amend our ways.
Lord, in your mercy,
   hear our prayer.

Grant us wisdom to know your will,
   courage to accept your guidance,
   and faith to build your kingdom.
Lord, in your mercy,
   hear our prayer.

Loving God,
we thank you for this opportunity
to bring you our worship.
Help us to use it,
through Jesus Christ our Lord.
Amen.

178

LIVING WORSHIP

Sovereign God,
   we come to worship you,
     setting aside these few moments
     to consecrate ourselves afresh to your service,
     to remind ourselves of your constant presence,
     and to learn more of your love.
   As we draw near to you,
     draw near to us.

We come as we have come so many times across the years.
Save us from coming out of empty habit or duty,
   from becoming stale or complacent,
     offering our worship simply as a tradition or custom,
     rather than as a joyful privilege and profound encounter.
As we draw near to you,
   draw near to us.

As your love is always new,
   your purpose always fresh,
   your hand always recreating,
   so also make our worship ever new in turn.
As we draw near to you,
   draw near to us.

Capture our imaginations,
   kindle our hearts,
   fill our whole being,
   so that we might come this and every day
   seeking new insights,
   learning new truths,
   experiencing new blessings
   and expecting new wonders.
As we draw near to you,
   draw near to us.

Sovereign God,
   we come to meet with you.
   Speak with us now,
      and send us out in the power of the Spirit
      and in the name of Christ,
      to live and work for your glory.
   As we draw near to you,
      draw near to us.

We ask it for Jesus' sake.
Amen.

179

SEEKING GOD'S PRESENCE

Eternal and everlasting God,
    you came to our world in Christ,
        sharing our humanity.
    You come to us each day through your Holy Spirit,
        sharing in our every experience,
    So now we come to you,
        to share together in fellowship with you and one another.
    Open our eyes to your presence:
        open our lives to your grace and power.

We come to acknowledge your omnipotence,
    to recognise your goodness,
    and to declare your wonderful works.
Open our eyes to your presence:
    open our lives to your grace and power.

We come in awe and wonder,
    to bring our worship,
    ourselves,
    and our world before you.
Open our eyes to your presence:
    open our lives to your grace and power.

We come to seek your forgiveness,
    to confess our many faults,
    and to receive your measureless mercy.
Open our eyes to your presence:
    open our lives to your grace and power.

We come seeking your strength,
    your guidance
    and your will.
Open our eyes to your presence:
    open our lives to your grace and power.

We come to read your word,
    to listen for your voice,
    and to discern your purpose.
Open our eyes to your presence:
    open our lives to your grace and power.

We come offering our discipleship,
    our gifts, talents and abilities,
    committing all once again to your service.
Open our eyes to your presence:
    open our lives to your grace and power.

Come afresh to us now in this time of worship –
    renew our commitment and vision,
    renew our faith,
    renew our love.
Open our eyes to your presence:
    open our lives to your grace and power.

For we ask it through Jesus Christ our Lord.
Amen.

PRAYERS OF PRAISE

180

ACKNOWLEDGING GOD'S GREATNESS

Almighty God,
    ruler over heaven and earth,
        Lord of space and time,
        creator of all that is and was and shall be,
        Alpha and Omega,
        we worship you.
    Hear our prayer,
        and receive our praise.

Everlasting God,
    all good,
        all truth,
        all love,
        all mercy,
        we honour you.
    Hear our prayer,
        and receive our praise.

Sovereign God,
    stronger than we can ever comprehend,
        greater than we can ever imagine,
        wiser than we can ever understand,
        kinder than we can ever dream,
        we acclaim you.
    Hear our prayer,
        and receive our praise.

Gracious God,
    always helping,
        always caring,
        always renewing,
        always blessing,
        we thank you.
    Hear our prayer,
        and receive our praise.

Living God,
> with joy and thankfulness,
>> awe and wonder,
>> devotion and dedication,
>> commitment and faith,
>> we acknowledge you.
> Hear our prayer,
>> **and receive our praise.**

Through Jesus Christ our Lord.
Amen.

181

COMING WITH GLADNESS

Almighty and all-loving God,
    we come together in the name of the living Christ,
        to confess our faith,
        to acknowledge your goodness,
        to celebrate your love,
        and to commit our lives afresh to your service.
    Greatly you have blessed us.
Joyfully we worship you.

We praise you for this opportunity to worship you,
    this time set aside week by week,
    this place of fellowship where we share something of your love,
    and, above all, we praise you for the assurance we have
    that, as we meet together,
    you are here amongst us!
Greatly you have blessed us.
Joyfully we worship you.

We praise you for your great love
    that has searched us out and enriched our lives,
    and for your care that constantly surrounds us,
    through joy and sorrow,
    hope and fear,
    light and darkness.
Greatly you have blessed us.
Joyfully we worship you.

We praise you for your sovereign power,
    your hand that has shaped the universe,
    your purpose that directs history,
    your grace that transforms lives,
    and your Spirit who sustains the Church.
Greatly you have blessed us.
Joyfully we worship you.

You have made us glad in so many ways,
    your love beyond anything we can deserve,
    your mercy inexhaustible,
    and your care for us never-failing.
Greatly you have blessed us.
Joyfully we worship you.

So now we bring you this time of worship,
    not so that we might withdraw from the world,
    but that we might serve it more effectively in your name;
    not so that we may escape from the daily routine of our lives,
    but that we may consecrate every moment
    and everything to you.
Greatly you have blessed us.
Joyfully we worship you.

Almighty and all-loving God,
    receive our praise,
    through Jesus Christ our Lord.
Amen.

182

A God, near and far!

Almighty and everlasting God,
   with awe and wonder we come to worship you.

You are higher than our highest thoughts,
      but always close by our sides;
      greater than we can ever think or imagine,
      yet made known to us in Christ;
      more powerful than anything or anyone,
      but nurturing us as a mother tends her child;
      constantly at work in the lives of nations and empires,
      yet having a special concern for every one of us.
We marvel at your love.
Receive our praise!

Though we stretch imagination to the limit,
      we barely begin to glimpse how wonderful you are.
Though we know you a lifetime,
      we scarcely start to fathom the depths of your love.
Though we have been blessed beyond measure,
      still you hold the best in store.
We marvel at your love.
Receive our praise!

Though we wander far from you,
      always you seek us out.
Though you sometimes seem distant,
      always you are near.
Though life seems to make no sense,
      still you are present, your purpose unchanged.
We marvel at your love.
Receive our praise!

If we ascend to heaven, you are there.
If we make our bed in Sheol, you are there.
If we settle at the farthest limits of the sea, you are there.
If we cover ourselves in darkness, even there you are with us,
    the night as bright as day and darkness as light to you.
We marvel at your love.
Receive our praise!

Almighty and everlasting God,
    give us humility to acknowledge our weakness
        beside your greatness,
        faith to trust in you
        despite our doubts and our blindness to your glory,
        joy in knowing you
        despite the limitations of our understanding,
        and peace in serving you,
        knowing that you are the Lord of all,
        a God both near and far.
We marvel at your love.
Receive our praise!

Through Jesus Christ our Lord.
Amen.

183

GOD'S INNUMERABLE BLESSINGS

Almighty God,
   we come together once more rejoicing in your love
      and celebrating your goodness.
   Richly you have blessed us:
      with grateful hearts we praise you.

We praise you for the constancy of your love,
      new every morning,
      for your handiwork in creation,
      the miracle of life in its infinite variety,
      and the beauty and wonder of the world around us.
   Richly you have blessed us:
      with grateful hearts we praise you.

We praise you for all you have done for us in Christ,
      opening, through him, a way for us to know you better,
      revealing something of your greatness and goodness,
      filling our lives to overflowing with your unfailing love.
   Richly you have blessed us:
      with grateful hearts we praise you.

We praise you for the way you have guided us
      across the years,
      and for the assurance that you will continue to lead us
      every step of our way;
      for the strength you have offered us in times of need,
      comfort in times of distress,
      encouragement in times of uncertainty,
      and joy in times of sorrow.
   Richly you have blessed us:
      with grateful hearts we praise you.

Accept now our worship,
   poor though it is
   and inadequate though our words may be.
Open our hearts to your sovereign presence,
   so that we may be filled
   with an ever-deeper sense of wonder,
   a greater feeling of awe,
   and a richer understanding
   of your purpose for us and all the world.
Richly you have blessed us:
   with grateful hearts we praise you.

In the name of Christ.
Amen.

184

THE WONDER OF OUR GOD

Great and wonderful God,
    we bring you once more our worship.
    We join with the great company of your people
        on earth and in heaven,
        to sing of your majesty,
        to marvel at your love
        and to rejoice in your goodness.
You are our God,
    and we praise you.

We acknowledge you as the Lord of heaven and earth,
        ruler of space and time,
        creator of all,
        sovereign over life and death.
You are our God,
    and we praise you.

We salute you as the beginning and end of all things,
        the one who is greater than we can ever begin to imagine,
        higher than our highest thoughts,
        beyond human expression.
You are our God,
    and we praise you.

We affirm you as all good,
        all loving,
        all gracious,
        all forgiving.
You are our God,
    and we praise you.

We bring you now our worship,
   our faith,
   our church,
   our lives,
   offering them to you in grateful adoration.
You are our God,
   and we praise you.

Through Jesus Christ our Lord.
Amen.

185

HEARTFELT PRAISE

Almighty God,
    we come together to praise you,
        to stand once more in your presence,
        to consider your handiwork,
        and to remind ourselves
        of all that you have done in our lives,
        all that you are doing,
        and all that you will continue to do.
    We would bring you our worship:
        receive our praise.

Help us, as we lift up our songs, to lift up our hearts also,
    as we read your word, to hear your voice also,
    as we unite in prayer, to be united with you in mind and spirit,
    as we hear your message proclaimed, to respond to your call
    and to accept your challenge.
We would bring you our worship:
    receive our praise.

Help us truly to praise you,
    not just in words and appearance,
    but in our hearts,
    our thoughts,
    and our lives.
So may we offer to you the truest expression of our praise:
    a life of faithful discipleship,
    a love for you and one another,
    and a living commitment to Christ.
We would bring you our worship:
    receive our praise.

In his name we ask it.
Amen.

186

GOD'S GREATNESS AND GOODNESS

Almighty God,
  we come to tell of your greatness,
    of all that you are,
    all you have done,
    and all you have given.
  Great is your name,
    and greatly to be praised.

We come to tell of your power and might,
    your mercy,
    love,
    and goodness.
  Great is your name,
    and greatly to be praised.

We come to tell of your faithfulness –
    the promise of your Word,
    the revelation of your Son,
    the living presence of your Holy Spirit.
  Great is your name,
    and greatly to be praised.

We come to lift up our voices,
    to proclaim your wonderful name,
    to rejoice in your faithfulness,
    and to offer you our worship,
    our thanks,
    our love
    and our service.
  Great is your name,
    and greatly to be praised.

Almighty God,
    receive this time set aside for you,
        accept the worship we bring,
        and speak to us through all that we share.
    Deepen our sense of wonder,
        increase our sense of joy,
        strengthen our sense of trust,
        encourage our sense of thanksgiving.
    Help us to know you more fully in our hearts,
        so that we may show your greatness more completely in our lives,
        and live always to your glory.
    Great is your name,
        and greatly to be praised.

Amen.

187

A JOYFUL RESPONSE

Great and wonderful God,
  we join today
    as part of the great company of your people across history
    to sing of your faithfulness,
    to celebrate your love,
    to acknowledge your mercy,
    and to marvel at your awesome power.
  Receive our praise,
    and accept our worship.

We rejoice in all that you are –
    higher than our highest thoughts,
    greater than we can ever imagine,
    sovereign over all,
    yet making yourself known to us in human form,
    sharing our humanity,
    and offering us your life.
  Receive our praise,
    and accept our worship.

We rejoice in the awesomeness of your love –
    in the fact that, even though we fail you,
    even though we make time for you only in moments of need,
    even though we use you for our own ends,
    still you have time for us,
    seeking us out, day after day.
  Receive our praise,
    and accept our worship.

We rejoice that you care for us as individuals –
  each chosen, valued and special in your sight,
  and we thank you that, as you have watched over us
  during this past week,
  so you are with us now and will be always,
  whatever the future may hold.
Receive our praise,
  and accept our worship.

We rejoice in the wonder of life,
  and we thank you for health and faculties to appreciate it,
  food and clothing to sustain it,
  pleasures and pursuits to enrich it,
  and families and friends with which to share it.
Receive our praise,
  and accept our worship.

We thank you for one another here,
  for the faith that we share,
  the fellowship we enjoy,
  the Lord we serve,
  and the call that unites us.
Receive our praise,
  and accept our worship.

Great and wonderful God,
  you have blessed us in more ways
    than we can ever begin to number,
    your goodness greater than we can ever hope to measure,
    your love beyond anything we can even begin to fathom,
    and yet we know you as a living reality in our hearts,
    as the one who gives shape and purpose to all of life.
So we come to you with grateful hearts in joyful homage,
  seeking, as best we can, to make our response.
Receive our praise,
  and accept our worship.

Through Jesus Christ our Lord.
Amen.

188

RESPONDING TO GOD'S GOODNESS

Loving God,
   once more you have blessed us,
      leading us through another week,
      forgiving our many mistakes and failings,
      blessing us in a multitude of ways,
      and so now, once more, we come to worship you.
   You have blessed us in so much:
      your name be praised.

We come with joy and thanksgiving in our hearts,
      to sing and pray,
      to read and listen,
      to think and learn,
      to give and receive.
   You have blessed us in so much:
      your name be praised.

We come to worship you as our creator,
      our Lord,
      our Father,
      and our friend.
   You have blessed us in so much:
      your name be praised.

We come to thank you for your goodness,
      your guidance,
      your love
      and your mercy.
   You have blessed us in so much:
      your name be praised.

We come to praise you for your purpose that will not be defeated,
   your power that brings good even out of evil,
   your grace that refuses to be denied,
   your strength which can never be exhausted.
You have blessed us in so much:
   your name be praised.

Loving God,
   as we worship you today,
      draw us closer to you,
      closer to Christ,
      and closer to one another,
      so that the faith we profess now
      may show itself in our lives always.
You have blessed us in so much:
   your name be praised.

Through Jesus Christ our Lord.
Amen.

189

THE LORD OF HISTORY

Almighty God,
    creator and ruler of the universe,
      we praise you for your great love,
      your faithful guidance
      and your sovereign purpose.
    Great is your name,
      and greatly to be praised.

We praise you that throughout history,
    and throughout our lives,
    you have been at work,
    bringing good out of evil,
    hope out of despair,
    love out of hate,
    and life out of death.
    Great is your name,
      and greatly to be praised.

We praise you for the way you have changed lives
    across the centuries –
    your call of Abraham to set out in search of a new land,
    of Moses to lead your people out of Egypt,
    of judges and prophets to speak your word,
    of disciples to follow Jesus,
    and of leaders and teachers to build your Church.
    Great is your name,
      and greatly to be praised.

We praise you that even when your people have gone astray
  you have been there,
    looking to lead them back to you,
    striving to restore the broken relationship,
    to put the past behind them and help them start again.
Though time and again your love has been betrayed,
  always you have remained faithful.
Great is your name,
  and greatly to be praised.

We praise you that with us too you have been patient,
    always willing to forgive and forget,
    slow to anger and abounding in steadfast love,
    your nature always to show mercy.
When we have lost our way,
    when we have lost sight of your goodness,
    even when we have lost our faith,
    still you have stayed true,
    seeking to draw us back to yourself.
Great is your name,
  and greatly to be praised.

Almighty God,
  Lord of human history,
    Lord of *our* history,
    we come to you with gladness,
    with praise in our hearts,
    and thanksgiving on our lips.
Renew us now through your gracious presence,
    assure us of your forgiveness,
    and equip us to serve you as you deserve.
Great is your name,
  and greatly to be praised.

In the name of Christ.
Amen.

PRAYERS OF PRAISE
AND CONFESSION

190

THE MAJESTY OF GOD

Eternal and sovereign God,
   with awe and wonder we come to worship you,
      to declare your praises,
      and offer our homage.
   Lord of all,
      in your mercy, hear us.

You are all-powerful,
   all-seeing,
   ever-present,
   shaping the pattern of history,
   at work in your Church,
   involved in our lives.
Lord of all,
   in your mercy, hear us.

You are all good,
   all loving,
   ever-merciful,
   showering us with your blessings,
   reaching out in our need,
   forgiving our faults and restoring us to your side.
Lord of all,
   in your mercy, hear us.

You are always true,
   always faithful,
   ever-constant,
   challenging us with what is right,
   standing by us when we go wrong,
   daily fulfilling your purpose with the same dependability.
Lord of all,
   in your mercy, hear us.

You are all holy,
   all pure,
   ever-perfect,
   acting in ways beyond our understanding,
   cleansing us from our imperfections,
   just and righteous in all you do.
Lord of all,
   in your mercy, hear us.

Forgive us that we have not worshipped you
   as often or as fully as we should,
   that we have not praised you with heart and soul and mind,
   that we have glimpsed so little of your greatness.
Lord of all,
   in your mercy, hear us.

Forgive us for failing to appreciate your mercy,
   for forgetting your countless blessings,
   and for losing our sense of awe and wonder before you.
Lord of all,
   in your mercy, hear us.

Open our eyes afresh to your splendour,
   our hearts to your love,
   our minds to your purpose,
   and our spirits to your presence,
   and so, assured of your forgiveness and your renewing power,
   help us to praise you not just in words,
   but in lives offered to you in glad and joyful service.
Lord of all,
   in your mercy, hear us.

In the name of the living Christ.
Amen.

191

DUE WORSHIP

Great and wonderful God,
 you deserve our heartfelt and constant praise,
  for you are all good,
  all loving.
We worship you now.
In your mercy, hear our prayer.

Our lives should be filled with gladness,
 our hearts brimming over with adoration,
 our lips overflowing with thanksgiving.
We worship you now.
In your mercy, hear our prayer.

Forgive us that all too often we take your many gifts for granted,
 losing our sense of privilege and wonder
 at your awesome generosity.
We worship you now.
In your mercy, hear our prayer.

Forgive us for singing praises with our lips
 without meaning it in our hearts,
 for offering worship out of a sense of duty rather than privilege.
We worship you now.
In your mercy, hear our prayer.

Help us rejoice in your love each moment,
 to bring our praise each day,
 and to offer our service always,
 faithful to you as you have been faithful to us.
We worship you now.
In your mercy, hear our prayer.

In the name of Christ.
Amen.

192

GOD'S LOVING HAND

Loving God,
  we praise you that we can put our hand into yours,
    knowing that you will lead, support and hold us
    throughout our lives,
    that you will supply all our needs and far more besides.
  You have touched our lives through your grace.
  In gratitude we respond.

We praise you for our experience of that truth across the years –
    the way you have always held firm to us
    despite our faults and faithlessness,
    never letting go of us even when we let go of you.
  You have touched our lives through your grace.
  In gratitude we respond.

Forgive us that we have let go so often,
    intent on going our own way;
    clinging to what ultimately can never satisfy.
  Forgive us for doubting you when times are hard,
    questioning your ability to lead us safely through.
  Forgive us for reaching out only when we have need of you,
    expecting you to lift us up from trouble of our own making,
    and to set us on our feet again.
  You have touched our lives through your grace.
  In gratitude we respond.

Help us to put our hand again in yours,
    in simple trust,
    quiet confidence
    and eager expectation,
    knowing that whatever we face
    and wherever we may find ourselves,
    you will hold us firm.
  You have touched our lives through your grace.
  In gratitude we respond.

In the name of Christ.
Amen.

193

A HOLY PEOPLE

Almighty and holy God,
  we gather as your people to worship you,
    to praise you for being here amongst us,
    and to thank you that, for all your goodness and greatness,
    you welcome us into your presence.
  We come, in all our weakness and with all our failings,
    rejoicing that in Christ we have been cleansed
    and made new;
    that, through him, you have set your mark upon us,
    and called us to be your people.
  Receive what we are,
    and direct what we shall be.

Forgive us when we fail you,
  our lives betraying our calling and your love.
Forgive us when people look at us,
  and, instead of seeing something of you,
  see only ourselves.
Forgive us when the things we say and do
  obscure and deny the gospel,
  rather than proclaim its message to all.
Receive what we are,
  and direct what we shall be.

Help us truly to be a holy people,
  reflecting your love,
  showing your compassion,
  and responding to your guidance.
Renew and restore us through the love of Christ
  and the inspiration of your Holy Spirit.
Touch our hearts through this time together
  and strengthen our faith,
  so that in the week ahead we may live and work for you,

to the glory of your holy name.
Receive what we are,
and direct what we shall be.

Through Jesus Christ, our Lord.
Amen.

194

FAILURE TO RESPOND IN THANKSGIVING

Gracious God,
   you have given us so much to enjoy and celebrate,
      to excite and thrill,
      to explore and challenge.
   Your goodness is beyond measure.
   Gratefully we respond.

We praise you for your wonderful love revealed in Christ,
      for the inner experience of your presence through your Spirit,
      and for the innumerable blessings received so freely
      from your hand.
   Your goodness is beyond measure.
   Gratefully we respond.

We praise you for loving us before we first loved you,
      for knowing us before we even knew you,
      and for caring about us, even when we stop caring about you.
   Your goodness is beyond measure.
   Gratefully we respond.

We praise you for your constant guidance,
      your faithful concern that never stops reaching out,
      and your amazing grace that is never exhausted.
   Your goodness is beyond measure.
   Gratefully we respond.

We praise you for the countless joys of life,
      the immeasurable beauty of our world,
      and the great mysteries of the universe.
   Your goodness is beyond measure.
   Gratefully we respond.

Forgive us that still we wander away from you,
 ignoring your guidance,
 forgetful of your love.
Your goodness is beyond measure.
Gratefully we respond.

Forgive us that so often we fail to appreciate
 all we have been given,
 more concerned with what we haven't got
 than what we have.
Your goodness is beyond measure.
Gratefully we respond.

Forgive us that we are so slow to give back to you,
 responding sometimes out of duty rather than joy,
 putting ourselves before others,
 more concerned with our own interests than your will.
Your goodness is beyond measure.
Gratefully we respond.

Assure us once more of your mercy and forgiveness,
 set us once more upon your way,
 and help us to follow your will,
 so that we may truly be your people
 and you may truly be our God.
Your goodness is beyond measure.
Gratefully we respond.

In the name of Christ.
Amen.

195

FAILURE TO APPRECIATE GOD'S GOODNESS

Gracious and merciful God,
    we come before you with joy and gladness,
        singing your praises,
        thanking you for your many gifts,
        celebrating your love,
        and offering you our grateful worship.
Lord of all,
    in your mercy, hear our prayer.

We come knowing you have made this day and every day,
    this place and every place,
    ourselves and all people.
We come conscious that once more
    you have blessed us beyond our deserving –
    that we have tasted your goodness
    and received richly from your loving hand.
Lord of all,
    in your mercy, hear our prayer.

But we come, too, conscious
    that we have not always appreciated your love,
    that we have been slow to thank you,
    yet quick to ask for more,
    dissatisfied with what we have,
    yet wasteful of the resources you have given us.
Forgive us for our failure.
Lord of all,
    in your mercy, hear our prayer.

Forgive us that we have not always been aware of your presence
and have closed our hearts to you;
that we have come sometimes to worship
with no enthusiasm or expectation,
more out of habit or duty than any real desire to praise you;
that we have committed our lives to your service,
and then had time only for ourselves;
that we have known your will,
yet repeatedly broken your commandments.
Lord of all,
in your mercy, hear our prayer.

Gracious and loving God,
assure us once more of your mercy,
renew us through the living presence of your Holy Spirit,
and so restore our relationship with you
that we may worship you each day
not just in words but through all that we are.
Lord of all,
in your mercy, hear our prayer.

In the name of Christ.
Amen.

196

FAILURE TO COUNT OUR BLESSINGS

Lord of all,
   in awe and gratitude we offer our praise.
   We come to sing of your greatness,
      to proclaim your wonder,
      to remind ourselves of your might and power,
      and to learn more of your will for our lives.
Loving God,
   in your grace, hear our prayer.

We come with glad thanksgiving
      for all the many expressions of your love –
      your mighty deeds and your simple everyday blessings,
      the beauty of the earth and the vastness of the heavens,
      the awesomeness of your eternal purpose
      and the unfolding of human history,
      the rich variety of life and the love that surrounds
      and encircles us each day.
Loving God,
   in your grace, hear our prayer.

Forgive us for sometimes being blind to it all,
   failing to see you or appreciate your goodness.
Forgive us for being unmoved by your presence
   and uninspired by your works.
Forgive us for worshipping you with our lips
   while being far from you in our hearts.
Forgive us for speaking of worship on Sundays,
   but failing to follow you the rest of the week.
Loving God,
   in your grace, hear our prayer.

Cleanse and renew us, we pray.
Meet with us again through the risen Christ,
    restore and inspire us through your love,
    and speak to us afresh through your word,
So help us to offer you the worship not just of words,
    but of hearts turned to you and lives reflecting your glory.
Loving God,
    in your grace, hear our prayer.

Through Jesus Christ our Lord.
Amen.

197

LOSING SIGHT OF GOD

Sovereign God,
   beginning and end of all,
   ruler over time and space,
     we acknowledge you as the one and only God!
Hear us, in your mercy.
Redeem and restore us.

We worship you in your majesty,
     we praise you for your greatness,
     we thank you for your guidance.
Hear us, in your mercy.
Redeem and restore us.

Forgive us for the way we fall into worshipping idols
     rather than you –
     putting you second to our other interests and concerns,
     imagining we know all there is to know of you,
     tying you down to our own limited understanding.
Hear us, in your mercy.
Redeem and restore us.

Forgive us for attempting to direct your will
     and dictate your actions,
     preferring our way to yours,
     as though we know better than you.
Hear us, in your mercy.
Redeem and restore us.

Forgive us for losing sight of your love,
     refusing your grace,
     overlooking your blessings,
     frustrating your purpose.
Hear us, in your mercy.
Redeem and restore us.

Forgive us the mistakes we make,
   the sins we fall into,
   the hurt we cause,
   through straying from your side.
Hear us, in your mercy.
Redeem and restore us.

Sovereign God,
   teach us more, day by day, of your greatness,
     of all that you are and all you have done,
     and so may we give you the worship and service
     that is rightly yours.
Hear us, in your mercy.
Redeem and restore us.

Through Jesus Christ our Lord.
Amen.

198

THE FAITHFULNESS OF GOD

Gracious and loving God,
   we thank you that, as we come to worship, you are here,
      waiting to greet us,
      speak with us,
      and teach us.
Meet with us now,
   go with us always.

You are here as you are always here,
   week by week as we come to worship you.
You are here as you are everywhere,
      at every moment,
      in every place,
      on every occasion,
      watching over us as a father watches over his children.
Meet with us now,
   go with us always.

Day by day, you have been by our sides,
      recognised or unrecognised,
      remembered or forgotten,
      obeyed or disobeyed,
      acknowledged or taken for granted.
Meet with us now,
   go with us always.

Though our response to you has been varied,
      our commitment uncertain,
      and our attitudes mixed,
      you have always been the same,
      ever-faithful,
      all loving,
      always true.
Meet with us now,
   go with us always.

Forgive us for the way we have responded –
　　failing to appreciate how much we owe to you,
　　and taking your love as ours by right.
Meet with us now,
　　go with us always.

Forgive us for so often forgetting you,
　　disobeying your commandments,
　　abandoning our faith.
Meet with us now,
　　go with us always.

Help us to love you as much as you love us,
　　to be as true to you as you are always true,
　　and to rejoice in your living presence not only now
　　but in every moment of our lives.
Meet with us now,
　　go with us always.

In the name of Christ.
Amen.

199

THE OTHERNESS OF GOD

Mighty God,
we come with gladness to worship you,
with joy to praise you,
with wonder to thank you,
and with awe to greet you.
Lord,
hear our prayer.

We come with all our weakness before your strength,
all our unworthiness before your holiness,
all our foolishness before your wisdom,
and all our smallness before your greatness.
Lord,
hear our prayer.

Yet we come knowing that you accept us, despite our faults,
that you love us, despite our failures,
that you wait to speak to us, despite our disobedience,
that you long to bless us, despite our ingratitude.
Lord,
hear our prayer.

Forgive us that we so often fail to recognise
how awesome you are,
losing our sense of mystery in your presence,
forgetting the constancy of your promises,
underestimating the extent of your grace.
Lord,
hear our prayer.

Open our eyes once more to your presence,
assure us of your redeeming and restoring love,
and send us out in the name of Christ
to live and work for your glory.
Lord,
hear our prayer.

Through Jesus Christ our Lord.
Amen.

PRAYERS OF CONFESSION

200

FAILURE TO SERVE

Lord Jesus Christ,
   we know we are less than perfect,
      our faith weak,
      our love poor,
      our motives mixed,
      our commitment unpredictable,
      but, despite our many weaknesses,
      we want so much to serve you,
      to live as the people you would have us be.
Forgive what we have been,
   and direct what we shall be.

We know that we have failed you in numerous ways,
      careless in our worship,
      half-hearted in service,
      concerned more about ourselves than your glory;
      our words saying one thing but our deeds another,
      the message we proclaim belied by the way we live,
      and yet, despite our failure, we hunger to know you better,
      to share in the work of your kingdom.
Forgive what we have been,
   and direct what we shall be.

Lord Jesus Christ,
   take what we are,
      flawed though it may be,
      and use it in your service.
   Take what we say and do,
      with all its blemishes,
      and use it to bring a little light
      into the darkness of our world.
   Through your grace,
      accept our imperfect discipleship,
      and work through us to share your love
      and to make known your goodness.
   Forgive what we have been,
      and direct what we shall be.

To the glory of your name.
Amen.

201

FAILURE TO RESPOND TO GOD'S LOVE

Loving God,
　once more we are reminded of our sinfulness
　　compared to your goodness.

We have broken your commandments
　in thought and word and deed,
　　pursuing our own ends rather than following your will.
We have missed opportunities to work and witness for you,
　lukewarm in our service and weak in our discipleship.
We have lost sight of your love and goodness,
　allowing you to be crowded out of our lives by other concerns.
We have grown stale in our faith,
　closing our minds to that which challenges and disturbs.
In so much we have failed you.
Forgive us.

You have offered us a new beginning,
　yet we have gone back to our old ways.
You have called us to shine like stars in the world,
　but instead we have walked in darkness.
You have sent us out to live and work for Christ,
　and we have turned in on ourselves.
You have welcomed us into your family as your children,
　but we have abused your trust.
In so much we have failed you.
Forgive us.

We thank you that you are a merciful God,
   slow to anger and full of constant love.
Though we have forsaken you,
   you never forsake us.
However often we may stray from your side,
   you keep on seeking us out,
   intent on restoring a relationship with us.
Yet despite your goodness, somehow we never learn,
   time and again making the same old mistakes.
In so much we have failed you.
Forgive us.

So we pray once more,
   forgive,
   cleanse,
   renew and restore us.
Open our hearts to your redeeming touch,
   open our eyes to your amazing grace,
   and so help us to amend our faults
   and to live more truly as your people.
In so much we have failed you.
Forgive us.

Through Jesus Christ our Lord.
Amen.

202

FAILURE TO APPRECIATE THE VALUE OF ALL

Gracious God,
    you tell us not to think of ourselves more highly than we should,
        but we find it hard to obey,
        and harder still to understand what that means in practice,
        for we can think both too much and too little of ourselves.

We have been full of our own importance and wisdom,
    preoccupied with self,
    harbouring vain illusions about who we are
    and what we can achieve.
We have not valued others as they deserve,
    allowing prejudices and preconceptions
    to colour our judgement and poison our attitudes.
We have looked down on those around us,
    failing to see the good in them,
    closed to the contribution they can make to our lives.
For all those times when we have valued ourselves too much
    and others too little,
    in your mercy,
    Lord, forgive us.

We have been too full of the importance of others,
    putting our trust in their example,
    placing our faith in their words and actions,
    allowing ourselves to be led astray.
We have not valued ourselves as we should,
    underestimating our potential,
    belittling our achievements,
    and failing to appreciate the gifts you have given us.
We have compared ourselves with those we consider successful,
    and felt worthless and inadequate as a result.
For all those times we have valued others too much
    and ourselves too little,
    in your mercy,
    Lord, forgive us.

Gracious God,
>we know that you value each one of us,
>>not for what we might become but for what we are.
>We thank you for having made every one of us unique,
>>precious in your sight,
>>and we rejoice that you love no one more or less than any other.
>Teach us what that means,
>>and help us to live each day in the assurance it brings.
>Give us a proper respect both for ourselves
>>and for those around us,
>>and if ever we lose that sense of balance,
>>in your mercy,
>>**Lord, forgive us.**

In Jesus' name we pray.
Amen.

203

FAILURE TO LOVE OTHERS

Merciful God,
  you call us to love our neighbour as ourselves,
    to testify to the reality of our faith
    through the love we show to others.
  It all sounds so wonderful in theory,
    but when it comes to practice we let you down so miserably.
  Forgive us.
Lord, in your mercy,
  hear our prayer.

Forgive us our failure to live up to your calling
  over this past week –
  the lost opportunities and wasted moments,
  the angry words and unkind comments,
  the thoughtless deeds and careless actions –
  all the ways we have denied you through our actions.
Lord, in your mercy,
  hear our prayer.

Forgive us for those times when we have ignored those in need –
  too preoccupied with our own affairs,
  too concerned about our own pleasures,
  too protective of our own interests –
  all the ways we have denied you through our failure to act.
Lord, in your mercy,
  hear our prayer.

Forgive us all the ways we have brought sorrow rather than joy,
  hurt rather than healing,
  despair rather than hope,
  doubt rather than faith.
Lord, in your mercy,
  hear our prayer.

Forgive us the love we have failed to show,
   the care we have failed to express,
   the support we have failed to give,
   the pardon we have failed to offer.
Lord, in your mercy,
   hear our prayer.

Merciful God,
   cleanse and renew us through your grace,
      cultivate what is good in our lives,
      and root out that which is bad.
   Restore us through your love,
      and recreate us by your power,
      so that we may learn to love others
      with the love you have so faithfully shown to us.
   Lord, in your mercy,
      hear our prayer.

In the name of Christ.
Amen.

204

FAILURE TO LIVE IN HARMONY

Loving God,
 you have called us together as your people,
  to serve you and one another,
  shoulder to shoulder,
  and heart to heart.
 Once we were estranged from you and one another.
Unite us now in love.

You call us to be a family of your people united in faith,
 walking in fellowship together,
 side by side,
 arm in arm,
 and hand in hand.
Once we were estranged from you and one another.
Unite us now in love.

Forgive us for all the ways we have failed to live as you desire –
 the times when we have allowed differences
 to come between us,
 the occasions we have acted behind people's backs
 in a way we would never dream of doing to their faces,
 the ways we have preferred to go it alone
 rather than stand together,
 refusing to heed any counsel other than our own.
Once we were estranged from you and one another.
Unite us now in love.

Forgive us for petty jealousies,
 intolerant attitudes,
 thoughtless words and careless deeds –
 the many expressions of selfishness
 which so easily and so often keep us apart.
Once we were estranged from you and one another.
Unite us now in love.

Forgive us that through our divisions
   we have broken again the body of Christ,
   causing him yet more pain and sorrow.
Instead of exhibiting the unity which he died to bring,
   we have shown the very discord which contributed to his death.
Instead of demonstrating the truth of the gospel
   through the love we share,
   we have caused people to ridicule and dismiss his claims.
Our words say one thing,
   our lives another.
And yet, despite it all, you go on calling us your people,
   striving to break down the barriers which keep us apart.
Once we were estranged from you and one another.
Unite us now in love.

Loving God,
   help us each day to know you better,
      to understand more of your will
      and to reflect more of your goodness,
      and so, in growing closer to you,
      may we grow closer to one another,
      growing together into a chosen race,
      a royal priesthood,
      a holy nation,
      your own people.
Once we were estranged from you and one another.
Unite us now in love.

Through Jesus Christ our Lord.
Amen.

205

FAILURE TO BE HONEST WITH OURSELVES

Sovereign God,
   from whom nothing is hidden
      and by whom all things are known,
      forgive us that we so easily and so readily deceive ourselves.
   Have mercy, O Lord,
      and make us new.

We concern ourselves with outer appearances
   rather than with inner reality,
      fooling ourselves into believing all is well
      when in our hearts we know that much is wrong.
   Have mercy, O Lord,
      and make us new.

We turn faith into something we do
   rather than something we are,
      a theory which we learn
      rather than a way of life we put into practice.
   Have mercy, O Lord,
      and make us new.

We talk of following Jesus,
   of committing our lives to him in joyful service,
      but it is ourselves we serve first,
      and our own inclinations that we follow.
   Have mercy, O Lord,
      and make us new.

We know we have done wrong,
   conscious of our weakness,
      yet we run from the truth,
      afraid to face facts,
      excusing or denying our mistakes.
   Have mercy, O Lord,
      and make us new.

Sovereign God,
    forgive us the faults that everyone sees
        and the faults known only to ourselves,
        the weaknesses we cannot hide
        and the weaknesses we conceal from everyone but yourself.
    Forgive us all the ways we let you down
        and betray our calling.
    Have mercy, O Lord,
        and make us new.

Fill our hearts with love,
    our minds with faith,
    our souls with power,
    and our lives with grace,
    so that we may love you better
    and serve you more faithfully.
Help us to see you in all your greatness
    and ourselves as we really are,
    and, through understanding both clearly,
    help us to become the people you would have us be.
Have mercy, O Lord,
    and make us new.

Through Jesus Christ our Lord.
Amen.

206

FAILURE TO CELEBRATE LIFE AS WE SHOULD

Loving God,
  we thank you for your great gift of life in all its fullness,
    for all the beauty, variety and interest
    of this world which you have made –
    so much to live for,
    so much to enjoy,
    so much to celebrate.
  You have blessed us so richly:
    forgive us that we fail to respond as we should.

We thank you for the message of the gospel –
    the good news of your unfailing love,
    your unchanging purpose
    and your unending mercy.
  You have blessed us so richly:
    forgive us that we fail to respond as we should.

Forgive us for so often failing to appreciate
    everything you have given,
    for becoming over-familiar and unmoved by it all,
    more concerned with what we don't have
    than with what we do,
    preoccupied by the negative instead of the positive things.
  You have blessed us so richly:
    forgive us that we fail to respond as we should.

Forgive us for so often turning the gospel
    into something inhibiting and restricting;
    for binding people with heavy burdens,
    for setting limits to your love of our own making,
    for being more concerned with what is wrong
    than what is right.
  You have blessed us so richly:
    forgive us that we fail to respond as we should.

Teach us to accept life in all its fullness,
    to celebrate your love in all its richness,
    and to share the joy you have given us in such abundance.
So may we make known the good news to those around us,
    that they too may understand your goodness
    and rejoice in your love.
You have blessed us so richly,
    forgive us that we fail to respond as we should.

Through Jesus Christ our Lord.
Amen.

207

FAILURE TO BEAR FRUIT

Gracious God,
    you have called us to bear fruit in our lives,
        to show the evidence of our faith
        by yielding a rich harvest of the fruits of the Spirit.
    Forgive us that all too often our lives have been barren
        or the harvest poor.
We have failed you in thought, word and deed,
    we have neglected opportunities for service,
    and we have been distracted by trivial concerns
    from our calling in Christ.
Lord, in your mercy,
    hear our prayer.

Forgive our weakness in discipleship,
    and, above all, our complacency,
    our lack of concern about it,
    our failure, so often, even to recognise that anything is wrong.
Forgive us for believing we have come far in faith
    when in fact we have barely started to grow at all,
    let alone bear any fruit.
Lord, in your mercy,
    hear our prayer.

Help us to place Christ at the centre of our lives,
    to make him the core around which all else grows,
    and so may our lives bear the harvest you long to see:
    joy, peace, patience, kindness,
    goodness, gentleness, faithfulness and self-control.
Lord, in your mercy,
    hear our prayer.

Gracious God,
   nurture the seed of faith within us.
   Renew our hearts,
      deepen our commitment,
      broaden our vision
      and open our lives to the power of your love.
   So may we bear a rich harvest to the glory of your name.
   Lord, in your mercy,
      hear our prayer.

In Christ's name we ask it.
Amen.

208

FAILURE TO LIVE AS PILGRIMS

Loving God
    you have shown us, in Christ, the way to life,
        the path of faithful service,
        and the meaning of your kingdom,
        yet sometimes we fail to see it.
    Have mercy upon us,
        and help us to walk in faith.

You are always leading us forward,
    eager to guide us into new experiences of your love
    and a deeper understanding of your purpose,
    yet so often we refuse to follow where you would have us go.
Have mercy upon us,
    and help us to walk in faith.

Forgive us for losing the sense of direction
    with which we began our path of discipleship,
    for finding it so hard to deny ourselves,
    yet so easy to follow our own inclinations,
    for trusting you when all goes well,
    but doubting the moment life fails to conform to our expectations.
Have mercy upon us,
    and help us to walk in faith.

Forgive us for losing sight of your kingdom,
    repeatedly measuring success and greatness
    by our standards rather than yours,
    confusing strength with weakness and truth with falsehood.
Have mercy upon us,
    and help us to walk in faith.

Forgive us our failure to live as your people –
    our repeated breaking of your commandments
    and disobeying of your will,
    our smallness of vision and shallowness of faith,
    our lack of love and feebleness of commitment.
Have mercy upon us,
    and help us to walk in faith.

Forgive us for preferring our own comfort and security
    to the way of faith,
    for putting ourselves and our interests before you,
    for so often putting ourselves out on our own behalf,
    yet so rarely on yours.
Have mercy upon us,
    and help us to walk in faith.

Renew us, we pray.
Rekindle our faith,
    revive our love,
    revitalise our vision,
    and restore our resolve to take up our cross
    and follow where you would lead us.
Show us the way,
    and give us faith to follow,
    looking always to Jesus, the pioneer and perfecter of our faith.
Have mercy upon us,
    and help us to walk in faith.

For his name's sake.
Amen.

209

FAILURE TO HONOUR OUR CALLING

Almighty and merciful God,
    we have done that which we should not have done,
        and failed to do what we know we should have done.
    We have thought that which we should not have thought,
        and failed to think of what is good and pleasing in your sight.
    We have spoken that which we should not have said,
        and left unspoken things we ought to have said.
    We have failed you in so much:
        forgive us.

We have sinned against you and one another,
    against many, known and unknown,
    in thought, and word, and deed.
We have failed you in so much:
    forgive us.

We are ashamed of our weakness and many faults,
    our greed, selfishness, pride and envy;
    the carelessness of our discipleship
    and the shallowness of our faith.
We have failed you in so much:
    forgive us.

We long to serve you better,
    to live as your people and bring honour to Christ,
    but though our hearts say one thing, our bodies say another,
    the spirit willing, but the flesh weak.
We have failed you in so much:
    forgive us.

Merciful God,
    deal kindly with us through your grace.
    Forgive us our failure to serve you,
        and put a clean heart and a right spirit within us.
    Assure us of your forgiveness,
        renew us through your love,
        and give us strength to follow you more faithfully
        in the days ahead.
    We have failed you in so much:
        forgive us.

Through Jesus Christ our Lord.
Amen.

PRAYERS OF THANKSGIVING

210

FOR THE JOY OF LIFE

Sovereign God,
    we come into your presence reminded of your greatness,
        your holiness,
        your beauty
        and your love;
        conscious that we come into the presence
        of one vastly greater than ourselves;
        the creator of life and sustainer of the universe,
        of everything that is and has been and shall be.
For all that we have received,
    we thank you.

You are a God of justice and truth, righteousness and purity,
    and yet we remember that you are also a God of love –
    a God who cares for each one of us,
    bringing joy out of sadness,
    hope out of despair,
    light out of darkness,
    wholeness out of imperfection.
Day by day you are with us,
    at work in the lives of all.
For all that we have received,
    we thank you.

We thank you for the many blessings you pour into our lives,
    for the innumerable gifts that enrich them –
    the love we share,
    the beauty we marvel at,
    the health we enjoy,
    the interests we pursue –
    so much to excite and enthral,
    to fascinate and savour;
    so much to give thanks for!
For all that we have received,
    we thank you.

We thank you that in Christ we are set free
    truly to appreciate your world –
    that the bondage of sin,
    the stranglehold of self
    and the grip of death have been broken.
We thank you that you want us to enjoy life at its fullest,
    and not just now but for all eternity.
Great is your name and worthy of all honour and glory.
For all that we have received,
    we thank you.

To you be praise and thanksgiving,
    power and dominion,
    now and for ever.
Amen.

211

FOR THE GUIDANCE OF GOD

Loving God,
    we thank you for your constant guidance throughout our lives,
        and for all that it means to us –
        the way you encourage,
        strengthen,
        challenge,
        and renew.
Day by day you are there to lead us:
    gratefully, we respond.

We thank you that you speak through your Word –
    that through the experiences of priests and prophets,
    judges and patriarchs,
    disciples and Apostles,
    you offer instruction for daily life
    and insight into your sovereign purpose.
Day by day you are there to lead us:
    gratefully, we respond.

We thank you that you speak through the Church
    and all that we share within it –
    through songs and prayer,
    preaching and worship,
    mission and service,
    fun and fellowship.
Day by day you are there to lead us:
    gratefully, we respond.

We thank you that you speak through creation –
    through the people we meet,
    the sights we see,
    the things we hear,
    and the experiences we go through.
Day by day you are there to lead us:
    gratefully, we respond.

We thank you that you speak through Christ –
>through his life and work,
>his preaching and teaching,
>his death and resurrection,
>and his living presence with us now.
Day by day you are there to lead us:
>**gratefully, we respond.**

We thank you that you speak through your Spirit within us –
>inspiring,
>comforting,
>teaching,
>and giving power from on high.
Day by day you are there to lead us:
>**gratefully, we respond.**

Loving God,
>for all the ways you have guided us,
>>and all the ways you continue to lead,
>>we thank you.
For the times we have found help through your presence,
>>the days when you have seen us through problems and difficulties,
>>and the moments when you have been there to watch over us,
>>we give you our praise.
Go with us now,
>>and direct our footsteps,
>>so that we may live and work for your glory.
Day by day you are there to lead us:
>**gratefully, we respond.**

In the name of Christ.
Amen.

212

FOR THE WAY GOD CHANGES LIVES

Loving God,
    we thank you that you are constantly at work,
        striving to fulfil your purpose –
        not just the course of history,
        nor only the destiny of nations,
        but equally the life of each one of us,
        everybody you have created precious in your sight,
        of infinite importance.
    You have done great things for us,
        and we are glad.

We thank you for the way you have moved in so many lives
    across the years –
    the way you have met with individuals,
    confronting them with your will,
    challenging them through your call,
    and leading them through your love.
You have done great things for us,
    and we are glad.

We remember Jacob, a trickster and a cheat,
    Matthew, a hated tax-collector,
    Legion, feared as a madman,
    Paul, formerly persecutor of the Church;
    and we remember how each experienced a life-changing moment –
    a vision of a ladder into heaven,
    a call to discipleship,
    a pronouncement of healing,
    a blinding light.
One touch of your hand,
    one word from your mouth,
    and life was never the same again!
You have done great things for us,
    and we are glad.

We thank you for the way you can change us,
   however much we may despair of it sometimes –
   that, despite our lack of faith,
   our many faults,
   and our sometimes wilful disobedience,
   you are constantly at work within us,
   nurturing the fruits of the Spirit,
   making of us a new creation,
   imparting the mind of Christ.
You have done great things for us,
   and we are glad.

We thank you that you can change anyone,
   however impossible that may seem –
   that the hardest of hearts
   and most twisted of people
   can be overcome by your grace,
   moved to turn away from their past life
   and commit themselves wholeheartedly to Christ.
You have done great things for us,
   and we are glad.

Loving God,
   we lose sight sometimes of your transforming power,
   becoming cynical, disillusioned and world-weary,
   frustrated by our repeated failure to serve you better,
   and disheartened by the continuing evil and heartache
   in our world.
Yet whether we see it or whether we don't,
   you are still present,
   still striving to fulfil your purpose,
   and still able to surprise us
   by the way you change what seems unchangeable.
You have done great things for us,
   and we are glad.

Joyfully we thank you,
   through Jesus Christ our Lord.
Amen.

213

FOR WORSHIP AND FELLOWSHIP

Living God,
  worthy of all praise and honour,
    great and wonderful,
    merciful and loving,
    we come to worship you,
      to lift up our hearts in grateful praise.
For all the ways you touch our lives,
  we thank you.

We thank you for this time and place set apart week by week,
    for these moments when we can regularly draw aside
    and enjoy your presence.
We thank you for the fellowship we can enjoy here with one another,
    with Christ,
    and with you.
For all the ways you touch our lives,
  we thank you.

We thank you that you want to meet with us,
    speak to us,
    move in us
    and work through us;
    that you are here now waiting to lead us forward
    in the journey of faith.
For all the ways you touch our lives,
  we thank you.

Help us to use this time you have given us
>to hear your voice,
>discern your will,
>and grow closer to you,
>so that we may return to our daily lives
>renewed in hope and vision,
>strengthened in our faith,
>and equipped to offer thanksgiving not just with our lips
>but through everything we are and do,
>to the glory of your name.
For all the ways you touch our lives,
>**we thank you.**

Amen.

214

FOR THE HOPE AT THE HEART OF OUR FAITH

Living God,
    we thank you today for the message of hope
        that lies at the heart of the gospel,
        the assurance that, whatever may seem to deny it,
        your love will emerge victorious.
    You have given us hope,
        and hope does not disappoint us.

We thank you for your word of hope that runs through the Scriptures –
    your promise to Abraham that, through his offspring,
    all the world would be blessed,
    to Moses, that you would lead the Israelites out of Egypt
    and into the Promised Land,
    to Isaiah, that your people's exile in Babylon would be ended,
    to your prophets, that the Messiah would come,
    to the followers of Jesus, that he would rise again on the third day,
    to the disciples, that, as he had departed into heaven,
    so he would return.
You have given us hope,
    and hope does not disappoint us.

We thank you that you fulfilled those promises,
    just as you said you would –
    your Son born from the line of Abraham,
    your chosen nation set free from slavery,
    your people returning joyfully to Jerusalem,
    your promised deliverer, born in Bethlehem,
    your power seen in the resurrection of Christ,
    and we thank you that in the fullness of time
    that final promise will also be fulfilled,
    your kingdom established when Jesus comes again in glory.
You have given us hope,
    and hope does not disappoint us.

We thank you for what that means for us today –
   that we can live each moment with confidence,
   and look forward with anticipation,
   whatever our circumstances may be,
   whatever times of testing may befall us.
Though dreams may be dashed and plans thwarted,
   though life may be hard and the future look bleak,
   we know that your steadfast love continues
   and your purpose endures,
   our trust not in things seen
   but in the assurance of things hoped for,
   the conviction of things unseen.
You have given us hope,
   and hope does not disappoint us.

Living God,
   we thank you that we can put our hand in yours,
   and walk where you will lead us,
   confident that, though all else may fail, you will not,
   though heaven and earth pass away,
   your words will endure for ever.
So we come in faith,
   with joyful hearts and in glad thanksgiving,
   to offer our worship,
   and to dedicate our lives once more to your service.
You have given us hope,
   and hope does not disappoint us.

Receive our praise,
   in the name of Christ.
Amen.

215

For God's many gifts

Almighty and everlasting God,
   we are here to celebrate your greatness,
      your power that created the universe,
      that sustains our lives,
      that dictates the course of history.
   For all you have given,
      Lord, we thank you.

We are here to celebrate your goodness,
   your love revealed in Christ
   that reaches out in forgiveness,
   that fills our hearts and minds.
For all you have given,
   Lord, we thank you.

We are here to celebrate your faithfulness,
   your covenant made with Abraham and your people of old,
   made afresh through Christ to his disciples and his Church,
   made new each day with us and all your people.
For all you have given,
   Lord, we thank you.

We are here to celebrate life in all its fullness,
   our faith in all its richness,
   our world with all its promise,
   our fellowship with Christ in all its wonder.
For all you have given,
   Lord, we thank you.

Almighty and everlasting God,
   you have blessed us beyond our deserving,
      filling our lives with good things,
      showering us with untold riches.
   Help us to show our gratitude by living as your people,
      and using your gifts wisely and responsibly
      to the glory of your name.
   For all you have given,
      Lord, we thank you.

In the name of Christ.
Amen.

216

FOR THE GRACE OF GOD

Gracious God,
 we come to declare your goodness –
  to celebrate again the awesomeness of your love
  and the wonder of your grace.
 Though we fail you, you never fail us:
  receive our thanks.

Undeserving though we are, you have shown us mercy –
 accepting our feeble faith and hesitant discipleship,
 understanding our weakness,
 putting our faults behind us and helping us to start again.
Though we fail you, you never fail us:
 receive our thanks.

However much we fail you,
 however far we wander from your side,
 you continue to seek us out and lead us forward,
 your patience never exhausted,
 your love refusing to be denied.
Though we fail you, you never fail us:
 receive our thanks.

We offer so little, yet you give us so much,
 our love is so weak, yet you respond so richly,
 our faith is so small, yet you bless us so constantly –
 your generosity towards us far beyond our deserving.
Though we fail you, you never fail us:
 receive our thanks.

Gracious God,
 your grace defies expression,
  too wonderful for us ever to understand,
  and yet it goes on being real, day after day.
 Gratefully we praise you
  and joyfully we celebrate your astonishing love.
 Though we fail you, you never fail us:
  receive our thanks.

In Jesus' name.
Amen.

217

FOR THE GIFT OF A NEW DAY

Loving God,
we thank you for this new day and all the opportunities it brings –
    a time to rest and unwind,
    to rejoice and celebrate,
    to reflect and worship,
    to share with family and friends,
    to meet with one another and with you.
For this and every moment,
    we bring you our grateful praise.

We thank you for having been with us over the days gone by –
    always there by our side
    to guide our footsteps,
    give light to our path,
    and lead us forward.
For this and every moment,
    we bring you our grateful praise.

We thank you for the assurance
    that you will be with us in the days ahead –
    that, whatever they may bring,
    whatever challenges we may face, or trials we may endure,
    you will be there to see us through,
    giving us the strength and the resources we need,
    and a joy that cannot be shaken.
For this and every moment,
    we bring you our grateful praise.

We thank you that you are God of past, present and future,
    the same yesterday, today and tomorrow,
    and in that faith we welcome this new day,
    receiving it as your gift,
    and consecrating it to your service.
For this and every moment,
    we bring you our grateful praise.

Through Jesus Christ our Lord.
Amen.

218

FOR A SOCIAL EVENT OR TIME OF FELLOWSHIP

Loving God,
   we thank you for this time we have shared together –
      a time of relaxation, fun, refreshment and celebration,
      but, above all, a time for coming together,
      for enjoying fellowship,
      for meeting friends old and new.
   It has been good to share.
   Lord, we thank you.

We thank you for everything that has made this day possible –
      the planning and preparation that lies behind it,
      the work that has gone on behind the scenes,
      the time and energy offered on our behalf.
   It has been good to share.
   Lord, we thank you.

We thank you for one another here –
      for our different characters and temperaments,
      gifts and interests,
      ideas and insights,
      for everything that enriches our coming together.
   It has been good to share.
   Lord, we thank you.

We thank you for the unity you have given us in Christ,
      the bond of love that holds us close,
      the encouragement we find through one another,
      the help and support we are able to share.
   It has been good to share.
   Lord, we thank you.

Go with us now,
    and may this time we have enjoyed together
    inspire us to reach out in the name of Christ,
    sharing his love and proclaiming his grace,
    so that others may come to know him for themselves
    and be welcomed in turn into the family of your people.
It has been good to share.
Lord, we thank you.

In Jesus' name.
Amen.

219

FOR THE JOYS YET IN STORE FOR US

Loving God,
> we have so many things to thank you for,
>> more than we can ever begin to number,
>> and there is so much we have not yet even started to explore!
> For all the joys that are yet in store,
>> **gratefully, we praise you.**

We thank you for the wonder of life –
> for the fact that it is able to thrill and move us in countless ways,
> constantly offering fresh experiences,
> new joys,
> unimagined opportunities.

No matter who we are or what we have done,
> there are still untold riches waiting to be tapped –
> places to visit, people to meet,
> pleasures to taste, possibilities to explore –
> far more than we can ever exhaust in this life's fleeting span.

For all the joys that are yet in store,
> **gratefully, we praise you.**

We thank you for the wonder of your love –
> for the fact that it too is able to thrill and move us
> in innumerable ways,
> once more offering fresh experiences,
> new joys,
> unimagined opportunities.

No matter who we are or what we have done,
> there are still untold riches waiting to be tapped –
> faith to explore, fellowship to enjoy,
> forgiveness to receive, fulfilment to discover –
> far more than we can ever ask for or imagine,
> and spanning all eternity.

For all the joys that are yet in store,
> **gratefully, we praise you.**

Loving God,
    we do not know what lies ahead,
        except that there will be a mixture of good and bad,
        joys and sorrows.
    But what we know for certain is that, in life or in death,
        you will be with us,
        always waiting to enrich our lives,
        always seeking to deepen our happiness,
        and ultimately bestowing on us untold blessings.
    For all the joys that are yet in store,
        gratefully, we praise you.

In the name of Christ our Lord.
Amen.

220

FOR OUR DIFFERENT EXPERIENCES OF GOD

Sovereign God,
    we thank you that you have made us all different,
        in character, temperament, background and experience.
    We thank you for the diversity this gives us,
        and for the opportunities it brings to share with one another.
    Help us to be open to all we might learn and offer,
        to recognise that our differences
        should not be a source of weakness but strength,
        not a cause of division
        but a chance to display the underlying bond that unites us.
    Though we are many, you have made us one.
Lord, we thank you.

We thank you that you meet us as we are,
    with all our quirks and foibles,
    everything that distinguishes us as individuals,
    the good and the bad,
    the pleasant and the ugly.
You speak in the concrete circumstances of our lives,
    responding to our prayers,
    meeting our deepest needs,
    speaking to our innermost selves.
Each of us has our own unique experiences of your love,
    yet we share the same faith
    and work towards the same goal.
Though we are many, you have made us one.
Lord, we thank you.

We thank you that you reveal yourself in different ways:
    through your still small voice,
    yet equally in the hustle and bustle of daily life;
    through exuberant songs of praise,
    but also through moments of quiet reflection;
    through traditional patterns of worship,
    yet just as much through spontaneous outpourings of your Spirit;
    through unforgettable moments of encounter,
    yet sometimes in the ordinary experiences of each day.
What moves one leaves another cold,
    what speaks to some says nothing to others,
    but each is equally real,
    each a way of expressing faith and responding to your love.
Though we are many, you have made us one.
Lord, we thank you.

Sovereign God,
    help us to see you in one another
        not despite our differences but because of them.
    Help us to overcome the fear of what is foreign,
        the suspicion of what does not conform with our own ideas,
        and so may we learn more of your purpose
        and more of your saving love,
        our understanding of you enriched
        and our fellowship deepened,
        through the diversity you have given us to share.
Though we are many, you have made us one.
Lord, we thank you.

In the name of Christ.
Amen.

221

FOR ALL WE HAVE RECEIVED

Gracious God,
  we have so much to be thankful for,
    so much to celebrate,
    but, to our shame, we all too often forget it.
  Hear now our thanksgiving for the many blessings we enjoy.
  For all we have received,
    we are truly grateful.

You give us all our daily requirements and far more besides –
    food in abundance,
    clothes of all kinds,
    homes rich in comfort and innumerable luxuries
    which those before us, and many still today,
    can scarcely have dreamt of.
  For all we have received,
    we are truly grateful.

We have so much that enhances the quality of daily life –
    schools, colleges and universities,
    shops and supermarkets,
    entertainment and leisure opportunities,
    healthcare and a welfare state,
    information at our fingertips
    and technology at our disposal.
  For all we have received,
    we are truly grateful.

We have a world of incredible beauty and variety –
    places to thrill and inspire,
    or in which to rest and relax;
    an abundance of wildlife –
    flora and fauna –
    to fascinate and delight us;
    people of different characters, backgrounds and insights,
    to meet with, talk with, share with.
  For all we have received,
    we are truly grateful.

We have the opportunity to love and be loved –
    whether as parent and child,
    husband and wife,
    brother and sister,
    relation or friend.
For all we have received,
    we are truly grateful.

And, above all, we have the knowledge of your care –
    your unfailing goodness,
    constant guidance,
    enduring purpose
    and inexhaustible mercy.
For all we have received,
    we are truly grateful.

Gracious God,
    we have so much to be thankful for,
        and today we make time to remember that –
        time to appreciate all we have been given,
        to rejoice in all the riches of this life,
        and to celebrate the treasures you have given us in Christ.
For all we have received,
    we are truly grateful.

Amen.

222

FOR SPIRITUAL FOOD

Gracious God,
   we thank you for the way you have touched our lives,
      the meaning and purpose you have given,
      the joy and fulfilment with which you have so richly blessed us,
      the strength and inspiration you have provided
      in such abundance.
   Blessed are they who hunger and thirst after righteousness,
      for they shall be filled.

   We thank you for the way you have nurtured our faith,
      offering guidance,
      challenge,
      comfort
      and encouragement.
   Blessed are they who hunger and thirst after righteousness,
      for they shall be filled.

   We thank you for the way you speak to us,
      through the words of Scripture,
      bread and wine,
      prayer and fellowship,
      worship and mission.
   Blessed are they who hunger and thirst after righteousness,
      for they shall be filled.

   We thank you for the way you make yourself known,
      through glimpses of your glory,
      through our encounter with the risen Christ,
      through the indwelling of your Holy Spirit.
   Blessed are they who hunger and thirst after righteousness,
      for they shall be filled.

Gracious God,
    we thank you for the way you have poured your blessings upon us,
        so that our cup brims over with good things.
    We thank you that we need never hunger or thirst again,
        since you have provided for our deepest needs,
        giving food to our souls.
    Blessed are they who hunger and thirst after righteousness,
        for they shall be filled.

Thanks be to God,
    through Jesus Christ our Lord.
Amen.

223

FOR THE WONDER OF CREATION

Creator God,
>we thank you for the world you have given to us,
>>so full of beauty,
>>so rich in diversity,
>>so much of interest,
>>so touched with wonder.
>You have given us so much,
>>**and we thank you for it.**

>We thank you for all the loveliness you have given us to enjoy –
>>the splendour of sunrise and sunset,
>>the variety of the seasons,
>>the beauty of hills and mountains, woodland and valleys,
>>the wonder of flowers bursting into bloom
>>and leaves rich in colour,
>>the grandeur of oceans and rivers,
>>the gentleness of a mountain stream,
>>the sound of birds singing and children laughing.
>>the smell of food cooking,
>>the joy of taste and touch.
>You have given us so much,
>>**and we thank you for it.**

Creator God,
>there is so much in our world to move, astound and refresh us,
>>so much that is good and lovely,
>>more to celebrate than we can ever begin to number.
>Forgive us that we so often forget it,
>>losing our first sense of childlike wonder and enjoyment.
>Forgive us that we fail to thank you for all we have received.
>Open our hearts today to the beauty of our world,
>>to all it has to offer,
>>and speak to us of the response
>>you would have us offer in return.
>You have given us so much
>>**and we thank you for it.**

Amen.

224

FOR ALL GOD'S BLESSINGS

Almighty and all-loving God,
  we come together in the name of Christ,
    as your people,
    your family,
    your children.
You have blessed us in so much:
  gratefully, we praise you.

We thank you for your love, so constant,
  your care, so faithful,
  and your guidance, so sure.
You have blessed us in so much:
  gratefully, we praise you.

We thank you that we can call you 'our Father';
  that our relationship with you
  is not one of fear, duty or subservience,
  but one of love, grateful response and freedom.
You have blessed us in so much:
  gratefully, we praise you.

We thank you for the wonder of creation,
  the beauty of the earth,
  and the awesomeness of the universe.
You have blessed us in so much:
  gratefully, we praise you.

We thank you for the joy of life,
  the love of family and friends,
  and the pleasure found in work and leisure.
You have blessed us in so much:
  gratefully, we praise you.

We thank you for food and clothing,
　　health and strength,
　　body, mind and spirit.
You have blessed us in so much:
　　gratefully, we praise you.

Almighty and all-loving God,
　　for the blessings we have received,
　　　the joy we experience,
　　　the love that surrounds us,
　　　and the hope that sustains us day by day,
　　　we bring our grateful praise
You have blessed us in so much:
　　gratefully, we praise you.

In the name of Christ.
Amen.

OFFERTORY PRAYERS

225

Loving God,
> whatever we give to you,
>> it can never match your offering to us in Christ.
> Through him you gave your all,
>> emptying yourself,
>> taking the form of a servant,
>> enduring even death on a cross,
>> so that we might share your life.
> Teach us,
>> as we offer our gifts,
>> to bring also our lives in joyful response,
>> ready for you to use us as you will,
>> for your kingdom's sake.
> **Amen.**

226

Gracious God,
> we cannot thank you enough for your great goodness,
>> yet the truth is we rarely thank you at all,
>> your gifts taken for granted,
>> your blessings scarcely even noted.
> We thank you for this opportunity to put that right –
>> this chance not only to say thank you
>> but to show our gratitude in action
>> through this offering of our money.
> You have provided for us so richly;
>> gratefully we respond,
>> in the name of Christ.
> **Amen.**

227

Loving God,
  take this money
    and use it for the work of your Church.
  Take our gifts
    and use them for the growth of your kingdom.
  Take our witness
    and use it for the spread of the gospel.
  Take our service
    and use it to make known your love.
  Accept all we bring you today
    and use it through your power and for your glory,
    in the name of Christ.
Amen.

228

Lord of all,
  as we bring this offering to *you*,
    teach us also to offer *ourselves* to *others*,
    to recognise that, wherever there is sorrow or suffering,
    hunger or hardship,
    you are there,
    sharing the pain
    and calling for our response.
  Teach us to offer what we can,
    where we can,
    when we can,
    conscious that, whatever we do for anyone,
    we do it also for you.
Amen.

229

Loving God,
> we bring these gifts
>> as a small way of thanking you for all you have given,
>> and as an outward expression
>> of all we want to offer you in return.
> We bring with them ourselves and our life together,
>> our prayers and our worship,
>> our words and our deeds,
>> our living and our loving.
> We bring ourselves, in grateful praise,
>> through Jesus Christ our Lord.
> **Amen.**

230

Loving God,
> you gave without counting the cost,
>> your sole desire to share your love
>> and bring us joy.
> So now we bring you our offering,
>> not as an afterthought or our leftovers,
>> nor as a routine collection of our money
>> given because it is expected,
>> but as a joyful privilege,
>> a giving of our best,
>> an offering from the heart.
> Consecrate it to your service,
>> through Jesus Christ our Lord.
> **Amen.**

231

Gracious God,
   you owe us nothing,
      yet you give us so much.
   We owe you everything,
      yet we give you so little.
   Forgive us the feebleness of our response,
      and teach us to give without reserve,
      not simply our money
      but our talents,
      our love
      and our service,
      each offered to you in the name of Jesus Christ, our Lord.
Amen.

232

Gracious God,
   it is in giving that we receive,
      in denying ourselves that we discover true riches.
   So we bring now these gifts,
      seeking no reward except to know you better
      and to serve you more faithfully,
      for in that is fullness of life.
   Receive our praise for that priceless gift,
      in Jesus' name.
Amen.

233

Sovereign God,
    though we offer our money
        and dedicate our lives to your service,
        it all seems so small compared to the needs of our world
        and the work of your kingdom.
    We wonder what our gifts can do
        or our lives achieve,
        so great are the needs
        and so small our resources.
    Yet you are able to take what seems insignificant
        and use it in ways far beyond our expectations.
    Receive, then, all we are and all we bring,
        and work through us to do your will
        and fulfil your purpose,
        through Jesus Christ our Lord.
Amen.

234

Gracious God,
    receive not only these gifts but also the givers,
        unworthy though we are,
        and poor though we know our response to be.
    Accept what we are,
        and shape what we shall be,
        and so use us to further your kingdom here on earth
        at it is in heaven.
Amen.

235

Gracious God,
   for your love which brought us into being,
      which surrounds us each day,
      and which will continue to hold us fast through all eternity,
      receive our praise
      and accept our glad thanksgiving,
      through Jesus Christ our Lord.
   Amen.

236

Gracious God,
   we bring you these gifts
      not to settle a debt or buy your favour
      but as an expression of our love,
      a token of our gratitude,
      an outpouring of our worship
      and a symbol of our commitment.
   Use them, and use us, in your service,
      through Jesus Christ our Lord.
   Amen.

237

Sovereign God,
  you need nothing from us,
    for all things are yours,
    held by us in trust
    and dependent ultimately on your goodness.
  Yet you invite us to give something back,
    to share in the work of your kingdom,
    and to contribute to the fulfilment of your purpose.
  For that awesome privilege we give you our praise,
    and, gladly, we make our response.
  Amen.

238

Sovereign God,
  we bring these gifts in adoration,
    as a visible sign of our homage.
  We bring them in praise,
    as a testimony to the faithfulness of your provision.
  We bring them in gratitude,
    as an acknowledgement of your awesome grace.
  We bring them in love,
    as a small way of showing how much you mean to us.
  Accept not only the gifts
    but the spirit in which we bring them,
    through Jesus Christ our Lord.
  Amen.

239

Almighty God,
　　all we have comes from you –
　　　　our world so full of beauty,
　　　　our lives so rich in blessing,
　　　　our faith so laden with joy.
　　Receive, now, these gifts we bring to you,
　　　　and teach us to use all you have given to us,
　　　　responsibly,
　　　　generously,
　　　　prayerfully
　　　　and lovingly,
　　　　to the glory of your name.
　　Amen.

PRAYERS FOR OURSELVES

240

THE CALL OF GOD

Loving God,
    your call comes to us in different ways and at different times,
        but to each one of us it inevitably comes –
        the call to faith, repentance and commitment,
        to sacrifice our time, money and energy,
        to explore new forms of service and positions of responsibility,
        to take up our cross and follow Jesus.
    Help us to hear your voice,
        and give us faith to respond.

You call us to things we enjoy,
    and to duties that are demanding;
    to responsibilities that are a pleasure,
    and to work that is hard;
    to tasks that ask little from us,
    and to love that is costly.
Help us to hear your voice,
    and give us faith to respond.

You call us when your will is clear,
    and when it is hard to fathom,
    through special moments when your word comes directly,
    and through more mundane times
    when it comes to us through the ordinary circumstances of life.
Help us to hear your voice when you speak,
    and to understand what you are asking of us.
Teach us to respond readily
    rather than hide from your challenge,
    to serve gladly
    rather than from any sense of duty or expectation.
Help us to hear your voice,
    and give us faith to respond.

You call us to be your hands and your feet,
  continuing the ministry of your Son Jesus Christ.
You ask us,
  through our caring and sharing,
  our loving and listening,
  our accepting and understanding,
  to bring hope, healing, strength and encouragement
  to a broken and hurting world.
Help us to hear your voice,
  and give us faith to respond.

Loving God,
  your call comes to us in different ways and at different times,
    but to each one of us it inevitably comes.
Help us to accept your call
  knowing that, whatever you ask of us,
  you will give us the strength to do it.
Help us to hear your voice,
  and give us faith to respond.

We ask it in the name of Christ.
Amen.

241

BEING STILL

Lord of all,
    you are a God of power,
        mighty and mysterious,
        and we thank you for that truth,
        for the knowledge that you are sovereign over all.
But we thank you also that you are a God of peace,
        a God whom we can meet in stillness and silence,
        and who speaks in a voice like a gentle whisper.
Draw near to us in the quietness,
    and may we hear your voice.

(Silence)

Teach us to make time and space for you –
    the opportunity to pause and ponder,
    to take stock of our lives,
    to reflect on your goodness,
    and to understand what it is that you would say to us.
Draw near to us in the quietness,
    and may we hear your voice.

(Silence)

Help us to be aware of your presence here among us,
    and, through meeting with you now,
    may we live each day,
    each moment,
    in the knowledge that you are always by our side.
Teach us to share every moment with you,
    confident that you are there,
    and that you care about our welfare.
Draw near to us in the quietness,
    and may we hear your voice.

(Silence)

Teach us to bring our prayers to you,
    not just today but every day;
    to speak freely, openly and spontaneously
    of what is in our hearts,
    knowing that you delight to hear us.
And teach us also to listen,
    humbly, reverently, attentively, eagerly,
    certain that you will respond to our cry,
    and that, in your own time, you will give us your answer.
Draw near to us in the quietness,
    and may we hear your voice.

(Silence)

Help us to use all times such as this,
    so that we may grow closer to you,
    and so that prayer may not be some occasional activity,
    still less some formal duty,
    but a joyful relationship
    and a constant experience of your renewing love deep within.
Draw near to us in the quietness,
    and may we hear your voice.

(Silence)

Lord of all,
    we have come in the quietness.
Go with us now into the turmoil of life,
    with all its noise and confusion,
    all its demands and responsibilities,
    and may your peace rest with us there,
    this day and for evermore.
Through Jesus Christ our Lord.
Amen.

242

SAYING YES TO THE CALL OF CHRIST

Lord Jesus Christ,
    we thank you for those you called to follow you across the years,
        and for those who have had the courage to respond in faith.
    Help us to be ready to respond in turn,
        willing to commit ourselves to your service
        and to walk the way of the cross.
    When you speak your word,
        living Lord,
        help us to say yes.

When you ask us to venture into the unknown –
    to be strong,
    courageous,
    obedient
    and faithful –
    living Lord,
    help us to say yes.

When you ask us to listen to your voice –
    to your word that confronts,
    challenges,
    teaches
    and inspires –
    living Lord,
    help us to say yes.

When you ask us to reach out in love –
    to the indifferent,
    the hostile,
    the unlovely,
    the unacceptable –
    living Lord,
    help us to say yes.

When you ask us to let go of self –
    to share,
    to care,
    to give
    and to sacrifice –
    living Lord,
    help us to say yes.

When you ask us to go out in your name –
    to speak,
    work,
    love
    and live for you –
    living Lord,
    help us to say yes.

Lord Jesus Christ,
    as you called the Apostles at the start of your ministry,
    and as you have called so many others since,
    so your call comes to us,
    urging us to respond in faith
    and to share in the work of your kingdom.
When you speak your word,
    living Lord,
    help us to say yes.

In your name we ask it.
Amen.

243

SAYING NO TO TEMPTATION

Lord Jesus Christ,
    we thank you that you held firm to your faith
        no matter what the pressure;
        that, despite the temptation to take an easier, less costly way,
        you refused to compromise your convictions.
    When we are tempted in turn,
        gracious Lord,
        help us to say no.

When we are tempted to follow the crowd –
    to shirk difficult decisions,
    to water down our principles
    and pander to popular opinion –
    gracious Lord,
    help us to say no.

When we are tempted to put ourselves first –
    to trust in our strength,
    to seek our own ends
    and to follow our own inclinations –
    gracious Lord,
    help us to say no.

When we are tempted to forget others –
    neglectful of their needs,
    dismissive of their opinions
    and unconcerned as to their welfare –
    gracious Lord,
    help us to say no.

When we are tempted to go astray –
    to indulge our desires,
    ignore your will,
    excuse what we know is inexcusable –
    gracious Lord,
    help us to say no.

Lord Jesus Christ,
  you were tempted just as we are,
      and yet you stood firm,
      even though the way you had chosen
      took you to death on a cross.
  Touch our lives,
      and grant us your faith, strength, vision and courage,
      so that, in the time of trial, we too may stay true to your way.
  When we are tempted in turn,
      gracious Lord,
      help us to say no.

For your name's sake.
Amen.

244

FELLOWSHIP IN ACTION

Gracious God,
 we thank you that you have called us into fellowship,
  to be part of your people not in isolation
  but as members of the Church,
  a family united in Christ.
 We thank you for that privilege and responsibility,
  and we ask for your help in fulfilling our role among your people.
 Bind us together, Lord:
  bind us together in love.

Help us to share with one another,
 not just our friends or those we get on with,
 but all in our own church family
 and the wider fellowship of the Church.
Bind us together, Lord:
 bind us together in love.

Help us to care for one another –
 to remember the housebound, sick and lonely,
 all those going through difficult times,
 and to take steps to show our concern and offer our support.
Bind us together, Lord:
 bind us together in love.

Help us to serve one another –
 ready, from our own experience of being helped by others,
 to encourage and strengthen others in turn;
 ready to put ourselves out on others' behalf,
 and to use our gifts in the cause of Christ.
Bind us together, Lord:
 bind us together in love.

Help us to show sensitivity –
    alert to each other's needs,
    awake to the silent cry of suffering,
    conscious of the problems some may be wrestling with,
    yet careful to keep a balance
    between intrusion into people's private affairs
    and indifference to their troubles.
Bind us together, Lord:
    bind us together in love.

Help us to be generous in spirit –
    to be tolerant,
    understanding,
    slow to take offence
    and swift to forgive.
Bind us together, Lord:
    bind us together in love.

Help us, in all dealings with one another,
    to show compassion,
    kindness,
    gentleness
    and patience.
Bind us together, Lord:
    bind us together in love.

Gracious God,
    teach us what it means to be your people.
    Broaden our vision,
        enlarge our understanding,
        unite us in care and prayer,
        in thought, word and deed.
Bind us together, Lord:
    bind us together in love.

We ask it in Jesus' name.
Amen.

245

DOUBTS AND QUESTIONS

Eternal God,
  all seeing,
    all knowing,
    all wise,
    all good,
    we come before you
    acknowledging our lack of understanding and knowledge.
Lord, we believe:
  help our unbelief.

There is so much we do not see clearly,
    so many things we are uncertain about,
    so many complicated and confusing areas of life.
Grant us faith to live with questions,
    and wisdom in coming to decisions.
Lord, we believe:
  help our unbelief.

We know you are at work in the world,
    and we believe in the final victory of your purpose,
    yet it is hard sometimes to see your hand,
    and harder still to make sense of the events that befall us.
We see so much that challenges
    and even seems to contradict our faith,
    and at times, despite ourselves, our trust is undermined
    and our confidence shaken.
Give us help to hold on to you,
    knowing that you hold on to us.
Lord, we believe,
  help our unbelief.

Teach us that doubts and questions are a part of faith,
  able to lead us to new insights
  and a deeper understanding of your purpose.
Give us the courage we need to be honest with you
  and with ourselves,
  open to that which stretches and challenges
  our comfortable preconceptions.
Help us to recognise that before building
  there must sometimes be demolition,
  before growth, a time of pruning,
  before receiving, a time of letting go.
Teach us, then, to bring both our faith and doubt to you,
  confident that you can use both
  to broaden our knowledge of your love,
  and to enrich our experience of your grace.
Lord, we believe:
  help our unbelief.

In Jesus' name we ask it.
Amen.

246

RENEWED COMMITMENT

Sovereign God,
  on this new morning
    we are made conscious of those many mornings,
    too many,
    when we have woken with a cold and dead heart,
    holding no enthusiasm for the new day,
    no vision of what it might bring
    or what you may do in it.
  So often we fail in our waking hours
    to emerge from the darkness of the night,
    our hearts burdened by fears, doubts and problems,
    unable to see beyond ourselves to you or others.
  Reach out, we pray, and touch again our lives.
  Restore us through your love,
    and renew us in your service.

We confess that sometimes our worship of you
    ceases to be a joy and privilege,
    becoming instead an empty routine
    which we perform out of a sense of duty.
  It is not that we consciously turn away from or abandon you,
    but simply that the spark which once fired us
    with hope and enthusiasm
    has been extinguished,
    damped by the cold realities of daily life.
  Rekindle the sense of joy that once thrilled us
    as we contemplate your love,
    so that we may awake to each new day
    with hope in our hearts.
  Move in the depths of our being,
    so that we may live every moment
    with fresh vision and purpose,
    and see the whole of creation in a different light,
    ourselves and our relationships transformed
    by our experience of your love.
  Restore us through your love,
    and renew us in your service.

Grant that we might become agents of your love,
   healing and helping the broken and the sick,
   the lonely and depressed,
   the poor and the weak,
   the oppressed and exploited –
   all who stand in need of your help and love.
Revive in us a picture of your kingdom,
   and an understanding of the part you would have us play
   in bringing it to fruition.
Send us out with joy and thanksgiving,
   to live and work for Christ,
   and to celebrate everything you have done for us through him.
Restore us through your love,
   and renew us in your service.

For we ask it in his name.
Amen.

247

ENCOURAGING OTHERS

Gracious God,
  you call us to support one another,
    to offer comfort in times of need,
    reassurance in times of fear,
    inspiration in times of challenge,
    and confidence in times of doubt.
  As you encourage us,
    so may we encourage others.

Forgive us for so easily doing the opposite –
    finding fault,
    running down,
    criticising and condemning.
  As you encourage us,
    so may we encourage others.

Forgive us for seeing the worst instead of the best,
    for believing the bad instead of the good,
    for so often pulling down
    and so rarely building up.
  As you encourage us,
    so may we encourage others.

Teach us to recognise people's gifts and nurture them,
    to understand their problems and share them,
    to acknowledge their successes and applaud them,
    to appreciate their efforts and affirm them.
  As you encourage us,
    so may we encourage others.

Teach us to help people believe in themselves,
    to discover their abilities,
    appreciate their worth,
    and fulfil their potential.
  As you encourage us,
    so may we encourage others.

Teach us, through the faith we show in people,
    to help them attempt great things
    and expect great things;
    to look at life seeing not the obstacles but the opportunities,
    not the things they can't do but the things they can.
As you encourage us,
    so may we encourage others.

Through Jesus Christ our Lord.
Amen.

248

PRACTISING WHAT WE PREACH

Almighty God,
  through Christ you have demonstrated the wonder of your grace,
    sharing our humanity,
    living among us,
    giving freely of yourself.
  You didn't just speak of love;
    you showed it in action.
  Help us to do the same.
  Take what we are,
    and make us what we long to be.

Forgive us for so rarely practising what we preach,
    for failing to show in our lives
    the faith we profess with our lips,
    our actions time and again belying our words.
  Take what we are,
    and make us what we long to be.

We talk of forgiving one another, yet we nurse grievances,
    of being content, yet we are full of envy,
    of serving others, yet we serve self,
    of loving truth, yet we deal falsely.
  Take what we are,
    and make us what we long to be.

We speak of commitment, but we are careless in discipleship,
    of faith, but we are full of doubt,
    of vision, but we are narrow in our outlook,
    of being a new creation, but we are the same as before.
  Take what we are,
    and make us what we long to be.

Forgive our weakness,
    assure us again of your forgiveness,
    inspire us with your love
    and renew us in your service.
Take what we are,
    and make us what we long to be.

Speak to us now as we meet together,
    and remind us again of the values of your kingdom –
    that in losing ourselves we find who we really are,
    in sacrificing much we gain everything,
    in weakness we discover strength,
    in sorrow we receive comfort,
    in dying to self we rise to you
    and discover life in all its fullness.
Teach us to base our lives on those principles.
Take what we are,
    and make us what we long to be.

Almighty God,
    help us not simply to talk about faith or speak of love,
        but to demonstrate both of these through the people we are
        and through the lives we live.
Grant that our words and our deeds may be one,
    and so may we be fitting witnesses
    to your renewing, redeeming power.
Take what we are,
    and make us what we long to be.

Through Jesus Christ our Lord.
Amen.

249

RESPONDING TO A BROKEN WORLD

Sovereign God,
  we bring before you our troubled world –
    a world of so much hatred, suspicion, greed and envy,
    so much poverty, exploitation, violence and suffering,
    and yet a world you love so much
    that you became a part of it through your Son,
    offering your love to bring it healing.
You call us to share in mending broken lives:
  help us to respond.

We bring before you our sense of frustration and hopelessness
    in the face of so much need,
    our awareness that there is so little we can do to help,
    so little we can even influence, let alone change.
And yet you call us to respond in whatever ways we can –
    to pray,
    to give,
    to serve,
    and to sacrifice in the cause of your kingdom.
Help us to do that faithfully –
    offering our love unreservedly,
    encouraging those who offer compassion and support to others,
    supporting all who work for peace and justice,
    and petitioning those with the power
    to shape the affairs of this world.
You call us to share in mending broken lives:
  help us to respond.

We thank you that, though it may sometimes seem otherwise,
    we are not alone,
    nor dependent solely on our own resources,
    for you are constantly at work,
    striving to change lives,
    to redeem situations,
    to shape the course of history.
We rejoice that you are able to speak and move
    through ordinary people like us,
    taking our feeble faith and hesitant discipleship,
    and using both in ways far beyond our expectations.
We praise you that, whatever may conspire against you
    and frustrate your purpose,
    your will shall finally be done and your kingdom come.
Inspire us with that knowledge,
    with the assurance that, in every situation of human need,
    you are there,
    and that in responding to these
    we are responding also to you.
You call us to share in mending broken lives:
    help us to respond.

In the name of Christ we ask it.
Amen.

250

GLIMPSING THE POSSIBLE

Sovereign God,
   creator and sustainer of the universe,
      present and active in our world,
      guiding and shaping the pattern of history,
      we praise you for your power.
   Open our eyes to your greatness.
   Open our lives to your power.

You are greater than our minds can fathom,
      able to achieve things beyond our imagination,
      working in ways that defy all our expectations.
   We worship you in your splendour.
   Open our eyes to your greatness.
   Open our lives to your power.

Forgive us that so often in our lives
      we lose sight of who you are and all you can do.
   We see things from a human rather than divine perspective,
      allowing our thoughts to be tied down to earth
      rather than soar up to heaven,
      failing to grasp the opportunities you offer us
      because we forget that what is impossible for us
      is possible for you.
   Forgive us for allowing what can still be
      to become what might have been.
   Open our eyes to your greatness.
   Open our lives to your power.

Too often we have been guilty of feeble faith,
   narrow horizons
   and negative thinking.
Help us to recognise all you would do in our lives,
   to be awake to the possibilities open to us,
   to have the faith to attempt and expect great things
   even though they seem beyond us.
Open our eyes to your greatness.
Open our lives to your power.

Through Jesus Christ our Lord.
Amen.

251

COMMUNITY IN CHRIST

Loving God,
  you have called us to be a living community,
    a people bound together as the body of Christ,
    a family united in love.
  Draw us closer to you.
  Draw us closer to one another.

Forgive us that we fall so far short of that ideal,
    that we allow division to grow between us,
    petty disputes and differences of opinion
    separating us one from another.
Forgive us that we are too much concerned for ourselves,
    so often forgetful of the needs within our fellowship.
Forgive us that we miss opportunities
    of supporting and strengthening one another,
    of sharing each other's joys and sorrows.
Draw us closer to you.
Draw us closer to one another.

Help us so to grow together
    that when one of us suffers we all suffer,
    and when one of us rejoices we all rejoice.
Help us to show that we care for one another,
    that we are truly one body,
    that we depend upon each other
    if we are to be the people you would have us be.
So may we be a people of love and acceptance,
    a healing, renewing fellowship,
    a community in Christ.
Draw us closer to you.
Draw us closer to one another.

In his name we ask it.
Amen.

252

AMBASSADORS FOR CHRIST

Lord Jesus Christ,
 we praise you that you are ready to call us your people,
  that, despite our weakness, faults and failures,
  you are happy for us to represent you here on earth,
  and to share in the work of building your kingdom.
We come now seeking your grace:
 may we go out proclaiming your love.

Forgive us that we are sometimes less ready
 to acknowledge you as our Lord,
 afraid of what people may think,
 embarrassed by the possibility of being misunderstood,
 concerned it may adversely affect our prospects,
 nervous about what it may lead to.
We come now seeking your grace:
 may we go out proclaiming your love.

Forgive us that we are sometimes poor ambassadors,
 all too often our lips saying one thing but our lives another.
We talk of being a new creation,
 yet there is little if anything different about us from anyone else.
We come now seeking your grace:
 may we go out proclaiming your love.

Move within us and nurture the seed of faith in our hearts,
 so that we may be a source of hope and comfort,
 love and compassion,
 to a needy world.
We come now seeking your grace:
 may we go out proclaiming your love.

Lord Jesus Christ,
    make us proud to declare your name
        and to identify ourselves with your cause.
    Help us to put you first in our lives
        even when it means putting our own interests second,
        to die to self so that we may live for you.
    So may your love be shown,
        and your kingdom brought a little closer.
    We come now seeking your grace:
        may we go out proclaiming your love.

To the glory of your name.
Amen.

253

FIRST THINGS FIRST

Lord Jesus, the servant of all,
    come among us and grant us the light of your presence,
        for we are weak and poor in faith,
        slow to follow and swift to stray.
Though we yearn to be your people,
    day after day we let you down.
Though we hunger to serve you better,
    time and again we serve only ourselves.
Teach us to put you at the centre of our lives,
    to focus on what really matters.

In all the stress and rush of life
    it is so easy to forget you and to lose our way.
In the press of each day we allow you to be crowded out,
    preoccupied instead with our own problems and concerns,
    our own plans and needs.
And then, suddenly, we stop and find that we are alone,
    burdened and troubled,
    laden with guilt and uncertainty,
    unable to cope with the demands put upon us.
Our thoughts are turned in on ourselves,
    rather than up towards you and out to the world.
Teach us to put you at the centre of our lives.
Teach us to focus on what really matters.

You tell us that the first shall be last and the last first,
    that it is in losing our life we shall find it,
    and that in giving to others we shall receive.
We know it is true,
    and we strive to live by those principles,
    but repeatedly we fall back into our old ways,
    unable to overcome the pull of self-interest.
Teach us to put you at the centre of our lives,
    to focus on what really matters.

Lord Jesus Christ,
  your call to take up our cross and follow you is frightening,
    for we find it hard to give up even a little,
    let alone to surrender our lives
    and put others before ourselves.
  Yet *you* sacrificed everything,
    enduring not only the agony of death on the cross,
    but the awfulness of our human sinfulness
    and the isolation that entailed.
  Give to us the faith and courage that sustained you,
    the willingness to spend and be spent in your service.
  Teach us to put you at the centre of our lives,
    to focus on what really matters.

  In your name we ask it.
  Amen.

254

PLAYING OUR PART

Living God,
we thank you that you are always with us,
whoever we are and wherever we may be.
We thank you that you make yourself known to us
in numerous ways,
not just when we gather to worship you,
but often in times and places we least expect.
And we thank you that you delight to meet with us,
taking pleasure in our company.
You reach out with unfailing love:
help us to respond in faith.

Forgive us that our relationship with you
is all too often one-sided,
that it is left to you to make the running.
We are casual and complacent in discipleship,
careless in making time to meet with you,
and forgetful of your love,
yet we expect you still to be there when we need you,
ready to answer when it suits us,
and swift to bless despite our slowness to serve you.
Day after day you have to seek us out
after we have gone astray,
and day after day you do just that.
You reach out with unfailing love:
help us to respond in faith.

Living God,
    teach us to be still in your presence,
        to listen to your voice,
        to seek your will,
        and to respond to your guidance.
    Deepen our relationship with you through Christ,
        so that we may know your presence with us more fully each day,
        and share your life more abundantly each moment.
    You reach out with unfailing love:
        help us to respond in faith.

In Christ's name we pray.
Amen.

PRAYERS FOR OTHERS

255

FOR THOSE FACING SORROW

Loving God,
    you have promised that those who mourn shall be comforted.
    So now we pray for all those facing sorrow at this time.
    Lord, in your mercy,
        hear our prayer.

We pray for those whose hopes have been dashed –
    their plans laid to waste,
    their dreams destroyed.
Rekindle their faith in the future.
Lord, in your mercy,
    hear our prayer.

We pray for those who have been let down –
    wounded by loved ones,
    betrayed by those in whom they put their trust.
Save them from succumbing to bitterness or cynicism.
Lord, in your mercy,
    hear our prayer.

We pray for those wrestling with depression –
    those for whom life seems empty
    and the future dark.
Show them a light at the end of the tunnel.
Lord, in your mercy,
    hear our prayer.

We pray for those who are unwell –
    afflicted by chronic disease,
    suffering from terminal illness.
Support them through all that they face.
Lord, in your mercy,
    hear our prayer.

We pray for those who grieve –
   those who mourn loved ones,
   those coming to terms with personal tragedy.
Cradle them in your everlasting arms.
Lord, in your mercy,
   hear our prayer.

Loving God,
   hold on to all who walk through the valley of tears.
   Reach out to them,
      and grant them the knowledge that you are with them,
      sharing their pain and moved by their sorrow.
   Minister the consolation that you alone can offer,
      and give them the assurance
      that those who mourn shall be comforted;
      those who weep will laugh.
   Lord, in your mercy,
      hear our prayer.

Through Jesus Christ our Lord.
Amen.

256

FOR THOSE WHO HAVE MADE MISTAKES

Merciful God,
    we pray for those who walk through life with a sense of guilt,
        burdened by past mistakes,
        overwhelmed by a sense of failure,
        troubled by feelings of shame,
        depressed by the knowledge of their own weakness.
    Help them to understand that in you
        they can find true forgiveness
        and a new beginning.
    Lord, in your mercy,
        hear our prayer.

We pray for those who commit evil with no sense of wrong-doing,
    no concept of sin,
    no hint of remorse,
    no sign of scruples.
Help them to glimpse what is right and good,
    and to be touched by the renewing, transforming grace of Christ.
Lord, in your mercy,
    hear our prayer.

We pray for those who have been wronged by others –
    those who have been hurt,
    deceived,
    betrayed,
    let down.
Help them to be ready to forgive others as you have forgiven us.
Lord, in your mercy,
    hear our prayer.

We pray finally for one another,
   in our relationships with family and friends,
   in our relationships at work or leisure,
   in our relationships in fellowship here,
   and in our relationships with other Christians.
Help us to recognise any divisions or grievances
   there may be between us,
   and help us work towards the healing of all such rifts,
   forgiving and seeking forgiveness.
Lord, in your mercy,
   hear our prayer.

Merciful God,
   help all in your world to discover the mercy you so freely offer,
      and to show that mercy in turn;
      to be ready to put the past behind them,
      and to begin again through your grace.
Lord, in your mercy,
   hear our prayer.

   Amen.

257

For our broken world

Loving God,
we bring to you our world of so much pain,
so much need and sorrow;
a world you care for so deeply
that you willingly gave your all for it,
living and dying among us through your Son, Jesus Christ.
Reach out again in mercy,
and heal our wounds.

We bring to you the causes of so much suffering –
the sin of greed,
denying the many their share of this earth's riches
to the benefit of the few;
the sin of waste,
wantonly squandering the resources you have given
with no thought of future generations;
the sin of intolerance,
dividing families, communities and nations
through a refusal to engage in dialogue;
the sin of pride,
thinking too highly of ourselves and too poorly of others;
the sin of indifference,
caring too little about you, too little about anything.
Reach out again in mercy,
and heal our wounds.

We pray for those who pay the price of human folly –
the poor and the hungry,
the homeless and dispossessed,
victims of war and violence, crime and cruelty;
the distressed, isolated, crushed and forgotten,
all who are deprived of love and denied hope.
Reach out again in mercy
and heal our wounds.

Loving God,
  come again to our world
      through your Son, our Saviour.
  Mend our divisions,
      forgive our folly,
      and guide all our affairs.
  Reach out again in mercy,
      and heal our wounds.

In the name of Christ we ask it.
Amen.

258

FOR THOSE FOR WHOM GOD SEEMS SILENT

Living God,
>we thank you that you are a God who hears and answers prayer,
>>and we praise you for those times
>>when you have responded to us
>>and granted our requests.
>But we confess that there are times, too, when you seem silent,
>>when, listen though we might, we cannot hear your voice.
>And so we pray now for all who cry to you
>>but who feel their prayers are unanswered.
>Lord, in your mercy, hear us,
>>**and all who pray to you.**

>We think of those known to us facing difficult times –
>>battling with illness,
>>wrestling with depression,
>>anxious about the future,
>>grieving for loved ones –
>>those for whom life seems a puzzle,
>>even a burden,
>>and who long to find hope
>>to make some sense out of their confusion.
>Lord, in your mercy, hear us,
>>**and all who pray to you.**

>We think of those who feel far from you –
>>burdened by doubt,
>>overwhelmed by temptation,
>>crushed by failure –
>>those who long to know you better
>>but who find it hard to get close;
>>who seek to serve you
>>but who are weighed down by a sense of their weaknesses,
>>their lack of faith
>>and their repeated mistakes.
>Lord, in your mercy, hear us,
>>**and all who pray to you.**

We think of those who seek guidance –
  who feel unsure of the way ahead,
  uncertain of their ability to face that future,
  unclear as to what you want from them,
  or what you plan for their lives –
  all who ask you to lead the way forward,
  yet who still have no clear sense of their particular calling.
Lord, in your mercy, hear us,
  and all who pray to you.

We think of the poor and the weak,
  the vulnerable and disadvantaged in society –
  those denied their rights,
  their dignity,
  their freedom,
  their livelihoods –
  all who long for a time when justice will be established
  but who have given up believing it ever shall be.
Lord, in your mercy, hear us,
  and all who pray to you.

Living God,
  we are conscious that so many in our world cry out to you
    yet seem to receive no answer –
    some because they do not expect to receive any,
    some because they are not ready or willing to listen,
    some because they do not understand what you are saying,
    but many genuinely and urgently longing to hear your voice,
    yearning for some response.
Speak to them, we pray.
Do not keep silent,
  but reach out into their pain and hurt,
  their need and hopelessness,
  and bring your word of comfort,
  of peace,
  of healing, love and renewal.
Lord, in your mercy, hear us,
  and all who pray to you.

In the name of Jesus Christ,
  your Word made flesh.
Amen.

259

FOR THOSE IN AUTHORITY

Living God,
  you call us to pray for our leaders,
    to remember those set over us,
    so we pray now for all those in positions of authority.

We pray for those in our Parliament,
  both government and opposition.
In all their decisions give them a proper sense
  of the responsibility entrusted to them,
  and grant that they may work not for themselves
  but for the good of all.
Lord, in your mercy,
  hear our prayer.

We pray for the Queen and the royal family.
Help them to cope with the constant glare of publicity
  and media interest,
  and to use their position wisely,
  offering inspiration and encouragement to the nation.
Lord, in your mercy,
  hear our prayer.

We pray for those in the police force,
  with all the dangers and difficulties their work involves.
Give them integrity, courage, patience and resolve,
  and grant them your strength and protection.
Lord, in your mercy,
  hear our prayer.

We pray for judges, barristers and jurors,
>for magistrates and solicitors;
>all those faced by complex moral and legal questions,
>and having the power to irrevocably shape people's lives.
Grant them honesty and wisdom,
>firmness yet sensitivity.
Lord, in your mercy,
>**hear our prayer.**

We pray for headteachers, lecturers
>and all those involved in education,
>entrusted with shaping the lives of young people.
Give them insight and understanding,
>the ability to communicate their knowledge
>in a way that enthuses their students.
Lord, in your mercy,
>**hear our prayer.**

We pray for managers and directors in industry and commerce –
>those whose decisions will affect not just firms or businesses
>but the lives of countless individuals, at home and overseas.
Give them the acumen they need to ensure financial success,
>coupled with a genuine concern
>for the welfare of their employees
>and of the wider community.
Lord, in your mercy,
>**hear our prayer.**

We pray for leaders in the Church –
>ministers, elders, bishops and deacons,
>all those entrusted with positions of oversight,
>and called to teach the faith through word and deed.
Grant them vision and discernment,
>a living knowledge of your presence,
>and a daily sense of your guidance.
Lord, in your mercy,
>**hear our prayer.**

Living God,
we thank you for those who are willing
to take on the often heavy burden of responsibility,
the onerous privilege of leadership.
Support them in their work,
and help them to fulfil their calling faithfully,
recognising that the day will come
when they have to answer to a higher authority,
and when you will pronounce your verdict on all.
Lord, in your mercy,
hear our prayer.

In Jesus' name.
Amen.

260

FOR THOSE WHO FEEL UNLOVED

Almighty God,
   we thank you for your great and never-ending love
      which never stops seeking us out,
      never fades,
      and never lets us go.
   We thank you for your care that we experience
      every moment of every day,
      for everything you have done for us and all the world in Christ,
      and we pray now for those who feel lonely,
      unloved,
      unwanted.
   Lord, in your mercy,
      reach out in love.

We pray for those whose relationships have been broken,
      whether through separation, divorce or bereavement;
      and we pray for those who have never enjoyed
      the relationships they might have had –
      children unwanted by their parents,
      parents alienated from children,
      family members estranged from one another.
   Lord, in your mercy,
      reach out in love.

We pray for individuals who feel rejected by society –
      those who have no confidence in their abilities,
      no place where they feel accepted,
      no sense of their own worth.
   Lord, in your mercy,
      reach out in love.

We pray for communities divided by prejudice, race or religion,
    for churches where there is disagreement,
    tension and disharmony,
    and for nations broken by war and violence.
Lord, in your mercy,
    reach out in love.

Almighty God,
    bring friendship to the lonely,
    reconciliation to the estranged,
    harmony to the divided,
    and comfort to the bereaved.
In our homes and our families,
    our schools and our places of work,
    our country and our world,
    may your love be shared among us,
    bringing hope and healing.
Lord in your mercy,
    reach out in love.

In the name of Christ we ask it.
Amen.

261

FOR ALL WHO WRESTLE AGAINST GOD

Gracious God,
    we pray for those who struggle against you,
        who through word and deed contend against your purpose.

We pray for those who knowingly flout your will –
    those who kill, maim and destroy,
    who exploit others,
    who ignore the poor and needy,
    who add to the total of human suffering.
Confront them with your searching presence.
Your kingdom come,
    your will be done,
    on earth as it is in heaven.

We pray for those who put their trust in false gods –
    who know there is something missing in their lives,
    but who try to deny it,
    seeking refuge in money, possessions
    or the trappings of success.
Reach out to them with your searching love.
Your kingdom come,
    your will be done,
    on earth as it is in heaven.

We pray for those who resist your call –
    who have heard your voice,
    recognised your challenge,
    and glimpsed something of your love,
    yet who hold out against you,
    refusing to take the final step of commitment.
Challenge them with your searching word.
Your kingdom come,
    your will be done,
    on earth as it is in heaven.

We pray for those who let you down despite themselves –
   ordinary believers like ourselves who each day betray your love
   and deny your purpose,
   the spirit willing but the flesh weak.
Restore them through your renewing grace.
Your kingdom come,
   your will be done,
   on earth as it is in heaven.

Gracious God,
   we look forward to a time when you will be all in all –
   when everything that conspires against you
   will finally be overcome,
   and your love will reign supreme.
Bring that day closer, we pray,
   through the indwelling of your Spirit
   and the living presence of Christ.
Your kingdom come,
   your will be done,
   on earth as it is in heaven.

In Jesus' name we ask it.
   Amen.

262

FOR THE VICTIMS OF UNFORESEEN CONSEQUENCES

Loving God,
   so often we act with little or no thought
      as to the potential repercussions of our words or deeds,
      only to find later that decisions taken,
      whether our own or others,
      are hard to bear.
   Hear now our prayer for all those suffering
      as a result of unforeseen consequences.
   Take what is and has been,
      and direct what shall be.

We pray for those who wish they could go back on their decisions –
      those whose consciences are troubled,
      who are burdened by thoughts of what might have been,
      who wish they had taken another course,
      or who simply find they have taken on
      more than they can cope with.
   Take what is and has been,
      and direct what shall be.

We pray for those who regret decisions they made
      or failed to make –
      unhappy in their relationships,
      their work,
      their homes,
      or in life itself.
   Take what is and has been,
      and direct what shall be.

We pray for those suffering the consequences
      of other people's decisions –
      those whose marriages have been destroyed,
      whose careers have been wrecked,
      whose confidence has been undermined,
      or whose feelings have been hurt.
   Take what is and has been,
      and direct what shall be.

We pray for those suffering the consequences of war –
　　their way of life overturned,
　　their livelihoods shattered,
　　their country destroyed,
　　their loved ones killed or injured,
Take what is and has been,
　　and direct what shall be.

We pray for the victims of economic systems and structures –
　　the poor,
　　the hungry,
　　the sick
　　and the exploited.
Take what is and has been,
　　and direct what shall be.

We pray for the casualties of thoughtless or careless actions –
　　victims of road or industrial accidents,
　　of misdiagnoses or inappropriate treatment,
　　of nuclear, biological and chemical testing,
　　of crime or miscarriages of justice.
Take what is and has been,
　　and direct what shall be.

Loving God,
　　there are so many whose lives have been changed for ever
　　　by the consequences of their own or other people's actions.
　　Give to each one the ability
　　　to live with decisions that have been taken,
　　　to reshape the results as best they are able,
　　　to pick up the pieces of their lives and to begin again,
　　　in the knowledge that you are able to make all things new.
Take what is and has been,
　　and direct what shall be.

Through Jesus Christ our Lord.
Amen.

263

FOR MATTERS GREAT AND SMALL

Loving and living God,
    we rejoice that this is your world,
        created by your hand,
        sustained by your power,
        guided by your purpose.
So now we bring it to you,
    seeking your blessing on all its affairs.
In mercy, hear us:
    in love, respond.

We pray for peace,
    that the leaders of all nations may work to reduce weaponry
    and promote dialogue.
We pray for justice,
    that the abundance of this earth's resources
    may be distributed more evenly.
We pray for liberty,
    that moves towards greater democracy and freedom may prosper.
We pray for harmony,
    that everyone, irrespective of race, sex, or creed,
    may be valued for what they are.
In mercy, hear us:
    in love, respond.

We do not just pray for the big things in life but also the little,
   rejoicing that all situations are important to you,
   all people matter in your sight.
So we bring the business of each day,
   small in the eyes of the world, but important to us:
   the responsibilities of family life and parenthood;
   the cost of buying and running a home;
   the problems of earning a living and making ends meet;
   the joys and sorrows of marriage and relationships;
   the well-being of our loved ones;
   our places of work and recreation, worship and relaxation.
We put these into your hands,
   knowing that they matter to you as much as they matter to us.
In mercy, hear us:
   in love, respond.

Loving and living God,
   we rejoice that you are involved in our world,
      and involved in our lives,
      not distant or remote,
      but seeking the good of everything you have made.
   Gratefully we put our trust in you.
   In mercy, hear us:
      in love, respond.

Through Jesus Christ our Lord.
Amen.

264

FOR THOSE BESET BY DOUBT

Living God,
  we pray for all those who find faith difficult or impossible –
    those beset by doubt,
      troubled by questions to which they can find no answer,
      unable to take the leap of faith,
      yet seeking, searching and thirsting for truth.
  Lord, in your mercy,
    hear our prayer.

We think of those unable to reconcile their own situations
    with the claims of the gospel –
    those whose dreams have been shattered,
    their love betrayed,
    their trust abused,
    and their best efforts gone unrewarded.
  Lord, in your mercy,
    hear our prayer.

We think of those for whom events in the world at large
    seem to deny your love –
    those confronted by natural disaster,
    sickened by war and violence,
    bemused by sickness, suffering and disease,
    perplexed by the apparent victory in so many places
    of evil over good.
  Lord, in your mercy,
    hear our prayer.

We pray also for those confirmed in their unbelief,
    unwilling to consider further the claims of the gospel,
    unmoved and unchallenged by the love of Christ.
  Lord, in your mercy,
    hear our prayer.

Living God,
   break through the barriers of doubt and unbelief.
   Open the hearts and minds
      of all who are troubled and confused,
      and all who are closed to your presence.
   Meet with those who find it hard to meet with you,
      and lead them to a living, life-giving faith.
   Lord, in your mercy,
      hear our prayer.

Through Jesus Christ our Lord.
Amen.

265

FOR THOSE WHO ARE WEARY

Loving God,
　we pray for those who are weary –
　　exhausted in body, mind and soul.
　Lord of life,
　　renew their strength and refresh their spirits.

　We think of those whose daily work hangs heavy upon them –
　　those in dull, soul-destroying employment,
　　in stressful and pressurised careers,
　　in labour that is heavy and physically exhausting,
　　or in jobs involving long and unsociable hours.
　Lord of life,
　　renew their strength and refresh their spirits.

　We think of those who have no job –
　　yearning for the opportunity to use their skills,
　　deprived of a sense of self-respect,
　　unable to provide for their loved ones as they would like to,
　　their life seeming empty and frustrating.
　Lord of life,
　　renew their strength and refresh their spirits.

　We think of those who are suffering –
　　battling against illness,
　　wrestling with infirmity,
　　crushed by physical disability,
　　or enduring long-term physical or emotional pain.
　Lord of life,
　　renew their strength and refresh their spirits.

We pray for those who have lost their enthusiasm for life –
  the depressed and downhearted,
  the mentally disturbed,
  the sad and disillusioned,
  the frightened and anxious;
  all those for whom just getting through another day
  has become an effort.
Lord of life,
  renew their strength and refresh their spirits.

We think of those who have nothing to sustain their hope –
  those whose dreams have been crushed
  by the harsh realities of life,
  who struggle with doubt and uncertainty,
  whose faith in you and the future
  has been battered beyond repair,
  their ability to bounce back finally exhausted.
Lord of life,
  renew their strength and refresh their spirits.

Loving God,
  draw near to all through Christ.
  Grant the peace of your presence,
    the healing of your touch,
    the blessing of your guidance,
    and the assurance of your constant love,
    so that all who are weary may walk in hope
    and look forward in faith.
Lord of life,
  renew their strength and refresh their spirits.

Through Jesus Christ our Lord.
Amen.

266

FOR THOSE DENIED THEIR FREEDOM

Sovereign God,
  we pray for all who are denied freedom –
    freedom to worship,
    to express their opinions,
    to vote,
    to determine their own affairs.
  Help them to make their voice heard
    and to secure the justice they seek.
  Set at liberty those held captive,
    and may the oppressed go free.

We pray for all denied the opportunity to live life to the full –
    the mentally and physically disabled,
    victims of accidents and illness,
    the depressed and broken-hearted.
  Give to each help to conquer that which can so easily enslave them.
  Set at liberty those held captive,
    and may the oppressed go free.

We pray for those whose freedom
    has been justly taken away from them –
    those who have knowingly broken the law,
    who have caused injury and hurt to others,
    who are a danger to themselves and society.
  May your love help them to find new life in Christ,
    and deliverance from their past ways.
  Set at liberty those held captive,
    and may the oppressed go free.

We pray for those whose spirits are held captive –
    poisoned by greed, envy, pride and selfishness,
    trapped in a vicious circle of hatred and bitterness,
    crushed by fear and anxiety,
    led astray by empty hopes and vain ambitions,
    false gods and superstition.
May they find in Jesus the way, the truth and the life.
Set at liberty those held captive,
    and may the oppressed go free.

Sovereign God,
    break through everything which denies your love
        and frustrates your will.
Reach out to your world in which so many
        are held hostage to fortune,
    and, by the power of your Spirit,
        grant release from all that imprisons us.
Set at liberty those held captive,
    and may the oppressed go free.

We ask it in Jesus' name.
Amen.

267

FOR CANDIDATES AND ELECTORS AT A GENERAL ELECTION

Sovereign God,
   you have called us to pray for those set over us,
     and to respect those in authority.
   So now we think of the coming election
     and of all those who will be standing in it.
   Lord, in your mercy,
     hear our prayer.

We pray for those standing as candidates –
   may they seek the good of others
   rather than be concerned with self-advancement;
   for those who will cast their votes –
   may they too look beyond self-interest
   to the wider needs of our country as a whole;
   for those who will be elected as MPs –
   may they strive to represent all their constituency members,
   irrespective of political affiliation.
Lord, in your mercy,
   hear our prayer.

We pray for whichever party forms our new government –
   may they see further than party and even national interest
   to the needs of the wider global community;
   for those who will sit in opposition –
   may they challenge complacency, injustice or abuse of power;
   for those who will be appointed to the Cabinet
   and other government positions –
   may they honour the responsibility entrusted to them;
   for the Prime Minister as *he/she* looks to lead this nation –
   may *he/she* be equipped for the onerous responsibilities of office.
Lord, in your mercy,
   hear our prayer.

Sovereign God,
 grant to all called to serve in any position, large or small,
  the gifts they will need –
  wisdom,
  patience,
  dedication,
  integrity,
  vision
  and humility –
  and help them to fulfil their calling faithfully,
  mindful of all, and mindful of you.
 Lord, in your mercy,
  hear our prayer.

Through Jesus Christ our Lord.
Amen.

268

For victims of racism

Lord of all,
  you have made us in your image,
    each one the work of your hands,
    a unique and precious creation,
    and we praise you for it.
  Yet we remember also how, across the centuries and still today,
    so many have endured prejudice and discrimination,
    rejected because of the colour of their skin,
    persecuted due to their creed or culture.
  Reach out in love,
    and heal our divisions.

Forgive the racism that still exists in our society –
    the automatic attaching of labels,
    the taunting and snide remarks,
    the denial of opportunities,
    the unconscious negative attitudes.
Break down the barriers that divide our world,
    the ignorance and suspicion
    which inflict such pain on so many.
Reach out in love,
    and heal our divisions.

Forgive the racism that exists within ourselves,
    recognised or unrecognised –
    the naïve assumptions and hidden biases –
    and forgive us those times we have remained silent
    when we should have spoken up,
    when we have ignored prejudice
    because *we* are personally unaffected.
Help us to see each individual in their own right,
    and to appreciate their true worth.
Reach out in love,
    and heal our divisions.

We pray for all who experience racism –
  victims of verbal abuse or physical assault,
  of social exclusion, deprivation and discrimination.
Give them courage to hold their heads high,
  perseverance in standing up for their rights,
  and support in times of adversity.
Reach out in love,
  and heal our divisions.

We pray finally for those who work for change –
  campaigning for equality of opportunity,
  striving to break down preconceptions,
  building bridges across divided communities.
Encourage them in their efforts,
  and grant that through bringing people together
  prejudices may be overcome.
Reach out in love,
  and heal our divisions.

Lord of all,
  you have made us in your image,
    each one the work of your hands,
    a unique and precious creation.
Break down everything that comes between us,
  and grant unity to our divided world,
  and a proper respect for all.
Reach out in love,
  and heal our divisions.

Through Jesus Christ our Lord.
Amen.

269

FOR THOSE WHO FEEL POWERLESS

Almighty and all-powerful God,
    we pray to you for the weak and powerless of the world,
        those who yearn for change,
        but who can find no opportunity to help themselves.
    Lord of all,
        reach out in love.

We pray for those in our own society –
        the homeless and unemployed,
        the disabled, sick and mentally ill,
        those caught up in circumstances
        which seem to be beyond their control
        and who feel unable to cope with the problems of life.
    Lord of all,
        reach out in love.

We pray for those in other countries and continents –
        the poor, underprivileged, hungry and dispossessed;
        those who are persecuted for their beliefs,
        or who have been driven from their homelands as refugees;
        those whose labour is exploited,
        or whose livelihoods have been destroyed
        by famine, disaster or war.
    Lord of all,
        reach out in love.

Almighty and all-powerful God,
   give strength to everyone who is powerless –
      strength to survive,
      to hope,
      and to work for a better future.
   Give help to those who campaign for freedom,
      for peace,
      and for a more just world.
   Grant that those who are strong may help those who are weak,
      so that the voice of all may be heard,
      and the rights of every individual be respected.
   Lord of all,
      reach out in love,

In the name of Christ.
Amen.

270

FOR THOSE WHO WORK FOR JUSTICE

Righteous God,
    we pray for those who work to promote justice in our world –
        those who campaign for fair trade
        and an easing of international debts,
        for a just sharing of the earth's resources,
        for freedom of conscience and basic human rights,
        for deliverance from dictatorship
        and the establishing of democracy.
Grant them encouragement and support
    in their struggle for change.
Lord of all,
    hear our prayer.

We pray for those who work to promote justice in our country –
    those who pass laws in our Parliament,
    who administer them in our courts,
    who deal with offenders in prisons, remand centres
    or the local community,
    and who strive to uphold law and order in our society.
Grant them wisdom in all they do.
Lord of all,
    hear our prayer.

We pray for those who work for justice in our society –
    who petition for the poor and disadvantaged,
    who fight abuse and exploitation in all its many forms,
    who support the cause of the wronged and the falsely accused,
    who stand up against crime and corruption.
Grant them courage and integrity.
Lord of all,
    hear our prayer.

Righteous God,
  we know that you want us to deal justly with one another,
    to work for the good of all rather than a few,
    and we thank you that there are those
    with sufficient courage to respond to that challenge,
    and with sufficient passion to devote their lives to those ends.
  Support them in all they do,
    and inspire us to pursue such goals in turn.
  Lord of all,
    hear our prayer.

Through Jesus Christ our Lord.
Amen.

271

For those who minister to others

God of love,
we pray for all those in our society
who minister to the needs of others.

We think of those in our hospitals,
the caring professions,
and the emergency services –
doctors, surgeons, nurses and ancillary staff,
paramedics, firemen, police,
psychiatrists, therapists, counsellors,
hospice, nursing-home and special-needs workers –
these, and so many others,
upon whose skill, compassion and dedication
we depend in time of need.
Support them in their work,
and show your love through their ministry.

We think of caring organisations –
those like Oxfam, Christian Aid and UNICEF
who work overseas,
like Shelter, Barnardos and Sue Ryder homes
who work in our own country –
a host of aid and relief agencies who bring hope to the poor,
support to the sick,
help to the homeless,
and comfort to the dying,
working in different ways
to support those facing times of crisis.
Support them in their work,
and show your love through their ministry.

We think of individual carers –
    those who offer their time and energy as volunteers,
    who look after elderly parents, disabled children
    or terminally ill loved ones at home,
    who each day perform small but vital acts of kindness
    for friends and family,
    neighbour and stranger –
    their acts unnoticed except by a few
    yet so valuable to those they care for.
Support them in their work,
    and show your love through their ministry.

We think finally of the family of the Church –
    of those entrusted with full-time pastoral responsibility;
    of chaplains in hospitals and hospices,
    industry and commerce,
    prisons and the armed forces,
    sport and education;
    of missionaries offering their skills abroad;
    and of individual believers seeking to express their faith
    through caring words and deeds.
Support them in their work,
    and show your love through their ministry.

God of love,
    we thank you for all who minister to the needs of others.
    Inspire us through their example,
        equip them in their continuing efforts,
        and enrich the lives of many through the service they offer.
    Through Jesus Christ our Lord.
    Amen.

272

FOR THOSE CARRYING HEAVY BURDENS

Great and gracious God,
  we pray for all those in life who carry heavy loads
    and long for rest.

We pray for people weighed down by remorse,
    carrying with them a burden of guilt –
    those who have made mistakes,
    who have said or done foolish things,
    who have acted unthinkingly,
    and who feel they can never find pardon.
Assure them of your constant forgiveness open to all.
Lord, in your mercy,
  hear our prayer.

We pray for those weighed down
    by a sense that life has lost its meaning,
    carrying with them a burden of despair –
    those who drift aimlessly through each day,
    who look to the future with a sense of weariness,
    who feel trapped in a rut from which there is no escape.
Assure them that you have a purpose for all.
Lord, in your mercy,
  hear our prayer.

We pray for those weighed down by injustice,
    carrying with them a burden of helplessness –
    the poor, sick and homeless,
    the oppressed, persecuted and wrongfully imprisoned –
    all who are deprived of their basic human rights
    and who feel powerless to do anything about it.
Assure them that you are able to transform all things,
    however hopeless they may seem.
Lord, in your mercy,
  hear our prayer.

We pray for those weighed down by advancing years,
    carrying with them the burden of age –
    those who wrestle with declining health,
    who are confused by the pace of change,
    who feel lonely and unloved,
    or who grieve for old friends who have passed away.
Assure them that your word and love endure for ever.
Lord, in your mercy,
    hear our prayer.

We pray for those weighed down by the burden of doubt,
    carrying with them a sense of shame
    at having lost their faith –
    those who feel cut off from you,
    troubled by all kinds of questions,
    unable to believe as they once did,
    alone in a cold and empty world.
Assure them of your involvement in every part of life,
    even when they cannot understand it.
Lord, in your mercy,
    hear our prayer.

Great and gracious God
    bring hope,
      bring joy,
      bring peace,
      bring trust –
      bring renewal of life
      to all who struggle under heavy loads.
May they find in Christ the one whose yoke is easy
    and whose burden is light,
    and through him find rest for their souls.
Lord, in your mercy,
    hear our prayer.

We ask it in his name.
Amen.

273

FOR THOSE WHO DO NOT UNDERSTAND THEIR TRUE WORTH

Gracious God,
  we thank you that you value each one of us,
    that we are all important in your eyes.
  We thank you that everyone matters to you,
    none more than others and none less.
  Hear now our prayers
    for those who have lost that sense of perspective.
  Lord, in your mercy,
    hear our prayer.

We pray for those who fall into the error **of pride,**
    thinking of themselves more highly th**an they** should,
    looking down on others,
    trusting in themselves rather than in **you.**
  Help them to recognise their weaknesses as well as their strengths,
    their need to receive as well as to give.
  Lord, in your mercy,
  hear our prayer.

We pray for those who have no sense of **worth,**
    who feel they are unimportant, unvalued, or unloved –
    victims of broken homes and broken relationships,
    the powerless and the poor,
    homeless and refugees,
    shy and depressed,
    lonely and rejected.
  Grant them the assurance that, whatever their circumstances,
    they are precious to you,
    each one your unique creation.
  Lord, in your mercy,
    hear our prayer.

Gracious God,
give to all a proper sense of their own value,
a true appreciation of the worth of others,
and, above all, an understanding of your greatness,
beside which we are nothing
yet through which you count us as your children.
Lord, in your mercy,
hear our prayer.

Through Jesus Christ our Lord.
Amen.

274

FOR THE FAMILY OF HUMANKIND

Living God,
   we praise you for all that is good and precious in human life;
     the value,
     potential,
     and uniqueness of every individual.
   For our family of humankind,
     hear our prayer.

We pray for all those whose humanity is abused and exploited –
     victims of violence, torture and rape,
     children drawn into the world of prostitution,
     people addicted to drugs,
     those living under corrupt and oppressive regimes.
   For our family of humankind,
     hear our prayer.

We pray for those whose humanity is diminished
     by prejudice and discrimination,
     subjected to insults, intimidation, hatred and suspicion,
     day after day denied justice,
     time and again deprived of the opportunity
     to prove themselves.
   For our family of humankind,
     hear our prayer.

We pray for those denied the chance to fulfil their potential,
     whether through lack of education,
     insufficient resources,
     limited opportunities,
     or a denial of their human rights.
   For our family of humankind,
     hear our prayer.

We pray for those whose lives are blighted by need,
  burdened by debt or unemployment,
  oppressed by poverty, hunger and homelessness,
  crushed by natural catastrophe or personal disaster.
For our family of humankind,
  hear our prayer.

We pray for those who have lost belief in their own worth,
  overwhelmed by self-doubt,
  beset by inner fears,
  their confidence broken,
  their faith in the future destroyed.
For our family of humankind,
  hear our prayer.

We pray for those who mourn at the loss of loved ones,
  life suddenly seeming empty of meaning
  and stripped of joy,
  and we pray for those who battle against sickness and disease,
  unable to live life to the full,
  and fearful as to what the future may hold.
For our family of humankind,
  hear our prayer.

Living God,
  grant that the day will come
    when the worth of all will be recognised,
    the rights of all respected,
    the good of all pursued,
    and harmony among all be enjoyed.
  Reach out in love,
    and show us how we can respond to the needs around us.
For our family of humankind,
  hear our prayer.

Through Jesus Christ our Lord.
Amen.

THE LORD'S SUPPER

275

INVITATION (1)

The table is prepared,
   the invitation extended,
   bread is broken,
   wine poured out.
Come now and share the supper,
   celebrate this most precious of gifts.
Eat,
   and find food for your souls.
Drink,
   and be filled to overflowing.
The table is ready,
   the Lord is here.
Come and share in this simplest of meals,
   this finest of feasts.
The offer is his,
   the moment is ours –
   Christ is waiting to touch our lives.
Thanks be to God.
Amen.

276

INVITATION (2)

Look up,
>   for God is here,
>   waiting to feed you through bread and wine;
>   waiting to nurture your faith
>   and nourish your soul.

Look in,
>   for he wants to meet *you*,
>   not the mask you wear for the world,
>   but the person you are,
>   with all your beauty and ugliness,
>   your potential for good and evil.

Look around,
>   for you are not alone –
>   your family is here,
>   your brothers and sisters in Christ,
>   sharing the same loaf,
>   bound by the same faith,
>   serving the same God.

Look out,
>   for the world is calling,
>   aching under a weight of sorrow,
>   a burden of sin that destroys and deprives,
>   robbing people of dignity,
>   denying them life.

Look back,
>   for Jesus is speaking,
>   tears in his eyes,
>   a tremor in his voice:
>   'This is my body, broken for you,
>   do this in memory of me;
>   This is my blood, shed for many.
>   Go on doing this to recall my presence with you.'

Look forward,
for Christ will come again,
the King of kings and Lord of lords,
returning to fulfil his purpose,
to establish his kingdom,
and to draw all things to himself.

Look now,
the bread is broken,
the wine poured out –
eat,
drink,
and be thankful.

Amen.

277

INVITATION (3)

Be still,
  look,
  for someone is reaching out,
  breaking bread,
  pouring out wine,
  sharing a meal with his friends.

Be still,
  listen,
  for someone is speaking,
  a voice breaking into the darkness of the world:
  'My body,
  my blood;
  do this in remembrance of me.'

Be still,
  touch,
  for the Lord is here,
  present among us,
  broken for you,
  poured out for many,
  waiting to transform our lives.

Be still,
  taste,
  for here is living bread,
  living water,
  the answer to our deepest hunger,
  the end of our thirst for truth.

Be still,
  listen,
  for someone is calling,
  a voice breaking into *your* darkness,
  speaking *your* name.

Come now,
    and feed in your hearts with thanksgiving.
Come now,
    and be filled to overflowing.

Amen.

278

APPROACH (1)

Lord Jesus Christ,
  we have no right to be here,
    for we are weak, foolish and sinful,
    our faults and failings part of the burden you carried on the cross,
    part of the reason for your death.
  We come at your invitation,
    conscious of our privilege.
  We come at your request,
    conscious of how little we deserve it.
  We come at your bidding,
    conscious of all that we owe you.
  We come at your instruction,
    conscious of our dependence on your grace.
  Draw near to us, in your mercy,
    so that we may draw closer to you.
  Fill us with your love
    and renew us by your Spirit,
    so that we may walk where you would lead us,
    and live more faithfully as your disciples
    to your praise and glory.
  Amen.

279

Approach (2)

Lord Jesus Christ,
  you invite us to share this meal;
    gladly we come.
You invite us to receive your love;
    joyfully we accept.
You invite us to unload our burdens;
    gratefully we let them go.
You invite us to follow where you would lead us;
    freely we respond.

Though our faith is poor,
    your grace is rich.
Though we deserve so little,
    you give us so much.
Though we daily prove false,
    you always stay true.

So, then, we come,
    as you have called us,
  to share together,
    to share with you.
Receive our praise,
    receive our thanks,
  receive our worship,
    for your name's sake.
Amen.

280

CONFESSION (1)

Lord Jesus Christ,
    we come to break bread and share wine in memory of you –
        a celebration which should sum up
        everything that binds us together.
    Yet the reality is different,
        this sacred supper one of the rare occasions
        we make time to think of you,
        one of the few concrete expressions of our faith.
    Loving Lord,
        forgive us.

We speak of proclaiming your death through this meal
    until you come,
        but the rest of our life fails to testify
        to your death and resurrection.
We claim that, as there is one loaf,
    so we, though we are many, are one body,
    but our fellowship is superficial, lacking depth or substance.
We say that whoever comes to you
    will never hunger or thirst again,
    but few of us are ever truly satisfied.
Loving Lord,
    forgive us.

We talk of following you,
    of taking up our cross and serving others,
    but the truth is that we are willing to sacrifice little,
    more concerned with serving ourselves
    than those around us.
Loving Lord,
    forgive us.

Lord Jesus Christ,
  in so many ways we fail you,
    the way we live denying the faith we proclaim at this table.
  We have no right to be here,
    no reason to expect your love,
    yet you call us to share together,
    your invitation dependent not on our goodness or obedience,
    but on your sheer and inexhaustible grace.
  So we come now,
    conscious of our sin but rejoicing in your mercy,
    praising you for your unfailing love
    which enables us to come in confidence
    and to seek once more your pardon.
  Loving Lord,
    forgive us.

Hear our prayer,
  for we ask it in your name.
  Amen.

281

CONFESSION (2)

Lord Jesus Christ,
 we come to this table deeply conscious of our unworthiness,
  for, though you died to bring us life,
   we continue to betray your goodness time and again,
   poor in our obedience,
   weak in our love for others,
   and feeble in our faith.
Yet still you invite us to share in your supper!
Feed, forgive and renew us.

We have such high ideals,
 such good intentions,
  our earnest desire being to serve you faithfully
  and to honour you through our discipleship,
  but each day we fall so far short.
We are mean and petty, thoughtless and weak,
 selfish and proud in our attitude,
 envious and intolerant of others.
There is so much about us that divides and destroys,
 and so little that brings wholeness and harmony.
Yet still you invite us to share in your supper!
Feed, forgive and renew us.

You want us to become a new creation,
 but there seems little evidence
 that anything is different about us.
You ask us to take up our cross and follow you,
 but we are reluctant to risk anything, let alone sacrifice all.
You call us to serve you as the Lord of our lives,
 but repeatedly we put your will second to our own.
Yet still you invite us to share in your supper!
Feed, forgive and renew us.

Lord Jesus Christ,
    you gave your life for us,
        nailing our sins to the cross,
        bearing the burden that should have been ours,
        but the only thanks we give you
        is to go on as though nothing has changed,
        our lives as flawed as they have ever been.
We are weak and foolish,
    faithless and disobedient,
    unworthy of your love,
    undeserving of your goodness.
Yet still you invite us to share in your supper!
Feed, forgive and renew us.

By your grace, hear us,
    and answer our prayer,
    for your name's sake.
Amen.

282

THANKSGIVING (1)

Lord Jesus Christ,
  we come as you commanded all who love you,
    responding to your gracious invitation
    to share in this sacred meal –
    to eat bread,
    and drink wine,
    in remembrance of you.
  For the wonder of this supper and all it represents,
    we thank you.

We are here not just to receive bread and wine
    but to celebrate everything that they symbolise –
    the breaking of your body,
    the shedding of your blood,
    your life poured out for us and for many,
    your death which sets us free
    from all that holds us captive.
  For the wonder of this supper and all it represents,
    we thank you.

We are here to celebrate the many gifts
    your life and death made possible –
    hope in our despair,
    joy in our sorrow,
    peace in our confusion,
    light in our darkness –
    the gift of your love flowing into our hearts
    and out through our lives.
  For the wonder of this supper and all it represents,
    we thank you.

We are here to receive your forgiveness –
   to rejoice again in your great mercy,
   your generous pardon,
   your unfailing willingness to pick us up
   after yet another failure,
   and offer us a break with the past,
   a new beginning,
   a fresh chapter in our history.
For the wonder of this supper and all it represents,
   we thank you.

Lord Jesus Christ,
   we come to this table in awe and wonder,
   with joy in our hearts
   and a song on our lips.
But we come, above all, with gratitude,
   recognising once more all you have done for us,
   and responding again to all you so freely continue to give.
For the wonder of this supper and all it represents,
   we thank you.

Amen.

283

THANKSGIVING (2)

Lord Jesus Christ,
    we thank you for this table spread before us,
        this unique meal and all that it represents.
    You have not just given us daily bread –
        you have given us the bread of life,
        inner nourishment,
        food which means we need never go spiritually hungry again.
    Though our bodies may be empty,
        our souls are filled to overflowing,
        brimming over with joy and thanksgiving.
    And so we have learned what it means to be content,
        the secret of true fulfilment.
    You came,
        you lived,
        you died among us,
        your flesh broken for us,
        and you rose again,
        opening up the way to new and everlasting life.
    Accept our thanks,
        receive our praise,
        and feed us now as we share together in your name,
        to your praise and glory.
Amen.

284

INTERCESSION (1)

Lord Jesus Christ,
    we remember that, before you died,
        you prayed not for yourself but for others,
        and not simply for your followers,
        but for all people, everywhere.
    You offered your life not just for the chosen few
        but for the whole world,
        your desire being that everyone
        should come to know your love for themselves.
    So now we pray for our world of so much good yet so much evil,
        so much joy yet so much sorrow,
        so much beauty yet so much ugliness.
    Come among us,
        and establish your kingdom.

We pray for those who have plenty and those who have little,
    those for whom life brings pleasure
    and those for whom it brings pain.
We remember all who celebrate and all who mourn,
    all who look forward with confidence
    and all who view the future with dread.
Come among us,
    and establish your kingdom.

We pray for those who know you and those who don't,
    those of other faiths and those of none.
We remember those who look for truth
    and those who feel they can never find it,
    those who seek purpose
    and those who believe life is devoid of meaning.
Come among us,
    and establish your kingdom.

We remember the rich and the poor,
    the healthy and the sick,
    the well-fed and hungry,
    the employed and unemployed,
    the free and the oppressed,
    the comfortably housed and the homeless.
Come among us,
    and establish your kingdom.

Lord Jesus Christ,
    we pray for our world in all its contrasts,
        and for the situations people face in all their complexity.
    Teach us that everyone, everywhere, matters to us
        because they matter to you,
        and so help us to respond wherever we are able,
        in the name of Christ.
Come among us
    and establish your kingdom.

For his name's sake.
Amen.

285

INTERCESSION (2)

Lord Jesus Christ,
   you know what it is to be broken in body,
      for your flesh was torn by the whip,
      pierced by a crown of thorns,
      skewered by nails in your hands and feet,
      and by a spear through your side.
   Hear, then, our prayer for all those broken today –
      the sick and the suffering, the old and the infirm,
      victims of accident, war, torture and abuse.
   Reach out to all in their pain,
      and bring your healing, renewing touch.

You know what it is to be broken in mind,
      for in the darkness of Gethsemane
      you faced the terror of the cross,
      and you endured what followed alone,
      betrayed, denied,
      abandoned by closest friends.
Hear then our prayer for all those broken today –
      the anxious, fearful, hurt or disillusioned,
      the lonely, bereaved, depressed or mentally ill.
Reach out to all in their pain,
      and bring your healing, renewing touch.

You know what it is to be broken in spirit,
      for you bore our sins, carried our burdens,
      endured the agony of separation from God,
      and the awful emptiness that entailed.
Hear then our prayer for all who are broken today –
      those who have lost their faith,
      and those who have never found it;
      those wrestling with hopelessness,
      failure, doubt, guilt.
Reach out to all in their pain,
      and bring your healing, renewing touch.

Lord Jesus Christ,
   you know what it is to be broken,
      and you know what it is to be made new.
   Grant your blessing today
      to all who are bruised and battered by life,
      and restore them in body, mind and spirit.
   Reach out to all in your love,
      and bring your healing, renewing touch.

We ask it in your name.
Amen.

286

DISMISSAL (1)

Go now in peace:
Christ died for us.
Go in joy:
he rose victorious.
Go with thanksgiving:
his Spirit is with us.
Go with hope:
he will come again.
Go in faith:
he calls us to follow.
Go in love:
he asks us to serve.
The supper is over but the journey continues:
our pilgrimage is barely begun.
Go then, in the name of Christ,
to live and work for his kingdom and to his glory.
Amen.

287

DISMISSAL (2)

Sovereign God,
  send us out in the name of Christ
    and the power of your Spirit.
  We have worshipped;
    now help us to serve.
  We have spoken;
    now help us to act.
  We have heard your word;
    now help us to make it known.
  We have rejoiced in your love;
    now help us to share it with others.
  Use us for your will
    and for your kingdom,
    through Jesus Christ our Lord.
  Amen.

288

DISMISSAL (3)

Living God,
>   go with us on our journey of discipleship.
>   Grant us faith to follow where you might lead,
>>   courage to step out into the unknown,
>>   grace to walk with humility,
>>   and commitment to travel on to our journey's end.
>   So may we take up our cross,
>>   and follow in the footsteps of Christ,
>>   to his praise and glory.
>   **Amen.**

289

DISMISSAL (4)

Go now with confidence,
   for the Lord is with you.
   May the joy of Christ shine in your eyes,
      the compassion of Christ reach out through your hands,
      the word of Christ fall from your tongue,
      the peace of Christ fill your mind,
      and the love of Christ flow from your heart.
   Reach out,
      and live for him,
      for his name's sake.
   Amen.

290

DISMISSAL (5)

You have come in faith;
  go now in peace.
  You have received from the Lord's hand;
    go now to give in his name.
  You have eaten bread and drunk wine;
    go now and share his love.
  You have proclaimed the Lord's death;
    go now and make known his life.
  The supper is ended but the journey continues;
    go then with confidence
    for the Lord is with you,
    now and always.
  Thanks be to God.
  Amen.

BLESSINGS

291

Loving Father, full of compassion,
    merciful Saviour, full of grace,
    life-giving Spirit, full of power,
    sovereign God, full of majesty,
    fill our hearts, minds and souls,
    and send us out to build your kingdom,
    for your name's sake.
Amen.

292

The God of grace forgive you,
    the Lord of creation remake you,
    the ruler of history direct your paths.
May God be a rock to support you,
    a shield to protect you,
    and a fortress to surround you,
    through Jesus Christ our Lord.
Amen.

293

Remember all God has done.
Rejoice in all he is doing.
Receive all he shall yet do.
Put your hand in his,
    the God of past, present and future,
    and walk with him wherever he may lead,
    knowing that he will walk with you,
    this day and always.
Amen.

294

Go now,
   redeemed in love,
   renewed in faith,
   restored in strength,
   and refreshed in spirit.
Return to your journey of discipleship,
   in the name of the risen Christ
   who goes before you.
Amen.

295

Whoever you are,
   wherever you go,
   whatever your strengths,
   whatever your weaknesses,
   God will be with you,
   to hold, to heal, to guide and to bless.
Go, then, in peace,
   assured of his love.
Amen.

296

To God, who is higher than our highest thoughts,
   yet closer than our closest friend,
   be thanks and praise,
   glory and honour,
   this day and for evermore.
Amen.

297

Go now,
    not to serve yourself,
    but to serve others;
    not to seek your glory,
    but the glory of God the Father;
    and so may all you are and do
    make him known,
    through Jesus Christ our Lord.
Amen.

298

Whatever today may hold,
    whatever tomorrow might bring,
    the future is secure,
    for Christ is with us,
    the same yesterday, today and for ever.
Live each moment with him
    in quiet confidence and joyful celebration,
    for he is ours
    and we are his
    for all eternity.
Amen.

299

The God who called us here
    is sending us out,
    to turn words into deeds,
    worship into service,
    and vision into reality.
Together we have celebrated the faith;
    now let us share it,
    in the name of Christ.
Amen.

300

To God, who blesses us beyond our imagining,
    who loves us beyond our dreaming,
    who forgives us beyond our deserving,
    and who uses us beyond our hoping,
    be praise and thanksgiving,
    honour and adoration,
    now and always.
Amen.

301

May the God of grace breathe health into your body,
    love into your heart,
    peace into your mind,
    and joy into your spirit.
Go now,
    your life filled to overflowing,
    and be poured out in his service,
    in the name of Christ.
Amen.

302

Return now to the world,
    for Christ is there,
    waiting to meet you and greet you.
Go back,
    with eyes open to see him,
    ears open to hear him,
    a mind open to receive him,
    and a heart open to serve him,
    for his name's sake.
Amen.

303

Let the grace of Christ redeem you,
    the power of Christ renew you,
    the example of Christ inspire you,
    and the love of Christ shine from you.
Go in faith,
    to walk his way
    and make him known
    to his glory.
Amen.

304

As the dew falls in the morning,
    so may the grace of God descend upon us.
As the sun bathes all in its life-giving light,
    so may the radiance of Christ shine in our hearts.
As the wind blows where it will,
    so may the breath of the Spirit move freely in our lives.
Living God,
    work in us
    and with us
    and through us,
    to your glory.
Amen.

305

The night is turning to day,
   darkness is turning to light –
   it is time to wake from our sleep.
Wherever there is sorrow,
   wherever there is fear,
   wherever there is need,
   wherever there is hurt,
   reach out in the name of Christ,
   and may his joy and peace,
   his healing and compassion
   dawn through you,
   until morning has broken
   and the day of his kingdom is here.
Amen.

306

Go now,
   with love in your hearts,
   light in your eyes,
   and life in your souls.
Go, in the service of Christ,
   to proclaim what he has done for you
   and share what he has given,
   to his glory.
Amen.

307

The seed is sown,
   the kingdom is growing,
   God is at work among us.
Offer him your love, your faith and your life,
   and, in bearing fruit in his service,
   may the time of harvest draw nearer.
Through Jesus Christ our Lord.
Amen.

308

Prince of peace, heal us.
Lamb of God, redeem us.
Shepherd of the sheep, guard us.
Light of the world, lead us.
Lord Jesus Christ,
   touch our lives by your grace,
   and help us to live and work for you,
   to your glory.
Amen.

309

Gracious God,
   take our faith, flawed though it is,
   our love, poor though it may be,
   and our commitment, for all its imperfections,
   and use us in your service
   to make known your gracious purpose,
   through Jesus Christ our Lord.
Amen.

310

In the brokenness of our world, God is there.
In the cry of the hungry,
　　the suffering of the sick,
　　the plight of the homeless,
　　and the sorrow of the bereaved,
　　he is calling your name.
In the misery of the lonely,
　　the despair of the oppressed,
　　the plea of the weak,
　　and the helplessness of the poor,
　　he is seeking your help,
　　asking for your response.
The world is bleeding,
　　and God is bleeding with it,
　　waiting for your hands,
　　your care
　　and your love
　　to help heal the wounds.
As you have come *to* him,
　　now go *for* him,
　　in the name of Christ.
Amen.

INDEX

INDEX

Index

References are to prayer rather than page numbers